W9-BYA-675

Praise for Kristen Lamb

Praise for *Rise of the Machines*

"In *Rise of the Machines*, Kristen Lamb has provided an invaluable compass for navigating the uncharted waters of 21st century publishing. I pity the writer working today who doesn't take advantage of the wealth of valuable insights and breakthrough methods contained in these pages."

—David Corbett,
award-winning author of *The Art of Character*

"For writers, the purchase price of Kristen Lamb's *Rise of the Machines* should easily become the best investment you'll ever make for your writing career. In Kristen's brilliant and easy-to-grasp book, not only will you learn how to become a successful marketer of your work—whether it's published by a legacy press or self-published—and achieve significant and ever-increasing sales of your work, but you'll learn how to without spending hours and hours each week to do so. *Rise of the Machines* is the standard—the cutting edge.

As a writer myself, I resent anything that takes time away from working on my manuscripts. Using Kristen's 'work smart and work efficiently' methods, I now only have to spend about three hours a week managing my social media for sales and can now devote the maximum time I have available to... you guessed it... *writing*. Yay! Get this book and start earning real money."

—Les Edgerton,
award-winning author of *Hooked*,
Finding Your Voice, and *The Bitch*

Praise for *Are You There, Blog? It's Me, Writer*

"It's a new world out there for authors—a new paradigm of marketing, communication, and interaction—called social media. It's the new digital Wild West. And while we're all out trying to reinvent the wheel, Kristen Lamb's informative and illuminating book, *Are You There, Blog? It's Me, Writer* is a brilliant roadmap through this new frontier. It literally changed my view of social media, my role in it, and my responsibility to my readers. If you're an aspiring or established author, this is a must-read for all."

—James Rollins,
New York Times best-selling author

"Packed with practical, humorous advice on how to do—and just as important, how NOT to do—social media. Writers of every stripe will benefit from this timely and fun to read resource.

—James Scott Bell,
nationally best-selling author

"Kristen Lamb is social media's Dorothy Parker for the 21st century. Laugh and learn. Kristen lays it on the line in a no-nonsense style that is sure to entertain as well as enlighten."

—Laurie McLean,
partner, Forword Literary, Inc.

"Rest your head and let the Gospel According to Lamb guide you crazy writers through the tangled (and often insane) labyrinth that is social media. Lamb will tell you how to build your writer's platform not by cobbling together globules of fatty spam, but rather by standing tall on your own two feet as a—GASP!—actual human being. Is this essential reading? Say amen and hallelujah."

—Chuck Wendig,
novelist, screenwriter and game designer

Praise for *We Are Not Alone—*
The Writer's Guide to Social Media

"I wished there had been a step-by-step guide for writers on how to not only do social media technically, but do it content-wise. This book is the answer to that wish."

—Bob Mayer,
New York Times and *USA Today* best-selling author

"Every author should read this book! Lamb teaches everything from using social media to help build a brand, to taking that brand and building a platform. Even how to write a stellar bio. Brilliant!"

—Candace Havens,
best-selling author

RISE OF THE
MACHINES

HUMAN AUTHORS IN A DIGITAL WORLD

KRISTEN LAMB

© Copyright 2013 by Kristen Lamb

All rights reserved.

No portion of this book may be reproduced or transmitted in any form or by any means, electronic or mechanical, including photocopying, recording, or by any information storage and retrieval system without written permission from the author, except for the inclusion of brief quotations in a review.

First print edition: June 2013

Cover design: Cory Clubb
Interior design: GreenE-books.com
Image used on page 288 courtesy of Ben Earwicker

eBook ISBN: 978-1-938848-31-5
Print ISBN: 978-1-938848-32-2

Published in the United States of America

TABLE OF CONTENTS

Section 5—Safe Social Practices

Dedication

This book is dedicated to the WANAs. Your love, support and service above self are a shining beacon of light in the darkness. You're more than writers, more than friends. You're my family. We truly are not alone.

Foreword

CONTRARY TO POPULAR BELIEF, Kristen Lamb is not a machine. She may be everywhere at once and online all the time, but she is definitely a human being. Hey, I've seen her get sick by mistakenly eating gluten-filled food at a writers' conference, so I know she's flesh and blood (and other things that I won't mention here).

I started following Kristen years ago online and was amazed not only by her depth of knowledge about the fledgling field of social media, I was astounded by the fact that she was freely sharing all her hard-earned knowledge with authors and writers and artists of all stripes.

The next obvious step after I'd been following Kristen's blog daily for about six months was to see if she was going to be at any conferences I was also attending. Lucky me. She's almost tenured at the Dallas-Fort Worth Writers' Workshop Conference, one of the best in the country. I quickly offered my services as a presenter. They really wanted me to come and take pitches from writers, but at least they let me talk about what literary agents want from self-published authors.

While there, Kristen and I talked and hung out and laughed a lot and, over time, that turned into a long-standing relationship of mutual respect and friendship. Kristen is tireless in her efforts to educate authors about how to succeed in what is the best time ever to be a writer. Even better than when Gutenberg invented the printing press. Even better than when typewriters automated everything. Even better than when Steve Jobs and desktop publishing taught us what fonts were.

Since 2008, with the advent of Amazon's Kindle eReader and its KDP self-publishing service, Mark Coker's free Smashwords ebook distribution site, and the rebirth of self-publishing as a viable publishing model, authors have more choices than ever before as to how they are going to get their stories and information to the hungry reading public. Writers are now known as hybrid authors, with each book or series given individual consideration as to its best path to publishing success. Nearly all my current clients have self-publishing, assisted publishing and traditional publishing planks to their branding platform.

With Kristen as a guide, writers do not have to be afraid to dive in the deep end. She'll tell you where the submerged stumps and shopping carts are lurking. So quit listening to me rave about her wisdom and start reading some of it. Then subscribe to her blog. And if you haven't tried any of the social media services out there, no more excuses. Once you finish this book, you'll be inspired and informed. Go forth and prosper!

Laurie McLean
Partner, Foreword Literary, Inc.

Introduction

MY FIRST BOOKS, *We Are Not Alone: The Writer's Guide to Social Media* and *Are You There, Blog? It's Me Writer* helped countless writers understand and even embrace social media. Ah, but times have changed and the paradigm has altered so much that a new kind of book had to be written to equip you for your brilliant future. This book will begin by teaching you where you fit within the context of these global shifts. By learning to think universally you'll become far more adaptable and thus, more successful. This is not a book about "marketing" nor is it an easy formula to become a rich, successful author. WANA (which stands for We Are Not Alone) is a different way of thinking, a unique approach to the digital culture that now dominates the world. We are now a global community. Technology is embedded into all we do. The machines are rising, but that doesn't mean we must forfeit our humanity. In fact, it is our humanity that will transform technology from a curse into a gift.

We'll begin our journey understanding this new world and then I'll walk you through the WANA 2.0 plan to build an author platform and brand. WANA platforms are capable of withstanding any changes or major upheavals in technology, and your brands and platforms will grow as you grow. We won't address every social site because we don't need to. The beauty of the WANA Way is it works on ANY social site.

Give a writer a marketing gimmick and he'll sell a few books today. Give a writer the keys to connect to her digital community, and she'll sell books for life. I'm honored to have an opportunity to serve you and to help you make your writing journey magical and enjoyable. It's an amazing time to be a writer.

We are not alone.

Section 1
BRAVE NEW WORLD

Chapter 1

THE CHANGING PARADIGM

I NEVER WANTED TO BE a social media expert. In fact, even though I saw where the world was headed, I had to be dragged kicking and screaming to use email. I've always had a love-hate relationship with technology. On one hand, I'm somewhat of a techno-geek. I bought one of the first digital cameras because I was tired of buying and developing film to end up with only three decent pictures out of a roll of twenty-four. I also owned one of the first MP3 players, primarily because I had a giant (and expensive) collection of CDs, many of which had only *one good song*. I used to joke that my laptop was a $3,500 typewriter (this *was* 2001).

I loved the intimacy of the written word, the enduring feel of the traditional print paradigm. I saw what the future had in store, but I held onto the old as long as I could. Like a mother who grieves for her baby who too quickly became a man, I mourned the world I saw disappearing before my eyes even as I held tighter. I knew the future would be filled with the impersonal and the meaningless, and I felt like Cassandra, trying to ignore the future she knew was inevitable. I tell you this because, unlike many social media experts, I'm hardly a technophile. Granted, I've been known to be an early adopter, but usually my motives were driven by my fondness for taking pictures or collecting music or reading books, not for the sheer novelty of a new gadget. I'm a writer and artist first, and I feel this makes me a lot more like you than other "technology experts."

I didn't plan to be a social media expert, but then the world changed and I had no other choice. Why? Because the only thing I love more than the written word is writers, so guiding you into the new paradigm has become my own passion and imperative.

In this book, we'll explore social media holistically to properly equip you for the challenges ahead. You will understand more than *what* to do, you will grasp *why you are doing it*. I want you to understand where you fit in the great tapestry of human history. **Tactics with no context are doomed to fail.**

Mastery is borne of total immersion. No matter what anyone tells you, we can't take each facet of social media as separate, breaking these components apart into tidy variables that we can plug into fancy algorithms guaranteed to bring us success. To approach social media this way is a formula for quick frustration. We cannot mix X number of followers, add a dash of automation, and a splash of vlogging to create a powerful platform capable of driving sales. We cannot use algorithmic alchemy to spin links, ads, and spam into gold. **Authentic success is never found using shortcuts.**

Instead, we must learn the component parts and use our minds and our artistic spirits as looms that weave all threads together. When we approach social media piecemeal, we become vulnerable to change and lose the predictive powers that help us to quickly adapt. We become slaves to tools and forfeit our ability to hear the hum and pulse of the virtual world.

Total Immersion

When it comes to harnessing the power of social media, we can envision ourselves like the indigenous peoples of Oceania (the Pacific Islands of Micronesia, Melanesia, Polynesia, Australia, and the Malay Archipelago) whose experiences are detailed beautifully in Robert Greene's phenomenal book, *Mastery*. In an area that is 99.8 percent water, the inhabitants were able to navigate between the islands in search of supplies, food, and water with remarkable ease for thousands of years. What made these people all the more astounding was that they navigated the vast distances between the islands in Stone Age canoes and without the aid of modern tools like charts and compasses.

Most of the Micronesian people, due to interference from Western culture, lost this primal ability to navigate, but a small population in the Caroline Islands maintained the ancient practices well into the 20th century. The first Westerners who traveled with the Islanders at sea were simultaneously terrified and astonished.

The Islanders sailed in primitive crafts with none of the modern instruments most Westerners depended on. The outrigger canoes had only a single sail and a tiny crew of three or four men, one who served as chief navigator. The Islanders could voyage day or night and were at ease even in immense stretches of open sea. The Westerners knew that any slight deviation in course due to minor miscalculations, weather shifts, or storms could mean death. Distances between the islands were so great that supplies could run out, yet none of this seemed to faze the Islanders. The chief navigator would chat idly with the others, and every once in a while, glance at the sky. The crew would lie on their bellies then report back information. They might even cup handfuls of water and smell, or look to the patterns of birds flying overhead. The Islanders had an uncanny ability to predict exactly how many supplies would be needed for the voyage, and, when they arrived at their destination, it was with the nonchalance of a taxi parallel parking. Fascinated, some Westerners asked if they could apprentice and learn this baffling system of navigating from the native sailors.

Westerners learned that the Islanders relied heavily on following the paths of stars at night. "Over the course of centuries, they had devised a chart comprising the path of fourteen different constellations, along with the sun and the moon, described arcs in the sky that could translate into thirty-two different directions around the circle of the horizon. These arcs remained the same, no matter what the season" (Greene, *Mastery* 313). By using the stars, the Islanders always knew their precise location. During the day, they would watch how the sun cast shadows on the mast and could tell whether reflections in the clouds were from water or land. They also paid attention to wildlife. Were the birds flying out to sea to feed or returning home to roost?

Newly-inducted navigators were taken out to sea and made to float in the ocean for hours upon hours. In time, these apprentices learned to distinguish currents simply by *feel*. The more deeply immersed the navigators became, the more in tune they became with all their surroundings: the feel of the wind on their skin, changes in the phosphorescence of the water, and the subtle changes in water temperature that could be measured simply with a touch of seawater to their lips. What seemed meaningless phenomena merged into a singular experience that was far simpler, easier, and more accurate than most modern tools.

What I found particularly fascinating about these "primitive" navigators was that they didn't envision their crafts as *moving through a medium*. Rather, they envisioned themselves as stationary, and everything around was moving, a grand symphony of natural events that played the familiar music if one could be still enough to listen.

I believe social media is very similar. Like the constellations that never change, no matter what the season, there are certain fundamental human characteristics that never change and are immune to trends, fashions, and technology. Love, community, connection, imagination, passion, family, and a desire for meaning are common to all humans, no matter what culture or generation. When we use the pillars of our humanity for guidance, we're more at ease, much like the Micronesian sailors who knew the stars never changed. Rather than chasing the latest technology or marketing trend we can envision our author brand as stationary, a fixed point of reference in a sea of ones and zeros.

Social media can overwhelm and terrify the best of us. In response to this fear, many writers want to know the bare minimum social media attendance required to sell books. They want to rely on tools, automation and algorithms. When they fail to gain real value from social media they blame the medium. *Social media doesn't work.* What they can't see is that they've relied too much on technology and failed to dip their toes into a digital ocean propelled by human currents. When we submit to the primitive, lie on our bellies feeling the ebb and flow of humanity around us, we reconnect to the elemental. When we are connected, we are more sensitive to change and better equipped to meet needs and overcome any challenges. Our brand isn't churning through a medium of cyberspace, darting from MySpace, to Facebook, to Tumblr, to Twitter, to the latest and greatest shiny whatnot. Instead, our author brand should be a fixed point in an ever-moving, ever-changing sea.

A Brief History of Technology

We are naïve to believe that technology can exist in a vacuum. Technology will always have consequences—just ask Henry Ford or Dr. Oppenheimer. To gain, we lose. Technology alters our lives, our habits, our language, and even the very structure of our brains. Neil Postman depicts this clearly in his timeless book *Technopoly*:

"On one hand, there is the world of the printed word with its emphasis on logic, sequence, history, exposition, objectivity, detachment and discipline. On the other, there is the world of television with its emphasis on imagery, narrative, presentness, simultaneity, intimacy, immediate gratification, and quick emotional response. Children come to school having been deeply conditioned by the biases on television. There, they encounter the printed word. A sort of psychic battle takes place, and there are many casualties—children who can't read or won't, children who cannot organize their thought into a logical structure even in a simple paragraph, children who cannot attend lectures or oral explanations for more than a few minutes at a time. They are failures not because they are stupid. They are failures because there is a media war going on" (16-17). To this I would add that the Internet and current multi-media climate have made the situation even worse.

Technology changes everything. Humans, from the dawn of time, ordered their lives around the sun and the passing of seasons, but then came a clever device. "The clock" made its first appearance in the Benedictine monasteries of the twelfth century, and it was invented to provide regularity to the monk's routines so they could be sure to slot enough prayer time in between gardening and doing cool stuff like inventing beer. Bells would ring, signaling each canonical hour. These holy men, however, could not foresee how this helpful device would alter the very course of human civilization, for the clock afforded more than the ability to keep track of time. It granted the ability to control it.

"In short, without the clock, capitalism would have been quite impossible. The paradox, the surprise and wonder are that the clock was invented by men who wanted to devote themselves more rigorously to God; it ended as the technology of greatest use to men who wished to devote themselves to the accumulation of money. In the eternal struggle between God and Mammon, the clock quite unpredictably favored the latter" (Postman, *Technopoly* 15).

If we were to hop into a time machine and zoom back to the year 832 A.C.E., we would find a world with no concept of "time" as we understand it. People didn't order their days by hours, minutes, and seconds, thus our ancestors would have no lexicon, no cognitive space, to make them capable of understanding our modern world. This is what technology does. It changes our vocabulary, how we order space, what our interests are and even how we organize our institutions. As Postman stated, "Technological change is neither additive nor subtractive. It is *ecological*. One significant change generates total change" (18). The world before the clock was very different than the one we know now. Temporal space had not yet been sliced, diced and parceled out.

The clock is only one of many inventions that forever altered our world. Agriculture and the domestication of livestock changed us from wandering bands of nomads to tribes who settled down, built permanent structures, and even invented the Pet Rock. The alphabet took words from the gods and handed them to mortals. Magnets opened the world for exploration, because sailors navigated far more successfully using a compass. I think it's also safe to assume that men didn't stop and ask for directions back then, either.

Later, the printing press transformed human civilization from an oral culture to a typographical one. The printed word slammed the doors on centuries of established Papal power while simultaneously throwing open the gates to public education and scientific discovery. For the first time, knowledge could be easily preserved, shared, disseminated, disputed, dismantled or expounded. Social hierarchies that had endured over thousands of years fell away, for what need did we have for the scribe in a world endowed with moveable type? The written word even changed the very biological structure of the human brain, for as we transitioned from an oral society to a typographical one, we traded our prodigious memories for far greater abstract thinking. Communication, the structure of language and grammar influences how humans think about time and space and even what they value (Postman, *Amusing Ourselves to Death*). Fast-forward and the telegraph made way for radio, then television, and civilization was once more transformed. Even Johann Wolfgang von Goethe, who died almost two centuries ago, predicted a time when technology would connect the globe, and when people would have instant access to unlimited information. "He called this future *the velicopedic age*, one determined by speed. He was concerned that it could lead to a deadening of the human spirit" (Greene 356). Goethe's prescience is nothing short of astonishing.

By the mid-nineteenth century, humans experienced another communication revolution, "the sudden and massive intrusion of the photograph and other iconographs into the symbolic environment" (Postman, *Amusing Ourselves to Death* 84). The photograph was the perfect partner for the massive influx of telegraphic news-from-all-places and served to further drown humans in a sea of meaningless and context-free information.

In a world dominated by print, the rules of logic, order, and epistemology reigned supreme. In the visual world, images, emotion and instant gratification took over. We began to rely on information gatekeepers more and more.

We had to if we hoped to keep sane.

With every change in technology, humans changed, too. In the 1800s, lectures were a standard form of entertainment. It wasn't at all uncommon for audiences to sit and listen for as much a five hours without a break, yet people of the 20th century—the radio/television generations—could barely sit still for a three-minute commercial break, and they certainly couldn't pay attention unless the colors were bright and the content condensed. These days? Most of us have the attention span of a meth-addicted squirrel.

You might be wondering what this has to do with a book about social media. Aren't I supposed to give you a nice easy formula?

X tweets + Y blogs = Success!

I wish I could, but if I had that kind of formula I'd probably charge a lot more for this book. No, the reason I took you through this brief historical tour is that we must understand the context of change if we are to navigate, adapt and thrive. If you don't understand this new world, then you will be dependent on a technology guru to hand you all the answers every time the technology updates. **I want you to understand more than what you are doing, I want you to grasp *why you are doing it*.** I want you on your bellies, feeling the changes in your bones, knowing storms are coming before dark clouds clot the horizon. I want you to be able to find your way home every time. I want your author brands to be resilient, stationary fixtures in a world that changes by the hour.

One of my great frustrations with other social media methods is that many of them seem to treat Facebook, Twitter, LinkedIn, and all other social media as if these sites are merely an extension of the TV-Industrial complex of the 20th century. The assumption seems to be that because gimmicks, commercials, ads, free stuff, giveaways, "exposure," and non-stop repetition worked for TV and radio they will therefore work on Facebook. Only on social media it is better, because we can do all this FOR FREE! We can pitch to thousands or even millions of people twenty-four hours a day all over the world without spending a dime and success will soon be ours, or so they promise.

Nothing could be further from the truth.

Social media is an entirely new world, with new rules, new expectations, new audiences, and new realities, and this is a lot of what this book will explore. I've spent the past few years trying to get writers and traditional publishers to understand that after the explosion of social media we don't have the same old USA plus social media. We have a different America. In fact, we have a *different world altogether.* We now operate with few boundaries and we are all part of the very real global village.

It isn't as if we have the traditional print paradigm coexisting with the digital paradigm. We've already slipped over the event horizon. The digital paradigm has forever altered the course of print media, as well as all the institutions surrounding them. Magazines, newspapers, advertising, and books have all been altered forever (or endangered). The digital paradigm, coupled with social media, has dismantled the TV-Industrial complex and summarily ushered in something completely new. We are not a typographical society, nor are we a television society. *We are a multi-media society and we don't resemble anything that's ever existed before.*

When I talk to writers, some have the idea that there is a choice whether or not they will participate in social media. But whether we like it or not there is no longer a choice. This is why I described how technology makes the choices for us. The genie is out of the bottle and our world has irrevocably changed. We cannot order our lives by the sun in a world governed by the wristwatch and expect to succeed. For the first time in human history, we have generations being born into a world where paper is a novelty and even a nuisance.

This is a wonderful time to be a writer, but a challenging one as well.

Orwell Was Wrong

My father was a voracious science fiction reader, and I practically cut my teeth on L. Ron Hubbard, Phillip K. Dick, Carl Sagan, and Isaac Asimov. I was a kid when the year 1984 came and went. The nightmare future George Orwell predicted in his novel *1984* seemed to remain in the realm of science fiction. I wasn't yet old enough to appreciate the idea of a police state, ruled by a government that tightly controlled and manipulated every message, every symbol, every thought, every choice, and every decision, even though the Lamb family (four generations of Texans) had many a dinner-table debate about the loss of free will and the encroachment of Big Brother.

As time went on, the world around me changed. At first the changes were slow and peculiar. My university required me to have a student email account. I somehow managed five years at a university without ever learning how to check my email and rarely using a computer. Then, the changes came faster and faster.

The Internet arrived on the scene with full force, bringing with it websites and online shopping. Then came Friendster, AOL, chat rooms, digital music, cell phones, online dating, YouTube, texting and unlimited data plans. Before long, it was clear that Orwell was very wrong. We weren't headed for domination by Big Brother. Rather, the Internet had diverted us to a Brave New World. Orwell's future might have come to pass for some countries but, in the Western world at least, Huxley seemed to predict our future with terrifying accuracy. Orwell feared a world that would ban books and deprive us of information, but Huxley feared a world where truth would become irrelevant, concealed behind the shiny, flashy allure of short-term gratification and consumer demands. We'd become a world so preoccupied by the orgy-porgy Feelies of the Centrifugal Bumblepuppy that we'd miss the meaningful. Pillars of Truth would be buried beneath Mountains of Trivial. "In short, Orwell feared that what we hate would ruin us. Huxley feared that what we love would ruin us" (Postman, *Amusing Ourselves to Death* 21).

This dystopian prediction isn't to scare you away from social media. Technology can't help but fundamentally change our society. It isn't a physical change. It's like a chemical change that can't be reversed, a cake that can never be un-baked. For most of human history, we didn't have enough information to solve our most basic problems. After the invention of the printing press, we experienced a very new kind of problem—too much information.

Telegraph, radio, movies and television only exacerbated this problem. Within less than a century, we were thirsting for knowledge, while drowning in a sea of information. Today in the 21st century, we have a new challenge. We have to find a way to make sense of our world, because we no longer have gatekeepers to do it for us.

The dark side of social media is that we are bombarded with millions of messages a day. Facebook, as I write this, has recently passed a billion active users. According to a recent article in *Tech Crunch*, "Facebook's system processes 2.5 billion pieces of content and 500+ terabytes of data every day. It's pulling 2.7 billion *"Like"* actions and 300 million photos per day, and it scans roughly 105 terabytes of data each half hour" (Constine). Twitter, which is estimated to only be roughly an eighth the size of Facebook, is on track to have more than 250 million active users by the end of this year (Bennett). According to comScore, there were over 200 billion online videos viewed globally in October of 2011 (Radwanick). These last statistics are over a *year and a half old* as I type this. Who knows how much larger those numbers are now?

Hundreds of millions of people engage in online gaming every day. HALO, Gears of War, World of Warcraft, Medal of Honor, The Sims, and on and on. Every time our attention wanes for one game, a newer, shinier Centrifugal Bumblepuppy appears to fill the vacuum. Many people spend more time in the digital world than in the real one, and Internet addiction is a growing problem. You might have heard the story of the Korean couple so addicted to virtual life that they neglected their real one, with fatal consequences. The couple became so engrossed in a video game taking care of a virtual baby that their real life newborn baby starved to death (CNN, 5 Mar. 2010).

This new virtual world is as fraught with dangers as the real one we're trying to escape. Online bullying is an escalating problem. Sexual predators comb the cyber-world like digital Big Bad Wolves disguised as Grandma, literally. Employers use our social circles to invade our privacy, and most of us accept that what happens in Vegas stays on YouTube. In a pre-digital world, advertising was a sound investment that could be controlled, tracked and manipulated. These days? Advertising alone is a placebo. In a world of people who've learned to un-see and ignore, advertising and marketing do little more than "make us feel" as if we are doing something meaningful.

I don't mean this to discourage you, as much as to acknowledge the reservations you might have about joining the madness. It does feel like we're losing ourselves, but the answer is not to pull back and divorce ourselves from technology. That's about as realistic an option as trading in our cars for horse-drawn carriages. What is realistic, however, is changing the way we engage the digital world. Our innocence might be gone, but our ability to choose our future remains. *Technology is the tool, not the craftsman.*

Many social media people I've encountered are technophiles, and only see the bright side of technology, yet there is this dark side that we must understand and guard against if we hope to enjoy the good. Yes, the clock forever changed society, and while most of us groan at having to "clock in" and "clock out" of a workplace, we probably wouldn't trade the spreadsheet in the cubicle for the scythe in the fields and the very real fear of starving to death over the winter. Yes, Facebook can suck people into a mindless world removed from others, but soap operas and sports channels have been doing that for decades. While computer technology is the largest cause of the information glut, it also happens to be the only cure.

The Problem We Face

I've been working with writers for over a decade. When I first came on the scene, self-publishing wasn't a viable option. In fact, many viewed it as the last ditch effort of the talentless hack. To say there was a stigma attached is an understatement.

Early on, I was skeptical of self-publishing because I knew it meant opening a door we could never shut. We were already living in a world that overwhelmed us with choices, but we at least had gatekeepers to stem the flow. To say one was a *published author* meant that a writer had passed an outside test of validation, had reached some benchmark for quality. I was aware that once self-publishing became affordable, easy and accessible, the world would be drowning in books. Discoverability would be a nightmare for all writers.

To quote the Pixar movie *The Incredibles*, "When everyone is special, then no one is."

Yet, I can't turn back the clock and neither can you. We can rail against the universe and shout to the heavens that we don't want self-publishing and it will remain. The technology is here. Same with social media. We can complain about Facebook until we're hoarse and it won't change reality. The only things we can control are our attitude, our approach, and our destiny. This is what WANA is about. The machines are here, but we humans were here first.

Chapter 2

THE RISE OF THE MACHINES:
Human Authors in a Digital World

HERE WE ARE—the future is now. The machines have taken over. Everything is computerized. People no longer talk, they text. What number do we have to press to get a flesh and blood HUMAN? It's easy to feel like we're losing our humanity when surrounded by computers, cell phones, and text messaging, but I'm here to bring you the good news. The same machines that seem to be stealing our humanity also have the power to restore it. Yes, you read correctly. The more we embrace technology, the more distinctly human we can become.

We're in control of the tool, not the other way around. The same Internet used by identity thieves, hackers, and pedophiles is the same Internet that allows members of law enforcement to locate dangerous criminals and lock them away. The tool itself has no intent. It is a thing. Humans, however, are not things. We have a higher consciousness and free will. Humans, unlike machines, are in a unique position to choose the future we desire.

The new author is a cyborg of sorts—part human, part machine. The machine part allows us to compose series of words, copy them, email them, and then send them across the globe with a push of a button. We can research faster and more accurately than ever before. We can communicate with people all over the planet real-time and virtually for free. The new power technology has given writers has made us, in effect, superhuman.

The Industrial Revolution was birthed by a society totally reliant on physical labor. Once humans created machines to do all the heavy lifting, we finally had time left to focus on the mind. If the Industrial Revolution was about brawn, then the Post-Industrial Revolution is all about brains. I believe that as we move deeper into the Digital Age, we are wise to open our minds and let go of the old ways of thinking. The new paradigm of publishing, coupled with the social media lessons I teach in this book forges a powerful alliance—the perfect merging of mind, soul, and silicon. But the WANA Way has a price. You must let go of the old ways of thinking, your old definitions of brand, and any rigid ideas of what a "platform" is.

Once we learn to bend and move, then we're in a position to use change to power forward momentum. Instead of standing paralyzed in the face of change, we can harness it for the lift necessary to navigate cyberspace with ease. If we walk into the new paradigm with old ways of thinking, we're obsolete before we begin.

Branding has broken free of marketing's shackles and merged with personal identity. If we want to thrive in our new environment, we need to adapt, to apply technology as an extension of our humanness. This is not a book to teach you 1,000 ways to blast people with advertising. The WANA Way is different than anything you've likely encountered. It is constructed using the timelessness of art, blended with the strength of human relationships. Technology is merely the force amplifier. In the old way of thinking, an author's platform was rugged, sturdy, built to endure because it was birthed from a disconnected world. Today, our virtual structures must take inspiration from nature, because the world we live in is shifting at an ever-accelerating pace.

All writers in this age must have platforms, but being boring has a steep price. Platform is more than a zillion ways to try to part readers from money; it is a living work of art that is meshed with the soul of the writer-artist. If we can think of a brand and platform as a living organism connected to its environment, the advantages become clear. A rigid structure of metal and concrete can't adapt when conditions change, and neither can a heartless brand with algorithms where a soul should reside. We are in a time of exponential change. The comet has struck and the climate is like nothing we've yet experienced. The Big Publishing dinosaurs are suffering. As sunlight dwindles and food is scarce, they can no longer sustain their bulk. The small, lithe creatures that can quickly adapt and seize opportunity are the ones that will thrive in this chaos.

Before we start talking about social media and technology, we need to first take a look at how history has transformed the publishing paradigm for better and for worse. These days, *everyone* can be published and that is a double-edged sword. To understand how to build your time-proof platform, though, I want you to understand both worlds the traditional and the indie. This is *your time* and *your future* so the path you choose has to be right for you.

Chapter 3

BRAVE NEW PUBLISHING

IT'S AN AMAZING TIME to be a writer. Though I've worked hard to remain neutral when it comes to what avenue of publishing is best, the paradigm has shifted to the point that you, the writer, should know the truth of what you're getting into. There are many roads that lead to Rome (aka being published), but not all roads are created equally. Each path has unique advantages and challenges, and which publishing road we choose can be one of the biggest decisions we'll ever make.

Writers have a lot more power and a lot more choices than ever before. In fact, there are only two reasons for failure in this new world—giving up or completely lacking talent. In the old publishing model, we could chalk up our failure to "agents who had no real taste" or "publishers who only wanted to print commercial drivel." We could hold onto one manuscript and edit it for years and years, convincing ourselves that our book was the next Great American Novel if only we could get our shot. In this new publishing model, we have our shot. If we use social media effectively, we also have the platform. If our books don't sell, then the blame is on us.

Let Go of the Myth

Back in the 90s, when I first dreamed of becoming a writer, I had a romantic image in my mind that looked a little like this: Me, wearing a white, flowing designer outfit and creating. I'm sitting on the veranda of my mansion by the sea typing out my latest *New York Times* best-selling novel as my long, blonde hair, wavy from the ocean's humidity, flows in the breeze. My butler only interrupts to bring me coffee or a message from my agent. When I'm not writing I travel the world, from one exotic location to the next, searching for fresh inspiration. I am an artist, and the art is paramount.

Never in this fantasy did I see myself sitting alone at a table in a bookstore while customers tried to get past me without ever making eye contact. In my vision, I never staggered in from a cross-country flight delayed ten hours for a mechanical problem. My fantasy never involved sending out newsletters, writing blogs, doing blog tours, or hoping I didn't hate my new book cover. Not once did my vision involve a two-star review by a reader who found three typos in 70,000 words or felt the publisher over-charged for my ebook.

I always hear writers wail silly things like, "I just want to cre-ate," "I just want to write books." Don't we all?

There is No Publishing Sugar Daddy

If you *just* want to write books, then forget about publishing them. The second we decide to publish is the second that this writing thing becomes a business. Chefs would love to just create new dishes, singers would love to just sing, painters would love to just paint, and actors would love to just act, but that is not re-ality for the creative professional. There is no career path where we just do our art and others tell us what to do and when to do it. We have to be brave, and we must take risks.

If you want to actually publish your books, then expect a lot of hard work that has absolutely nothing to do with writing books. You will need to collect and organize receipts for tax pur-poses. You will likely need to research, edit, travel, teach, speak, create newsletters, blog, and do social media to cultivate a thriving fan base. Odds are you will have to hire and fire people, work with a website designer or learn to do it yourself, and you will work long hours for no pay for a long time before you see any payoff. Sounds awesome, right? Are you ready to jump in?

Ah, but here is where the choice gets tougher.

Which Publishing Option is the Best?

In my opinion, big traditional publishing is a terrible option for new writers. Please understand that I am saying this as carefully as I can because I do respect the New York publishing houses and what they do, but in my opinion their current business model will eventually kill them off, and we might not even be asking ourselves this question in five years. They're large, with massive overhead and payroll, and this makes them less likely to take risks. With their bulk and size, they can't change rapidly as the climate shifts, so, **unless something radically changes**, they're doomed to always be behind. Big publishing is modernizing, but there are a couple of problems.

Problem #1

First, the two recent mergers (Random-Penguin) tell me they didn't update their operations fast enough. Recently, I noticed that Amazon's home page was filled with books priced at around $6.99, when eighteen months ago (2011), that same home page was stocked with books priced at $1.99 and below.

Why is this important?

The higher price on books tells me that Amazon (at least as of November 2012) no longer considered traditional publishing a viable threat. Additionally, back as early as 2009, I recommended that the Big Six learn from some of the successful indies and embrace a hybrid-publishing model by creating imprints specifically for e-publishing. Ebooks—with the introduction of the iPad, Nook, and Kindle—were exploding in popularity and the e-format was an excellent way of vetting untested authors with minimal risk.

In a true hybrid-publishing model, big houses could gamble on good books by new authors. I have many agent friends who found books they loved, but couldn't sell. The risk was too high and New York was uncertain people would buy. Okay, fair enough, *but it was still a good book.* In a hybrid model, the author's agent could at least score her writer an ebook deal, betting that the author would generate enough sales (demand) to open the door for a paper deal at a later point in time. Everyone wins.

New authors with good books and a solid work ethic could be given a chance at the gold ring. Publishers could mitigate risk because an ebook is far less expensive to produce than a paper book (no printing, paper, shipping, shelf space, etc.). This would also mean that traditional publishers could take on Amazon in regards to pricing and gain lost traction in the ebook marketplace. Since a hybrid model would have been true publishing (meaning an agent/editor vetted the work first), this would have maintained brand confidence for the major houses. Brand confidence would have been a major advantage because these imprints could offer consumers a promise of *quality.*

If the ebook didn't happen to be a runaway success? No big deal. But if it was? Happy dance for all—author, agent, publishers all win. Stonehouse Ink uses this model and they are making a killing. Authors and the publisher all sing Kumbaya around the glow of healthy sales numbers.

I *did not in any way* recommend what Big Publishing actually did.

Problem #2

New York is modernizing, but how they've been "modernizing" is cause for great concern. Finally, in 2012, one of the major houses realized self-publishing was profitable and that some authors might even be diamonds in the rough. This publisher decided to partner with an established vanity press with a notorious reputation for defrauding authors. This new traditional-vanity hybrid now offers a series of packages that range from $2,500 to almost $26,000. No vetting. You pay, you play. This *isn't a hybrid model* (which is what I proposed and what smaller indies have already done). It is *vanity press*.

Other traditional houses have launched digital-only imprints to give the impression that they are forging ahead and helping authors by offering sweet 50/50 ebook publishing deals, but their boilerplate contracts, threaded with Hollywood accounting, were nothing short of raw predation. **This wasn't publishing. It was indentured servitude.** Had it not been for sites like *Writer Beware* and author bloggers like John Scalzi, these imprints (which I will not name) would have gotten away with highway robbery. Yet, here's the deal. The publisher only reworked their parasitic contracts *because they got caught*.

Please keep this in mind.

Yes, the Internet is overwhelming, but without active blogging watchdogs, new authors everywhere could have been filleted. The Internet can also steer you to traditional publishers with reputations for being good to their authors. Part of our responsibility as authors is to pay attention and read before we sign. If you don't understand, don't sign. Get an agent. Hire an attorney. Don't be so desperate that common sense gets tossed out the window.

Before you think I'm being a big fat sour-grapes meanie who is just out to bash traditional publishing, I want to make this clear. I love authors more than publishers. My loyalty is to you guys, first. They don't call me the WANA Mama for nothing, and I am like a ticked off mother bear when anyone tries to mess with my kiddos. If a traditional publisher is interested in an *equitable partnership* that is fair to the author and in her best interests? Yay! 1000% support from me. Not every traditional publisher is out to get us. There are great traditional publishers that treat their authors professionally and that do what publishers should do. Some are modernizing in ways *favorable* to all parties. This is why it is critical for us to research and again it's why we need a good agent or a good publishing attorney.

I've worked my tail off trying to offer solutions for traditional publishers to remain a viable force in the marketplace. I'm here to help all kind of authors, no matter which path you choose to take and I really do hope my predictions about traditional publishing don't come true. I love gatekeepers, and I know that many writers simply aren't well suited for the life of an indie. I want all writers to have the home that fits them best. Also, to be fair, **there are indie houses out there that are just as predatory**. Amazon is no angel either, but the best way to keep Amazon playing nice is for New York to reinvent and offer viable competition. It's why I still root for traditional publishing to succeed. Last I checked? Monopolies were bad juju for everyone but the owner of the monopoly. Traditional publishing brings balance to The Force. Other businesses have astonished the world by pulling out of a death-spiral last minute, so it ain't over 'til it's over. I have been impressed with some smaller houses like *Entangled*, so maybe the old dogs can learn new tricks. Apple nearly died and now it's a force to be reckoned with, so I never lose hope that New York can make a turnaround, and do so in a way that treats their writers in a way that is professional and respectful.

Our contracts shouldn't come with a Rufie. Basic expectations here.

This said, we're going to go over some of the fundamentals so that whatever decision you make is an educated one. In the end, all writers *who want to sell books* need a social media platform. Period. Whether you self-publish, go indie, or still take a traditional road, it doesn't matter. There are too many choices out there and writers are drowning in a sea of competition. A platform is your lifeline. Why you need to be educated about your publishing options is so you can customize you social media platform. I don't offer One Size Fits All, and your publishing path directly affects your platform.

Sparks Notes for Traditional Publishing

Big publishing has long subsisted on what is called *the consignment model*, which is a system that is grossly inefficient and entirely unnecessary in the Digital Age. This model has never been ideal; there were no other alternatives.

Until now.

But, for those of you who are new to the ways of how the consignment model works, this will be a valuable lesson, and hopefully it will help you make an informed decision when it comes to choosing a publishing path. All of us would love Random House printed on the inside cover of our books, but the question is, "Is the designer label worth the cost?" That is a question only you can answer, and a decision only you will live with. I am merely a guide here to help you.

Bookstores and Publishers

Most of us, before we become writers, drift through publishing as spectators. We don't see the man behind the curtain, and have no idea of the inner workings that create the beautiful displays of books we see at the Barnes & Noble in our local mall. This section is your indoctrination into the professional world of being a traditional author.

Bookstores and retailers never *buy* books from a publisher. They never did. Bookstores and retailers are part of a consignment model that was created over a century ago to minimize risk and thus encourage retailers to carry books. Bookstores could order books they thought customers would like, but if the customer didn't buy, the retailer could ship the books back to the publishers at no cost to them. Sweet deal if you're a retailer, though it kinda sucks if you happen to be the publisher (or the writer). This is why publishing relied heavily on agents to find the talent and editors to cultivate that talent. This was to minimize risk.

Here's a brief summary of how the consignment model works. A writer writes the books, then queries, then probably gets a stack of rejection letters and then wonders why she didn't become a dental hygienist like her mother recommended. After some tough revisions, the writer continues to query and, ideally, finds an agent who believes this writer's work has merit. An agent sells an editor on either a completed novel or an outline/proposal for a book. When the publisher decides to take on a book, that book is then produced, however many steps that might take. For a novel it might be a series of edits, rewrites, more edits, then cover design, interior design, and printing. For a non-fiction, it might involve holding the hand of a writer from an outline and proposal until the work is complete.

Before that book is released, salespeople go out to retailers and negotiate placement for the book. Whenever you go into a bookstore, make no mistake. Those books stacked neatly on the front table? An agent, and the publisher's sales team negotiated that book to be there, which is awesome if one of those books is your book, right? Don't get too excited. Those front tables and displays can only accommodate a small fraction of the books published each year, and those spots are generally VIP only.

The hard reality is that prime retail real estate—front displays at bookstores, airport bookstores, checkout aisles of drug stores—is most frequently occupied by the *New York Times* or *USA Today* best-selling authors. These prime spots are for the authors who are household names, *whose name alone* can sell hundreds of thousands or millions of books. Why? Well, because, as you will soon see, the consignment model is so bloated and full of needless waste, that publishers only make money off their big brand name authors. Publishers *need* the mega authors to sell a lot of books to keep afloat so that they can pay the rent and bring in new authors.

New authors? What about you?

First of all, new authors will likely not make it into the retail establishments that sell the most books. Costco, Wal Mart, the front tables at Barnes and Noble, and airport bookstores are pretty much beyond our pay grade. When a new author does make it into a bookstore, then likely she can expect to be spine-out on a shelf and only for a short window of time. Hopefully the author's name falls on a fortuitous letter that places her book at least at the potential reader's eye level, because Browsing Roulette is the best this author can hope for. This seems so unfair! Yet, it really isn't when we look at how the consignment model works.

Retailers only make profit off the books that sell. Not rocket science, right? Ah, but this is the largest reason why the mega authors are the most predominantly carried and displayed. J.K. Rowling, Stephen King, Dean Koontz, Lee Child and Janet Evanovich have massive followings and will sell a lot of books. They will sell far more books than Jane Newbie's first novel. Jane Newbie doesn't have Tom Cruise playing her lead character in a blockbuster movie. It isn't personal. It's business.

Once the clock runs out, the retailer gathers up any unsold inventory, and then rips off the covers. They box the unsold books and ship them back to the warehouse at the publisher's expense. The books are then pulped and turned into other paper products like toilet paper.

Tragically poetic if you think about it.

Make no mistake, for generations this model worked well enough. It had to work. There was no other way of doing business. Farmers used horses pulling plows for thousands of years because they had to. But, in a world where most other farmers are using giant tractors? Probably a good idea to trade in the horses for a John Deere.

Publishing and the Author

Publishing, from the author's side, generally worked like this. The only way to ever get published and have a career as a writer was to write and then write more and write even more and then query until you finally landed an agent who liked your book and felt it was something he could sell to a publisher. With a lot of hard work, praying and tears, your agent sold the book to an editor and then negotiated rights and print run (how many copies the publisher plans to print). A writer can tell almost immediately how much faith a publisher has in her work by looking at the print run. A low print run generally means the publisher isn't very confident that a lot of copies will sell. Ironically, publishers mitigate risk on new authors by having a low print run, but low print runs actually increase the odds the new author will fail. Super high print runs mean the book will have better placement in more stores, thus giving potential readers the sense that this book is a really big deal, and thus a good buy. In fact, I believe one of the methods traditional publishers employ to promote the next generation of best-selling authors is to order a higher print run in hopes the massive exposure will help the author "break out." The publisher is gambling that the higher the print run, the more times consumers are likely to be exposed to the book, and thus the greater the odds of hitting the tipping point for success. High print runs are a calculated risk to help improve the chances an author and her career will flourish. Conversely, the lower the print run, the higher the odds *against* an author breaking out and the higher the probability the writer will fail. Thus, the conundrum soon becomes clear.

The Ugly Truth about Advances and Multi-Book Deals

Some of you might be like I was at the beginning of my career. I dreamed of the three-book deal and the million-dollar advance. That is, until I learned the ugly truth about advances. First of all, in recent years, due to the gross waste that is part and parcel in the consignment model, most advances have dried up, shrunk, or all but disappeared. Beginning novelists almost never get advances, and the handful of non-fiction authors who manage to get an advance can't expect big bucks (those are pretty much reserved for celebrities). Not that this matters all that much, because most writers who are paid an advance never earn out that advance.

What does that mean?

Say a publisher wants my next technology book and they are willing to give me a $25,000 advance. Yay for me, right? Eh, don't get too excited. Remember the consignment model we talked about? The bad part about this model is a lot of people need to be paid before we ever bother paying the writer. The publisher, the agent, the cover designers, the line editor, the copy editor, the binder, the printer, the salespeople, the marketing department, and then there are the costs of warehousing, shipping, gas, the butcher, the baker, and the candlestick maker. A lot of people with their hands in the book pie.

On a $10.00 book, a traditionally published author only makes roughly $1.27, and this is *before* an agent gets his or her 15%, which amounts to a whopping .19, making the author's portion $1.08 before state and federal taxes, which will take at least a third of that, leaving the writer .72 a book. This also means that I the author must sell 23,149 copies *before I ever make a cent above my initial advance.*

The sad reality is that writers are paid so little per copy that the odds are against them from day one. They fail to sell out their print runs and they fail to earn out their advances. Thus, most writers never see a second book in print because this system is tooled to produce "failures." Retailers then rip the covers off the books and ship them back where the books are then pulped and turned into posters of Justin Bieber. Great you had a three-book deal but, due to a flawed system, you now have to negotiate the rights back to the other two books. The publisher doesn't want to publish them because, well, you're a failure, but they still own the other two books and now you're trapped. Not saying *all* publishers act this way, but I've heard way too many horror stories like these for this behavior to be an anomaly.

Case in point, Dorchester Publishing started running into money troubles in 2010 after a steep drop in demand for their mass-market paperbacks. They made an ill-fated decision and switched to digital and print-on-demand in hopes of regaining market traction they lost with the demise of the mass-market paperback. As the company continued to bleed out, authors were not being paid. Some authors were owed anywhere from $10,000 to $50,000 in royalties and many hadn't seen a check in over a year. Think this is bad? Wait. Not only did Dorchester fail to pay its authors, the writers then had to hire attorneys to get the rights back to their books. Some authors had multi-book deals and they couldn't go forward so long as Dorchester (who wasn't paying them) held the rights. This was further complicated because clauses in the contracts stipulated an automatic reversion of the rights *if the publisher claimed bankruptcy*, which it didn't. According to literary agent Chris Fortunado who spoke to *Publisher's Weekly*, "As far as my author is concerned, they (Dorchester) are not communicating with him or paying royalties…The owners of Dorchester are not even fulfilling their obligations to foreign publishers by providing PDFs of manuscripts for which the rights have been sold. They are not fulfilling any of the normal functions of a publisher, yet they continue to pocket receipts for ebooks and foreign royalties" (Deahl). This was certainly a case where the dream of landing a multi-book deal turned into a nightmare for many writers. Amazon finally bought the rights to a thousand of Dorchester's titles, but this story elucidates how the three-book deal is certainly no magic bullet. Amazon might be a great publisher, but the authors of those thousand titles sold on the auction block had no choice in the matter. Either the books went to Amazon or the authors would never be paid. And what about those authors who weren't among the thousand chosen? What about them? Do you see how the three-book deal can quickly become a three-book noose?

I'm trying to be as objective as I possibly can in this section, but the reasons writers once had for choosing the traditional route are getting thinner by the day. Traditional publishing continues to embrace an antiquated, bloated system that pays writers last and the least, and this was all well and good when writers had no power and no other alternative. For example, the Pony Express was awesome in 1860, but who could realistically conduct business using the Pony Express today, when the competition is using email and FedEx? Traditional publishing has clung to print and the consignment model because 1) it's all they've ever known and 2) change is scary. Change means that people lose jobs or change jobs. Change means that not everyone is as relevant as they are accustomed to being. It isn't that I don't have compassion for New York. It must be hard to realize that change will cost people jobs, people you *know*. Yet, economics doesn't generally have as much compassion as I do. *Fail to plan and plan to fail.*

Seeing a gap in the market, indie publishers stepped in and reduced waste and improved speed and production. Technology allowed the entrepreneur to crack the iron curtain of the publishing monopoly. New York no longer holds the only keys to distribution. In the traditional model it takes months, even *years*, to get a book to market. In a world that expects instant gratification, there is no way to remain competitive with this model, especially since there are a lot of talented writers capable of writing to demand. **For the first time, we are seeing fiction authors make six and seven figures without New York's involvement.**

In the Digital Age, ebooks and online sales are starting to equal and even outpace paper sales. Bookstores are closing and Barnes & Noble is hanging on by a thread and scrambling to reinvent itself. According to a *Wall Street Journal* article, "Nook revenue plunged 26% to $316 million for the fiscal first third quarter ended January 26. The Nook segment, which includes e-readers, tablets and ebooks, posted a loss of $190 million, measured before interest, taxes, depreciation and amortization, compared with a loss on the same basis of $83 million a year earlier. Why is the Nook suffering? Because Apple's iPad mini resonated better with consumers. Additionally, revenue at Barnes & Noble stores fell 10.3% to $1.5 billion, in stores open at least a year" (Trachtenburg). Retailers like Amazon are devouring the market, and one core reason is they saw the potential in the self-pub and indie market early and made sure they were digitally entrenched so they could capitalize on this explosive new market when it finally took off.

Unlike Amazon, traditional publishers have a lot of overhead. The book price needs to cover all those people who expect to be paid, and all that high-priced Manhattan rent. Paper books need to be shipped, and so the skyrocketing cost of gasoline has to be factored into the price. In the traditional model, many *New York Times* best-selling authors make so little, they *still* can't afford to quit their day jobs. Every day there are fewer and fewer reasons any writer should desire to take the traditional route to publication. Still think I'm being mean? Okay. Time for a little myth busting.

Myth #1—If I traditionally publish, then I can just write while my agent does the business stuff and the publisher markets my books. Then, all I'll have to do is write books.
Yeah, um...NO. Again, there are no Publishing Sugar Daddies. Or unicorns. I was bummed, too. Whether a writer traditionally publishes, self-publishes or goes with an indie publisher, the onus for marketing, PR, and business is on the author. Most traditional publishers expect writers to have an existing social media platform. These days, when a writer queries an agent, most agents will google the writer's name to see if the writer has a decent on-

line platform and a cohesive and marketable brand. This is part of how an agent will sell the book to a publisher. Once published, the publisher expects the writer to do exhausting and practically useless blog tours, send out newsletters, run contests, and have zillions of meaningless Facebook "Likes" on the author fan page and Twitter followers...all while writing more books. A handful of the mega authors don't have to do this stuff because they're tenured and also from another paradigm. For those of you who are new and considering traditional publishing because you don't want to blog or tweet? Guess again. Publishers not only will expect you to be actively engaged on social media, but they will also want a say in how you do it, even if it means chasing valueless numbers. I've assisted *New York Times* best-selling authors who practically needed Xanax because the publisher was concerned that *this author didn't have as many Facebook "Likes" as Such-and-Such-Author.* Thus, not only do traditionally published authors still have to do social media, often their social media is micro-managed and directed down ineffective paths that might look great on paper, but do nothing in the long-term for the author unless you count wrinkles and gray hair.

Indie authors have to do a lot of social media too, but we earn more than $1.08 per book.

Writers are entrepreneurs no matter which path we take. This idea that we can sit in a room and never worry our pretty little heads about business and marketing is a myth. If your only reason for going traditional is that you want to be able to focus on writing books, you've been warned. The workload is virtually the same.

Myth #2—Traditional publishing produces better quality books.

One of the main arguments I get from those in favor of the traditional paradigm is that the quality of the book is somehow so much more superior. For a while this was true, but as more traditionally vetted authors are leaving traditional publishing, that's changing. I remember when I met *New York Times* Best-Selling Author Bob Mayer. At the time, he was at a hard crossroad in his career. He had roughly forty titles under his belt, many of them best-sellers. Yet when I met him he was seriously considering giving up on a career as an author. Stunned, I asked him why. This was only my second writing conference and I dreamed of being a successful author and Bob was walking away from his dream. Okay, MY dream. How could this be?

I was shocked when Bob replied, "Authors can't make decent money. There's no money in writing fiction." Fast-forward a few years. Bob is now happily making a better income than he ever did in the traditional model, and he has total control over his career. Other authors who've been traditionally vetted are also going indie. Authors like Bob Mayer, Joe Konrath, CJ Lyons and Barry Eisler helped take the stigma away from self-publishing. They also exposed the pointless waste of the traditional system and how this waste was adversely affecting the earning abilities of authors. As more respected writers have become bold enough defect from the traditional model and self-publish, others who offer services have stepped in to improve the quality of the product. As little as a year ago, I could look at a book and tell if it was self-published. These days? There are some self-published books that look *better* than what traditional publishing is producing. Cover designers, book designers, printers, formatters have all seen a market open up and have jumped in and upped the game. When I was at *Thrillerfest* in the summer of 2012, the self-published books were some of the best looking books on the table.

A lot of writers believe that handing their "baby" to a traditional publisher is a formula for a far better product, yet I've met many romance authors who couldn't even expect the *ethnicity* of the hero on the cover would match the hero in the book. They couldn't expect the heroine to have the correct hair color. The author's love story could be set in Scotland and yet the book cover might have pyramids *and there was nothing the writer could say about it.* Having race, setting, and *hair color* reflect the author's story seems like a pretty basic expectation to me. Creative control is one of many reasons that indie is appealing to a lot of authors.

Myth #3—Traditional authors do better because of the gatekeeper seal of approval.

Writers who are traditionally published have the validation of being backed by a publishing house. True. But this doesn't hold near the weight it used to. We've already discussed how writers who are willing to do some homework and hire the right people can produce a product that looks as good if not better than books from the major houses. Ah, but the reader of the Digital Age is more prone to search for books on a computer or other digital device, an iPad, Nook, Kindle, etc. Potential readers browsing Amazon don't know a Random-Penguin from an indie book unless the indie cuts corners and the cover screams *Hey, I hired my nephew who used a pirated copy of Photoshop.* Good books are good books, and most consumers look to the price and the free sample pages to help them choose.

Again, remember that much of the emerging market is in ebooks. In the Digital Age, traditional publishing has been consistently behind when it comes to even basic formatting. Many of the indies knew they could never compete in a bookstore, so they took the fight where they could win.

The ebook.

New York, still scope-locked on print, failed to put as much effort into being innovative with ebooks. To this day, I buy traditionally published books and find sloppy formatting with spacing and pagination that doesn't make sense, yet the indies? Not only are many of them superior in their formatting skills—smooth, even, no errors, and have the look of the inside of a print book—but many indies are also taking advantage of hyperlinks, multi-media (video, sound, visual effects), and QR codes. They're also creating apps to pair with the books (or hiring people who can). I recently saw a children's book for the iPad. When the reader reached the page with a bear looking up to the night sky, crickets began to chirp (the sounds were embedded in the formatting). Little kids are growing up reading books on iPads and Kindles. They are accustomed to multimedia, yet traditional publishing still clings to paper books and is failing to keep pace with innovation. As schools start issuing iPads instead of textbooks and kids grow up on laptops and smart phones, we will see the gradual extinction of the traditional reader. Remember, when I mentioned how we transformed from an oral society to a typographical one? The bard is as irrelevant in the Gutenberg World as the print model is in the Digital Age. We have eaten of the Apple and it opened our eyes. We can never go back.

This means that New York waited too long to change their business model and, as a consequence, they've hemorrhaged talent that Amazon was only more than happy to offer a book home and a higher royalty rate. See, writers are bad at math, but we aren't *that bad*. Instead of traditional publishing getting into the digital game early and dominating the field, they continued to embrace the outmoded notion that, readers will always want paper. While they were doing this, new hungry indies came along and did what entrepreneurs are really good at doing. They took a scalpel and removed fat, bloated inefficiency, improved the publishing process for the writer and enhanced the reading experience for the reader. They also realized that content producers (code for "writers") were the beating heart of profit. Apparently science has proven that well-paid writers are happy and productive writers.

Myth #4—Traditional publishing is looking out for an author's long-term career.
Writers need time to mature, to grow an audience. Writers are

like fine wine. I said wine, not *whine*. In the olden days, publishers were better at leaving an author's backlist on the shelves for readers to discover. Remember this is back before the days of the megastore and discount outlets. Bookstores like *B. Dalton* and *Waldenbooks* were common in shopping centers and malls and, in a slower-paced society not addicted to checking its Facebook status every thirty seconds, people took time to browse bookstores and discover a new favorite author. Authors could make decent royalties because they weren't merely making money off the book they'd most recently released; these authors were also making money off their backlists, which often were their bread and butter and allowed them to make a respectable living.

Most of us have seen the movie *You've Got Mail* and saw the mega-bookstore beating out the poor little independent in a Darwinian survival-of-the-fittest kind of way. This market transition not only all but devastated independent bookstores, but the shift also had serious consequences for authors. First of all, mega book outlets didn't always hire employees who knew anything about the books or the authors. The intimacy between bookstore and author was replaced with the faceless tyrant—Bulk Sales. Then, numbers and "moving inventory" started taking priority over anything else. In order for the big booksellers to offer the deep discounts, they needed to sell, sell, sell and always have a "new shiny" to offer. As a consequence, less and less shelf space could be dedicated to an author's backlist, because the retailer had to always make way for the new. Also, many retailers like Barnes & Noble made more money off selling cards, journals and knick-knacks than selling books. Why dedicate floor space for author backlist when you can sell cute ceramic kittens reading Shakespeare? Now that e-readers have exploded in popularity, why waste prime front-of-the-door real estate for paper books when you can use that space to display Nooks and Nook accessories?

This loss of shelf space for backlists is bad for a couple of reasons. If you happened to be a multi-published author, then that backlist paid a lot of the bills and allowed you to write full time. Unfortunately, the mega-stores didn't generally devote shelf space to backlist unless you happened to be a mega-author. This meant a serious cut in pay for many authors. Doesn't sound like a great long-term career plan to me.

For new authors, having books remain on the shelves longer offered an advantage. It gave more time for readers to discover your work and allowed you as an author to cultivate a readership. Once the bargain bookstores came on the scene, books experienced increasingly shorter shelf lives because metrics determined everything. This eventually translated into lower sales numbers overall. Lower sales numbers equaled failure in a world of spreadsheets. Unless some stroke of blind luck or magic intervened to make a first book a runaway success, often authors were left in the cold with un-renewed contracts. In a nutshell? No career at all.

Myth #5—Traditional publishing values the craft more.
Yes, and no. Yes, traditional publishers value quality writing but, unfortunately, they're beholden to their business model. They *have* to make a profit. This means there are many good works traditional acquisitions editors will pass up simply because they don't feel they can sell enough copies. I don't say this with any judgment. It's simple math. Traditional publishing is caught up in the commercial paradox. They have to make money, so they have to cater to what will sell a lot of copies. We see a similar situation in Hollywood. These mega-studios are busy filming *Transformers 7* and *Friday the 13th Part 75* at the expense of great screenplays. Is it because *Transformers 7* and *Friday the 13th Part 75* constitute great filmmaking? Or is it because *Transformers 7* and *Friday the 13th Part 75* will fill movie theaters with teenage boys who are the most likely demographic to pay full price to see a movie in theaters multiple times and then later *buy* a copy of the movie? Instead of producing great films, Hollywood is looking to the bottom line and the most profitable markets—teen boys and kids.

Suddenly, Hollywood is gearing its films to where it knows it can *sell*, and that's how we end up with gems like *The Smurfs*. In the world of publishing, it's how we end up with Snooki's memoir, *Confessions of a Guidette*.

Really? Just, really?

Another point to consider is the profound limitations of the print paradigm. Many types of writing had dwindled to the brink of extinction because they weren't profitable for a publisher to produce. In the Digital Age, we're seeing a resurgence of poetry, novellas, and short stories, because now there is a way to reach the audience and create a market without going in the red. These niche markets would have all but disappeared if we judged all writing based on profit in the print model. If traditional publishers were true patrons of the arts, then they should have embraced the ebook model for these non-traditional works at the very least.

But they didn't.

A final point I will make is that traditional publishing is *slooooowwwww*. One of the reasons it's been over two years since my last book is that I wanted to traditionally publish. The problem? Time. Social media is the most fundamentally significant change in human history since the invention of the Gutenberg Press, but the fastest any traditional publisher could get my (any) social media book to market was *a year*. I find this so strange. Traditional publishers all use social media and *require their authors to use social media*, but, ironically, they can't even print the manual. That's a problem.

We live in a world of email, instant messaging, text messages, delivery pizza and UPS. Consumers are spoiled. They hunger for information and entertainment as quickly as possible. How long can New York compete with a minimum lead-time of a year?

I'm not here to say we need to throw out the standards and not strive for excellence, but I am saying that the modern consumer will take a less-awesome product NOW over a "perfect-and-twice-the-price product" later.

The Unvarnished Truth

As it stands, traditional publishing has two main advantages. One, they have the power to get lots of your books into bookstores and retailers at no *monetary* cost to you. Two, they take care of all the production. You write a book, query, land an agent, get a contract and then the publisher takes control and pays for everything—editing (what editing gets done), book design, cover design, etc. Ideally, you will have a team of kind professionals to help you, though there is no guarantee, and you can't fire them. You will be told what to do, how to do it and when to do it. Ah, but there's always a tradeoff. "If you want a job where it's okay to follow the rules, don't be surprised if you get a job where following rules is all you get to do" (Godin, *Linchpin*, 29).

The good news is that the cost and effort involved in book production will be lifted from your shoulders. The bad news is that your social media workload will probably be just as heavy, and you'll lose most, if not all, creative control. Also, because a lot of other people get paid ahead of you, you'll make less money. There is a huge difference between 17% and 70%. Another point of consideration is that the indie authors who are making the big money are selling a lot of titles and writing to demand. In traditional publishing, an author is pretty much limited to a book a year. This means that writers have to gamble everything on one book being a runaway hit, especially since shelf space is rarely dedicated to backlists. Therefore, authors lose the advantage of compounded sales. John Locke didn't sell a million copies of *one* book in five months. He sold a million copies of *multiple books* in five months. He had the major advantage of combined sales.

As traditional publishing hemorrhages, it's cutting advances and the size of the sales force. Many are also grabbing up author backlists. These days, most of what a traditional publisher does for an author can be outsourced. Yes, if you the writer choose to publish nontraditionally, you will bear upfront costs of production, but those people can also be fired if you don't like the quality. There won't be any excuse for a blonde-haired Viking on the cover of your Caribbean pirate romance.

I get that self-publishing isn't for everyone, but consider this: there are a lot of indie publishers popping up and they can be far more author-friendly, often because many of them are run by authors who were fed up with being run through the corporate machine. There are also some exciting hybrid publishers. Spend some time researching before making a decision. I'm not here to convince all authors to self-publish, or all go indie, but I am an author advocate and facts are facts. **The paradigm is changing at light-speed and many of the big publishers aren't.**

One More Consideration for Traditional

Distribution is one reason to go traditional. Also, there are publishers out there who are becoming more and more author-friendly and offering support. You can write without worrying about hiring and firing editors, overseeing cover design, formatting, sales, distribution, etc. I'm not narrow-minded, and I know indie isn't a good fit for everyone. Going indie is a lot of work, and maybe being a full-time entrepreneur and artist is simply too much. WANA's mission is to help *all* authors, no matter which path you choose. My goal here is to simply ensure that you make an educated decision. If you want to go traditional, go for it, but be certain you have a great agent or hire a publishing attorney who can make sure that the contracts are in your favor. A lot of the mess that writers experienced with Dorchester could have been completely avoided with some initial changes to the contract that stipulated a reversion of rights once the publisher ceased functioning as a publisher. A good agent or attorney can make sure you have the right to publish in a variety of ways and that a publisher doesn't have complete and total control over you and your work for all eternity. We have rights, but it's our responsibility not to leave them on the table. Get educated and hire people who can garner you the most advantages.

One of the great changes we are seeing is that authors finally have a career path. They can begin indie, and then once they've demonstrated success, traditional houses will come calling and can offer a greater reach (e.g., foreign markets). There have been self-published authors who've used their sales numbers to negotiate highly favorable contracts. For instance, John Locke maintained full control over his ebooks, but handed the print side to traditional. As writers gain more power, publishing houses will be encouraged to reinvent and offer deals that benefit all parties.

The Digital Wild West of Indie: The Good, the Bad and the Holy $#%!

We live in a wonderful time, when all kinds of writer dreams can come true, but it would be foolish of me to present indie and self-publishing as some kind of author's panacea. Not all dreams are good dreams; some are nightmares. I have helped literally thousands of writers, and I will attest that there are many who believe they have the next big thing when really what they have is a mess. I've been there myself. I always joke that my first novel was being used in Guantanamo Bay to interrogate captives. Well, at least it was until the UN banned it under the Hague Convention.

"I'll tell you where the bomb is, just not another chapter of that booook!"

The thing is, I didn't know any better. I sat down one day in the '90s and started writing. Finally, after a couple years, I hit 176,000 words and figured that was long enough.

The end.

Give me a break. Since I made A's in English I was naturally qualified to be a best-selling novelist, right? My book was a memoir-thriller-romantic-suspense-comedy that appealed to all demographics, young and old, and even small pets and some artificial houseplants. My novel was so brilliant it shocked me how the medium of paper and ink could contain the power of such awesomeness.

New York set me straight. Gatekeepers provide a public service. They protect society at large from bad novels that will eat the furniture and multiply (especially if you get them wet and feed them after midnight).

Historically, agents and editors have been the gatekeepers to keep these unholy creatures at bay. They're humanity's last line of defense against really awful writing. This is one of the reasons I've worked so hard to help them innovate. They did and still do offer value. These unsung warriors sift through the 176,000 word memoir-thriller-romantic-suspense-comedies and send polite rejection letters in hopes that the author of the 176,000 word memoir-thriller-romantic-suspense-comedy, experiencing sufficient rejection, might get a clue and take time to learn the craft of writing fiction.

Some of these authors do actually get a clue. I did. I finally received enough "does not fit our needs" letters that it humbled me enough to read every writing book I could find and then later, to join a critique group. And then even later, to attend confession even though I'm not Catholic, so I could seek absolution for making family and friends read my novel. I'm thankful every day for those wonderful gatekeepers who didn't let me go out into the world with the back of my literary skirt tucked in my literary underwear.

I have a printout of my first novel in a box in the garage. Its presence seems to keep burglars at bay. Sometimes at night I can hear it clawing at the door. I think it wants inside.

Where was I? Oh, yes.

For generations, the gatekeepers have been able to keep bad writing sealed in the murky realms of the *Unpublished Dimension*. Granted, in trying to protect the unsuspecting public, a lot of great writing became collateral damage. Yet my point remains— the gatekeepers protected us from a lot of horrible novels.

Ah, but then vanity presses were born.

Many vanity publishers quickly swooped in to tell the writer of the 176,000 word memoir-thriller-romantic-suspense-comedy that, for a few thousand dollars, their company had the power to spring the writer's baby manuscript from *Publishing Purgatory* and make the author a star. They could even offer this ~~sucker~~ lucky writer an assortment of affordable packages with easy payments to transform this ugly duckling aspiring writer into a published author swan. Also, with the right cover and binding (for a tad extra, of course), New York was sure to pay attention and launch the novelist to fame and fortune.

Boy, New York is sure going to be sorry they overlooked this little jewel.

Or not.

Often what happened was the hopeful writer ended up with a garage full of books, a maxed-out credit card, and an ear full of "I told you so" from friends and family who warned against cashing in the 401K to publish *The Chiropractor's Assistant—A Tale of Love, Betrayal and Orthotics.* Yet, thankfully, the high cost of vanity publishing kept a lot of bad books sealed in the *Unpublished Dimension* because most writers didn't have a few thousand or even a few hundred dollars to publish their books. I know I didn't, and I thank God for that every day. Ah, but times are different and now we are in the era of e-publishing. Anyone with a computer or access to a computer can become a published author for free or pretty darn close to free.

Many aspiring writers, upon rejection from traditional publishing, rush to self-publish. Is this a bad thing? Yes and no. I tend to be an optimist. First we will look at the bright side.

The Good

If an unpublished writer with no author platform self-publishes a really dreadful book, the outcome, in some ways, is actually better than it used to be. How? If a book dies in the forest but no one is around to hear the guttural death-throes . . . .

You get the point.

The bad book will be able to die a quiet death and no one will be the wiser except, with luck, the author. This might be exactly what he needs to finally appreciate that all the agents who rejected him knew what they were talking about, after all. With no existing platform, this author is likely to sell only a handful of copies, mostly to family members. Ah, but this is an improvement already over vanity press in that now the writer's family members are only out $.99 or $2.99, not $35 for a fancy hardback. The writer might also be less desperate because he isn't trying to earn back the ten grand he put out on gold-leaf copies of his first novel. Since there isn't this massive financial investment, the writer might be quicker to admit defeat and go back to the drawing board and write more books and better books.

At least we can hope.

This type of writer can keep trying to hawk his book, but odds are he'll eventually wear out and give up. He can also keep writing more bad books that only sell forty copies, or he will actually get better and maybe, one day, will write something people want to buy.

I meet people like this every day. Certain that all agents were functionally retarded and didn't know a masterpiece if it bit them, these writers, in a flurry of enthusiasm, ran out and uploaded their books. Then, they waited patiently for the website to crash because so many readers were trying to buy books all at the same time.

insert cricket chirping noises here

Hey, I'm not judging. I would have been there myself if timing and poverty hadn't saved me from myself. The good news is that if we self-publish, we get to keep all the royalties. The bad news is if we jump in too soon with a shoddy platform and an iffy product, we are making 70% royalties off nothing, or darn close to nothing.

Running our heads into a wall over and over is not a recommended career path, but it is certainly an option. Don't say I didn't try to stop you.

This even applies to the traditionally published author. Stephen Shapiro, in his blog, *Sobering Statistics About the Book Industry* reported the 2006 BEA (Book Expo of America) statistics. "According to the BEA, there are 172,000 books printed each year in the United States. Of these, only 1,000 books sell more than 50,000 copies in retail channels. Fewer than 25,000 sell over 5,000 copies, and 93% of all books published sell less than 1,000 copies" (Shapiro). Is it because 160,000 books were that bad? Maybe. I strongly doubt it. I want you to remember these tough statistics whenever you're tempted to think about "the good old days" before writers had to worry about author brands, platforms and social media. Without the digital tools we now have at our disposal, those numbers are the hard reality of the writer's lot.

Go indie with no platform and the odds of success are almost nonexistent. No one knows about the book, even if it is good. Maybe the unsuccessful book isn't bad, it's that no one knows about it.

Sometimes a book might be good, but the author was VERY misguided when it came to building an author platform. It could happen. There is a lot of faulty information out there. It could simply be that the writer has taken the incorrect approach (e.g., non-stop spamming on Twitter and form-letters on Facebook). I would venture to say that is not usually the case but, hey, anything can happen. But if this is the case, then I have good news. All this writer needs to do is adjust her approach to social media, keep writing books, and the sales should pick up.

Case in point. There was a writing duo in the UK, Mark Williams and Saffina Desforges, who'd queried for years with no success. Finally, they decided to self-publish. Their sales were dismal. In Mark's words, "After five weeks, we weren't even in the top gazillion." Mark and Saffina happened to follow my blog and decided to buy my first book *We Are Not Alone—The Writer's Guide to Social Media* and put WANA methods to the test. Within months, a book no one had noticed was dominating the top of the British best-seller charts with (as of summer 2011) sales not far short of 100,000 ebooks. Mark and Saffina continue to be very successful. I feel this is a really good case against the "all you need to succeed is a good book" myth. I hear this a lot, and yet the same book that sold one copy a week is the same book that later catapulted to the top of the charts and became the 11th best-selling ebook in UK history.

Regardless, we must always keep writing more books. Don't bank everything on that first manuscript. The more you write, the more skilled you become. Keep pressing on with writing and building that platform and one day you will hit a tipping point.

The Bad

This is all great if the book is actually an overlooked treasure, but what if it's a book that never should have seen print? That's another story altogether and, sadly, a far more common one, especially for indie authors. Herein lies the conundrum: if a writer self-publishes but doesn't have a social platform then the book will almost certainly fail. This means all writers—self-published and traditionally published—need a social platform. Social platforms improve the odds of success, true. But a large platform means more people will gasp in horror if the book is a train wreck.

The traditional routes to publishing are harder, and there are many more barriers to success. Yes. But one historical advantage has been that writers had time to toughen up and mature *privately*. These days, authors finally have a career path that is directed by readers. Unfortunately, the slush pile has been handed off to the unsuspecting public. This is all the more reason to make sure our product is as good as, if not *better than,* anything out of New York. If you rush out and publish a bad book, it isn't the end of the world, but it can make it harder to regain reader trust. Also remember, we are artists and few things can make us suicidal like pages of one and two-star reviews from ticked off readers. Publish too soon and we earn our rhino skin the hard way.

The Holy $%#!

The danger of rushing out to self-publish is that gatekeepers exist for a reason. Gatekeepers are there not only to help readers, but also to keep us writers from humiliating ourselves. It is highly likely that a writer's self-published book could crawl off and die a quiet death that no one but its creator mourns, but some manuscripts have been known to go out more like Frankenstein and take a bunch of villagers and some small farm animals with it. The demise of some novels is the stuff of Internet legend. How? There are some self-published authors who finally met up with an actual online critic and couldn't take the heat. The public meltdown that ensued sealed the writers' fates, and their careers crashed like a meteor strike.

Why do I bring this up? Because those of you who decide to traditionally publish will have people on your side to assist, guide and protect you. Yes, we live in a wonderful time with many new publishing opportunities, but these new routes are fraught with danger. If you *do* decide to self-publish, then invest in your success. You can have the same team as a traditional author. In fact, you can actually have a *better one*, but you're going to have to budget money, be open to honest feedback, and be willing to work your tail off.

There are a lot of social media gurus out there teaching new and improved ways to sell a million books in so many months, which I affectionately refer to as "How to Kill a Writer in Less Than a Year." In this book, I will touch on why mass marketing methods don't work for most writers. Unless you happen to have a background in high-pressure sales and can commit full-time to rocking the spreadsheets, this approach leaves little time for much else. Also, aside from traditional marketing's lack of effectiveness, the other major downside of an impersonal marketing strategy is that it leaves the worked-half-to-death author vulnerable.

All writers need a community of support, yet those who decide to go it alone without the shelter of an agent or publishing house need a vested community more than any other type of writer. We need more than people willing to plunk down a few bucks for a book. We need people who care about us, our futures, and our reputations. This was largely the reason that I created the WANA movement and later built the social media site WANATribe. Writers need a community of support, especially since we're all braving new and perilous terrain. Together we are safer and stronger.

When you create a platform the way I teach you, you'll be surrounded by peers who can offer tips, advice, feedback, and maybe even tough love. If we are plugged into a community, then we have connections who will gladly be our sounding board. They care and so they won't let us humiliate ourselves by publishing bad books with horrid covers, no proper editing, and formatting that looks like it was performed by a drunk one-eyed chimpanzee.

Also, I will warn you that any marketing plan that focuses on email lists and technology is very vulnerable to any major changes in technology. If a social site adjusts an algorithm or an email provider improves spam filters, all that hard work can disintegrate in an instant.

Good News for All

Yes, self-publishing and indie publishing have a lot of good to offer. There are a lot of opportunities that haven't been explored simply because there was no cost-effective way to get content to the consumer.

For those of you who still love the traditional model, take heart. Self-publishing also weeds out the talentless hacks and makes the stack of queries a little less daunting for the gatekeepers. This means that agents might actually stand a better chance of finding great talent because they aren't wasting time rejecting the 176,000 word memoir-thriller-romantic-suspense-comedy… that is part of a ten-book series (yeah, I left that part out). So for those of you who want to query an agent, thank the stars for self-publishing. Your odds of an agent seeing your query have dramatically improved.

Chapter 4

WHY TRADITIONAL MARKETING DOESN'T SELL BOOKS

ONE OF THE BIGGEST QUESTIONS we must ask ourselves is, "Is it possible to market fiction?" No . . . and yes, but not in the traditional way. Some people believe that social media is breaking all the paradigms, shifting us into a future world we barely recognize. I actually believe the opposite. Technology is returning us to what it means to be uniquely human. Thousands of years ago, we gathered, shared stories and bonded as people with common dreams, hurts, and challenges. We cared about the small things, and what our peers thought and said mattered most. Today, I think the fireside chat is making a comeback in a big way. Only, now it's a global chat with no limits and no boundaries. This is the largest reason I called the WANA social site WANATribe. Tribes were the original social networks and we humans are returning to our roots. This is wonderful news for the publishing industry in particular. Why? We'll get to that in a moment.

To succeed, we need to think in new ways. Often, our instincts mislead us. We have to expand our vision. But before we probe any deeper, let's talk a little about marketing.

I've been told time and time again that it is impossible to market fiction. I agree. It's impossible to market fiction in the traditional way. Good thing WANA is anything but traditional. Shiny bookmarks, flashy author flare, ads, and book trailers all make a writer feel productive but, alone, offer little to drive book sales. Anyone who's been in publishing more than a minute knows there are only two secrets to healthy book sales—good story and positive word of mouth. Period.

Yet, historically, most books encountered staggering failure rates. Let's take a moment to think about those depressing BEA statistics. I refuse to believe all 160,000 books that sold poorly were junk. I believe this staggering rate of failure had more to do with the fact that writers could only control half of the formula for success. All we could do is write really great books and hope the stars aligned just right so that our work would get seen by the right people at the right time to spark a blitzkrieg of buzz.

On the other side of the fence, publishers did what they could for their writers, but reality dictates that they are not fountains of never-ending cash. The publishers only have so much money, and it makes business sense to funnel the lion's share of that money to the major hitters. Why? Um, the big names sell books, which generates the revenue for publishers to take a chance on new writers. Publishers have (high) overhead and payroll. It makes zero sense to sink big marketing bucks into an unproven product. Yet, in the end, that really doesn't matter anyway. Why? **Traditional marketing does not sell fiction, especially now**. Fancy ads and all that jazz are little more than placebos meant to help authors feel their publishers are on their side. At the end of the day, even those well-intended efforts do very little to impact sales.

Marketing worked in a world where gatekeepers stemmed the flow of information. In a world without gatekeepers, marketing merely adds to the noise we've grown to hate. Remember, at the beginning of this book we discussed how our world has become inundated with the irrelevant. Humans must lean on coping mechanisms so their heads don't explode from all the influx. Early humans could thank the oral culture they lived in for their re-markable memories. Then, once language merged with a phonetic alphabet, we traded our formidable memory for greater abstract thinking. As we shifted into the 20th century, we lost the ability to focus for long periods on one activity. But, we *gained* an unprecedented ability to multi-task. As society continues to change, produce more gadgets, and pile on more multimedia, attention spans grow proportionally shorter.

But our ability to process chaos improves.

Ah, but there is a price for the ability to process chaos and that price is our vision. We literally *don't see* a lot of the information shoved up our noses. We can't. It's too much data for the human mind to process and remain efficient. Thus, when faced with this dilemma, **the visual cortex learns to only pay attention to what we're intentionally looking for.** Our brains learn to read blogs and never notice the ad space in the header. We scan our Facebook page for pictures of Darth Vader and Grumpy Cat and literally *never see* all the sales in the sidebar. **Advertising alone can't work in a Huxleyan world because the human brain views it as part of the problem.**

Marketing Norms Versus Social Norms

Marketing has long sought to blur the line between social and market norms. Early in the TV-Industrial complex, those with stuff to sell learned that using emotions sold more stuff. By tapping into our primal centers, companies could gain connection. Connection equaled sales.

> *Like a good neighbor, State Farm is there.*
> *Allstate. You're in good hands.*
> *What's riding on your tires?*

When we rely solely on market norms, price is a major factor. This usually means a race to the bottom and who can give away the most goodies for free and be the cheapest. Companies that don't want to compromise on price try to gain an advantage by convincing us that we are in a relationship. The plus side is the company can charge more. The down side is that if they screw up, consumers take it personally.

Don't call me family, then not be there when I need you, is how we all feel.

Social norms are the rules that govern relationships. There is no balance sheet. If I help you move your couch, there is no expectation that you will help me move mine. As Dan Areily explains it in his book, *Predictably Irrational*, "Social norms are wrapped up in our social nature and our need for community. They are usually warm and fuzzy... It's like opening a door for someone; it provides pleasure for both of you, and reciprocity is not immediately required" (Ariely 68). Social norms dictate that when I open the door for you, I don't stick out my hand and expect a tip.

Market norms are a different matter. "There's nothing warm and fuzzy about them. The exchanges are sharp-edged; wages, prices, rents, interest, and costs-and-benefits" (68). Market norms are not a bad thing or even necessarily evil. A day's wages for a day's work, fair and square. We pay the price on the sticker. Clean, simple, and the rules are clear.

Social norms and market norms are all fine and good if they operate in their own spheres. Problems usually arise when we try to mix the two. We run the risk of violating rules and committing taboos. Mom cooks breakfast every morning, but she doesn't bring your bill at the end of the meal.

When I say it this way, it's easy to laugh, but social media has made navigating the mixed waters of social and market norms very treacherous. This has been a major reason most social media sites have struggled to monetize. They lure people in for the social experience and it's like a grand global cocktail party. But how would we view a guest at our cocktail party setting up a table and credit card machine and selling books? Selling anything for that matter? When an environment is governed by social norms, offering to take cash or credit is gauche and a good way to get shunned. Facebook ads don't work. General Motors pulled its advertising on Facebook because it wasn't effective, but why is this shocking? We're on Facebook to be social, not shop. If we wanted to shop, we'd go to the Home Shopping Network, not the *social* network. When social sites try to monetize, they inevitably find out their advertising is either ignored or resented. This is why "marketing" on social media is busy-work with very little return on investment. In fact, advertising on social media can create BIG problems for authors who abuse social norms to sell books.

Beware of Friends with Benefits

I've seen rampant abuse of social norms by writers. *I tweeted about your book, now you need to tweet about mine. I gave you a 5-star review because I know you; now go write a 5-star review for me.* Do you see how an unhealthy blending of social and market norms not only hurts relationships, but how it can also tarnish a brand? People are smart and it won't take long for them to figure out that this kind of promotion is based less on our personal evaluation of a good quality book or blog and more on our misguided sense of reciprocation. After a while, we become white noise because others filter us out as part of the information glut. When we make friends online, we need to be authentic and we need to set aside our agendas. We must make friends because we value people, not because we want to *get something* out of the relationships. People don't like to be manipulated and they don't like to be lied to. All of us have come to lean on one another for guidance in this new paradigm. We have to be able to trust the opinions and recommendations of others. Friends who want you to promote them simply because you are pals are misguided and wrong.

I once had a writer friend of mine who became very angry with me because I wouldn't tweet his blog posts when he "always tweeted" mine. Problem was, his blogs needed work. He needed time to grow. I adored him as a person, but he had a lot of maturing to do as a writer and blogger. This behavior is akin to, "I helped you move your couch and now you owe me." In the Digital Age, our names are among our most precious possessions, so we need to be prudent where we put them. Do not let others guilt you into support. It hurts everyone.

Authenticity is paramount.

This is one of the reasons I am so strongly opposed to automation, particularly misleading automation. I've seen writers preprogram tweets to not only constantly push their books for sale, but to also give the impression there are flesh-and-blood people on the other end of those tweets. This is *very* dangerous. Why? **Because this behavior seeks to take advantage of social norms, without fulfilling the obligations that go with them.**

I was at a writing conference last year and a writer became irate with me. She strongly disagreed with my opinions about automation. She felt that I was doing a great disservice to writers by not telling them about this wonderful time-saving tool. She took great pride in the fact that she *wrote* all her tweets and carefully crafted them. Okay, so she was *eloquent* spam. The problem with "crafting" tweets is this: they still violate social norms. People are on Twitter to talk and connect, not to be blitzed with non-stop advertising. When we allow computers to tweet for us, we are essentially saying that others have plenty of time to be on Twitter, whereas we have far more important things to do with our time. We want friends with benefits. We want all the fuzzies that go with a real friendship, but none of the work or sacrifice.

We should NEVER ask from others what we, ourselves, are unwilling to give.

Yes, it means that we might not be on every social site every hour of every day, but that's fine. These days, less is more. Others would rather see us less often, but our interaction be authentic. When we rely on automation, we are quickly rendered invisible. Why? Remember that the visual cortex is very good at ignoring the irrelevant. If others suspect no one is behind our tweets, their brains will filter us out. Why? Because most people are participating on social media for the purpose of connection and community. Anything outside that purpose is disregarded or disdained... just like the ads in the Facebook sidebar.

These days we can use community to our advantage. We can also use emotions to our advantage. We simply need to make sure we're using an approach that is congruent with the unspoken social rules that govern our cyber-villages.

The Power of Emotion

Emotion is powerful, especially when it comes to creating an author brand that will translate into sales. If we fail to appreciate and apply the power of emotion, the only way we can stand out from the competition *is price*. This is a big reason a lot of authors find themselves having to slash their book price to $.99 or give their work away for free. Without the leverage of relationships and the power of emotions, we're back at market norms. We find our "marketing" consists of slashing prices and resorting to ridiculous giveaways to capture attention.

Come, buy my book and be entered to win a free book okay a gift card—okay a Kindle—okay, an iPad...OKAY, A CAR!

Sometimes I shake my head at these contests because the ROI (return on investment) simply isn't there. How many $.99 or even $4.99 books does one have to sell to make a free iPad a good idea? This isn't to say that price isn't *a* factor, just that it stinks when it's the *only* factor. This is why creating an author brand is critical for successful sales. But *brand* isn't exactly what it used to be.

Why We Buy

Martin Lindstrom, in his book *Buyology: Truth and Lies About Why We Buy* explores how emotion, rituals, superstitions and our past experiences govern what we buy. Many of you reading this are old enough to remember the Pepsi Challenge. Back in 1975, the executives at Pepsi-Cola launched a nationwide campaign to try to make a dent in Coca Cola's unrivaled dominance of the estimated $68 billion soft drink industry. Their plan was pretty basic. Set up tables in grocery stores and shopping malls across the country and ask every warm body who passed by to take a Central Location Test (CLT) also known as a "sip test." The Pepsi folks were simultaneously astonished and baffled when the results finally rolled in. Over half of the participants claimed to prefer the taste of Pepsi over Coke. Yay! Right? Not so fast. If consumers preferred the taste of Pepsi over Coke, why weren't the sales numbers reflecting this?

Coca Cola was equally perplexed. When Pepsi started touting the results of their Pepsi Challenge, Coke decided to do their own blind test…and 57% favored Pepsi. Of course, Coca Cola was horrified, and there was a real fear that maybe their time had passed by. Coca Cola suddenly fell into target-fixation on taste, and that's where they got genius ideas like New Coke. Their scientists tinkered with the taste to make Coca Cola sweeter and more like Pepsi, and when the executives looked at the results from the blind taste-tests, people seemed to now prefer New Coke over Pepsi. Success! Uh, no. New Coke was the largest failure in the company's history. In Malcolm Gladwell's book *Blink*, he offers a theory about why people chose Pepsi in the taste-test but then still bought Coke. He also explains why New Coke did so well in blind taste-tests, but then bombed once on the market. How does Gladwell do this? He brings in an expert. According to Carol Dollard, who worked product-placement for Pepsi for years, there is a huge difference between drinking a sip of something and downing a whole *can*. People generally will prefer a sweeter drink when it's just an initial sip, but when they commit to drinking an entire can? The drink becomes *too sweet* (Gladwell, *Blink*).

But is taste the only reason that Coke still continued to trounce Pepsi in sales?

Lindstrom, on the other hand, offers up another theory. In 2003, twenty-eight years after the first Pepsi Challenge, Dr. Read Montague, the director of the Human Neuroimaging Lab at Baylor College of Medicine, decided to put the Pepsi Challenge to the fMRI challenge. By using an fMRI brain scan, Montague could see if the gray matter of the participants matched their stated preferences. In the initial blind test, the results were the same as the original taste-test results. Most of the 67 participants said they preferred Pepsi, and their brains concurred. "While taking a sip of Pepsi, this entirely new set of volunteers registered a flurry of activity in the ventral putamen, a region of the brain that's stimulated when we find tastes appealing" (Lindstrom 26). Okay, no great shockaroo here.

Ah, but the second test is when things got interesting.

In the second test, Dr. Montague permitted the participants to know which beverage they were tasting *before* they tasted it. The results were astonishing. 75% of the participants claimed to prefer Coke, and the region of the brain that lit up was completely different. In the blind test, the ventral putamen sparked to life, but when the test was no longer blind? The medial prefrontal cortex (region of the brain responsible for higher thinking and discernment) lit up as well. Two areas of the brain were now in a wrestling match, and emotions eventually won. Pepsi could only compete with taste, but in Coca Cola's arsenal? Every pizza party the participants went to as kids. Birthdays, celebrations, ads, the logo, the commercials, cute polar bears, Norman Rockwell Americana, and family cookouts all overpowered the participants' taste preference for Pepsi. According to Lindstrom, "emotions are the way in which our brain encodes things of value, and a brand that engages us emotionally will win every single time" (Lindstrom 27).

What does the Pepsi Challenge show us about social media and author branding? First, the quality of the product might not necessarily be as big a factor as we believe. Think back to the Cola Wars. In taste tests, participants *preferred* the taste of Pepsi in the initial sip test. We as writers conduct sip tests all the time. They're called sample pages of our books. Yet, though Pepsi rocked the sip test, it was grossly lacking in its emotional arsenal when going head-to-head with Coca Cola. This experience can also be applied to the world of books. We might buy a slightly less awesome book from an author we *like* over a superb author who we don't feel emotionally connected to. The "slightly-less-awesome" author brings more to the table than simply the book. She brings every funny picture she's posted, every compliment, every encouraging tweet, and all the fun and positive experiences we've collected while following her online. All of that positive emotional branding can tip the sales scales in her favor.

The other thing the Pepsi Challenge shows us is that emotions will trump price every time. A brand is more than blitzing out a message to all who can see. Our brand must be tethered to positive emotions and pleasant experiences in order to have power, which brings me to another study that will take my point a step further.

Name Recognition is NOT Brand

Brand goes beyond being recognized in a line-up. I've been to many conferences and listened to many different teachings about how writers should market. Some of the prevailing wisdom is that audiences need to see us MORE. We need to be on Twitter and Facebook all the time. We need to post on ten different social platforms and blast our message from the rooftops. This is one of the main reasons a lot of these experts have no problem with automation or even having others do our social media *for* us. We do need computers and minions to help if we feel we need to be omnipresent.

In case you hadn't already gleaned this, you *don't*.

Branding is more than name recognition, it is also how people *feel* when they see or hear our name. Our brand is more than books, and includes everything we do on social media as well.

Every tweet, every "Like," every blog, every vlog, every conversation. Every interaction on social media is another piece of the whole we call *author brand*. Having four different Twitter accounts so we can spam the same hashtags is actually damaging to our author brand.

First a little more neuroscience to help you better understand. When I was five, I went to stay with my older cousin (she was a whopping *ten*!). My cousin made me a bowl of spaghetti for lunch and asked if I wanted Parmesan cheese. I said yes. She told me to tell her "when." I was busy watching cartoons and not paying attention, and I swear she put half a can of Kraft Parmesan on my spaghetti before I snapped back to reality. She forced me to eat it…and I puked spaghetti everywhere. For *years* I couldn't smell Parmesan cheese without feeling like I needed to throw up.

Another example. You're young and in college and you meet the guy or gal of your dreams. Sparks fly. Every time you're around this person, it's like you're high. You have a favorite love song that embodies the feelings you have for each other. The two of you eventually part and build separate lives and marry different people, but even though *years* have passed, every time that song plays, your heart flutters and you feel nineteen all over again. Memories gush forth. You recall events you haven't thought about in ages. What happened?

Subconsciously your neurons assembled and linked together concepts that previously were unrelated. The song is linked to the euphoric feeling of your first love. It's a neurological shortcut, the exact same shortcut that teaches us not to touch hot stoves when we're kids. The brain links together Berlin's *Take My Breath Away* with "passion" and "excitement" the same way it ties together the notions of "hot," "pain," and "stove," or even "Parmesan," "sick," "tossed your cookies, so stay away." It's what scientist Antonio Damasio calls a **somatic marker**. "Sown by past experiences of reward and punishment, these markers serve to connect an experience or emotion with a specific, required reaction. By instantly helping us narrow down the possibilities available in a situation, they shepherd us toward a decision that we know will yield the best, and least painful outcome" (Lindstrom 131). Eventually we collect enough of these somatic markers and they become what we refer to as *instinct*. The same *behavior plus reward* that teaches toddlers that sharing toys equals praise is the same *behavior plus reward* that can give our brands positive and lasting power (or crater them altogether if we're unwise).

Somatic markers have always been around, namely to keep us alive, intact, and reproducing. In an age where we are being deluged with information, products, video, tweets, bargains, emails, ringtones, etc. the brain now has to efficiently process a lot of chaos quickly and in a way that yields ideal results. How does it do this? By leaning more heavily than ever on somatic markers to filter what we pay attention to. In short, we must ask: how do others *feel* when they see our names?

Layers of Filtration

The first layer of content that will disappear is the irrelevant. This is why loads of tweets with no interaction are for all intents and purposes invisible. It will not help us to *do more* or to *join even MORE social sites* because no one is seeing what we're posting anyway. I see writers tweet link after link, day after day, thinking this is a good idea. Social media is more than attendance, and links are the most likely content to be ignored on a social site. Why? Giving us a reading list or the equivalent of digital flyers on our windshield is not being social.

The second layer the brain will sift out is any information coupled with negative somatic markers. The brain will move this content into the STAY AWAY file. This is why using tools to tweet about our books, book signings, blog tours, free deals, and giveaways non-stop will actually harm our brands. If every time others see a certain name their subconscious minds *feel* something negative, they'll steer clear, unfollow, or otherwise ignore. At best, the offending author will be invisible, but if this writer persists in being obnoxious (tweeting MORE, from MORE identities) then he drifts into the Land of Annoying, and is filed under STAY AWAY. Remember that social media is ruled by social norms, which presume there is an unwritten rule of *quid pro quo*, give and take.

Negative somatic markers are powerful. They can be even *more* powerful than positive markers. This is one of the reasons that I am adamant about writers staying out of religion and politics in a negative way while online. I've had to unfriend countless writers on Facebook because every time they posted, they were ranting or calling me and my belief system stupid. We all have beliefs, and most people are respectful that we have a right to be different. Freedom of speech is no excuse to be disrespectful and unkind. There is a *huge* difference between:

God loves marriage.
God hates fags. (Courtesy of the Westboro Baptist Church haters most of us want to hit with a truck).

I want everyone to live in a safe world and together we can find an answer to keeping guns away from bad people.
People who own guns are domestic terrorists and traitors.

Every time I study evolution I'm amazed. What an intricate and wonderful universe.
If you believe in God, you're a caveman idiot with no brain.

With each of the statements in **bold**, the person's belief system is clear. Those who agree can "Like," share or even comment and join in a discussion. Those who believe differently can simply move on, because the message just becomes part of the white noise, namely because the person's brain filters it out as something uninteresting. For those who happen to agree, there is a positive somatic marker. For those who don't? They likely moved on and really didn't "see" the content anyway.

The hateful posts in *italic* font are another matter entirely.

First of all, there might be people who normally would agree with the politics, but the sheer nastiness and disrespectful nature of the posts creates a negative somatic marker. For those who are the target of the attacks? Negative somatic marker to the power of a thousand! At best the offended party will ignore or unfollow, but don't expect any book sales or good word of mouth no matter how good our books happen to be. There are some authors who are so vicious and disrespectful on Facebook and Twitter that I will die before I part with money to purchase their books.

Most reasonable people don't buy books only from clones of themselves. We'll buy supernatural romances written by a practicing Wiccan even if we don't practice paganism, and purchase woman's fiction by a lesbian author even if we happen to be heterosexual. Politically liberal readers will still purchase good spy-thrillers from conservative military authors. The beliefs alone are not the problem. Rather, *how we choose to share those beliefs* creates the problem. If people are bombarded with insulting, threatening messages, they steer clear, and can we blame them? We all have enough doom and gloom. Why spew negativity during our social time? We can all support our causes, our faiths, and our beliefs in ways that are respectful of others. If we wouldn't shout out these things in our workplace, why do we think it's acceptable in social media? It isn't. If the very *sight* of our name creates heartburn we're doing something horribly wrong. Later we will talk about how to fuse your beliefs into your platform in a nonthreatening way. We can't change the minds and hearts of insulted, angry people who hate us.

Politics aside, another way to create negative somatic markers is to spam others. Five different Twitter accounts that blast out the same message every so many hours, unsolicited direct messages pestering for a sale, making people validate they are a real person in order to "follow" us, sending form-letters, adding people to Facebook groups without permission are all major offenders. If every time we see an author's name she's trying to *take* from us without giving, she is tarnishing her brand. Yes, I want social media to be effective for all writers, but a great start is to avoid the cerebral spam folders of those in our following. Just because everyone *knows us* doesn't mean that's a good thing.

Here's a little illustration from *Buyology*. In 2007, Nokia was one of the most popular cell phone brands in the world. With approximately 400 million cell phones in circulation at the time, Nokia commanded 40% of the market, making it a global success. To this day, most of us are familiar with Nokia's default ringtone because most users never changed it. If prompted, I bet a few of you could even still hum it. One would think that a ringtone going viral would be awesome for Nokia. The ringtone was even used in movies. Wow, look at all that *exposure* (Lindstrom).

Think again. Lindstrom details the study better in his book (buy it, it's AWESOME), but here's the short version. Remember that fMRI test used to demystify the Pepsi Challenge? Lindstrom teamed up with Dr. Gemma Calvert who holds the Chair in Applied Neuroimaging at the University of Warwick, England, and is the founder of Neuroscience in Oxford, to test some popular brands and the somatic markers that, theoretically, should make a brand popular. They tested several major brands from phones to software to airlines using the fMRI test. Most of the major brands performed well, but the results from the Nokia test were particularly interesting.

Dr. Calvert's team separated the participants into two groups. One group was only shown Nokia products, and they consistently rated the products favorably. Why wouldn't they? They were good cell phones. The other group was shown Nokia's products in tandem with the default ringtone, and they consistently rated the products lower. What went wrong? "The fMRI results showed that there was a negative emotive response to Nokia's famous ring. So much so, in fact, that merely hearing the sound actually suppressed the generally enthusiastic feelings (the other) volunteers' brains showed for the sight of Nokia's phones alone...In short, Nokia's ringtone was killing the brand" (Lindstrom 163).

How could this be? The ringtone was viral. It should have been awesome. Everyone had *heard the ringtone*. Exactly. Everyone had *heard* that ringtone, and that was precisely the problem. The volunteers had all heard the ringtone. They'd heard it in the middle of a meeting, in church, and during Grandma's funeral. That ringtone had broken up intimate moments, ruined dates, resulted in a burned meatloaf, heralded bad news and even alerted them that their job was calling them in to work the weekend shift. There is a great video on YouTube of a Nokia ringtone interrupting a classical music concert. Can you imagine how embarrassed the owner of the phone was? How irate others in the audience were?

Note: There is no YouTube *video of the later crucifixion of the cell phone owner.*

These negative experiences, coupled with negative emotions, built up over time rendering the popular ringtone a major disadvantage to Nokia's brand. Maybe it didn't hurt sales, but it certainly didn't help them either.

Whenever I go head-to-head with other social media experts, one of our main disagreements is over the notion of *exposure*. My opinion? Exposure is overrated.

This past year I had a heated battle online with an author guru. This woman had multiple accounts on Twitter. All the profiles had her picture, but different variations of her name. On top of this, she clearly used Social Oomph (a social media tool) to automate her tweets to post every few hours, 24 hours a day, seven days a week. To make matters worse, she included the same hashtags (which we will talk more about later). I am the founder of the WANA movement, and to give authors a digital water cooler, I created #MyWANA. What this means is any author could join in a conversation with authors from all over the world instantly. Hey, writing can be a lonely job and we need people to talk to. Have a moment after making word count? Come chat with real people. Real *writers* at #MyWANA.

****The # symbol is called a **hashtag** and we will discuss how this sucker works later in the book. For now, just roll with it.*

#MyWANA was created for community, not advertising. This woman, however, insisted on using #MyWANA in all her tweets from all her multiple identities. What then happened was that her tweets (the same messages) would show up in the #MyWANA column and overwhelm all the other tweets. We would get the same *Buy My Book* or *Sign Up for My Marketing Classes* messages twenty and thirty times a day. She mustn't have been monitoring her Twitter, because, 1) she would have easily seen she was spamming entire hashtags, and 2) she would have received the polite, then the stern, then the downright ticked-off messages from others.

Remember we talked about social norms and social media? This woman in interviews has excitedly declared that Twitter is so awesome because your message can be seen by millions! Yet, Twitter was so wonderful she couldn't be present? Plain and simple, she wanted the advantages of Twitter without any of the work, and that's at the core of what went wrong.

The WANAs quickly became angry. They tweeted her and asked her to stop. I tried direct messaging her to privately and politely ask her to cease and desist, but of course she wasn't following me so I couldn't (back to that "all take, no give" thing again). I tried emailing her, but couldn't send a message unless I allowed her site to "capture" my information. Yeah, I was being spammed enough. Thanks. I even blogged a polite message to give her a hint. She persisted. No matter how many of us messaged her asking her to stop, nothing changed. So, we reported her to Twitter as a spammer, and here's the doozy. After Twitter shut down her accounts, she reopened NEW accounts and did the same exact thing. She was absolutely wrecking the #My-

WANA experience. No one could chat or even *see* posts from other people, because all we saw was this woman's face over, and over, and OVER. Her non-stop marketing consumed the community. It wasn't until we brought the fight to her Facebook page that the woman finally stopped. She claimed she never used the #MyWANA and we were being irrationally mean. Fortunately, a screenshot of her multiple identities taking up the entire #MyWANA column *that very morning* ended the argument. I haven't seen her on #MyWANA since.

Here's what I want you to take away from this. Countless people had been exposed to this woman. Countless people *knew* her, her name, the name of her books, her business and her services… and they hated her. When I blogged about the problem, I didn't even refer to this person by name, (because I'm classy like that), but *everyone* knew exactly who I was referring to. When they saw her name, they saw red. This wasn't limited to #MyWANA. She was doing this to *all* the popular author hashtags. Perhaps she did mean well, but that didn't change the results. She wanted to offer services to writers, but all she ended up doing was making her target market despise the digital ground she walked on.

Social media is a social experience with rules dictated by social norms. When we fail to respect this, we create negative somatic markers that are hard (if not impossible) to erase. If we wouldn't go to a cocktail party and call people names and insult their beliefs, we shouldn't do it online. Who among you would walk into a party and start handing out flyers and coupons instead of talking to people? If we know it's uncool to act this way in person, then it's a pretty good bet that it won't fly online either.

We have to be *present* on social media. Like the Micronesian navigators, we have to be on board the craft. We must smell the water and feel the winds of change. The woman who blitzed #MyWANA could have easily spotted bad storms on the horizon had she not been trying to navigate Twitter from the safety of Social Oomph. Algorithms and reports couldn't accurately show her how she was being received. The irony is that less than fifteen minutes a day of her being present would have protected her brand, yet her "time-saving" tools cost her how much time repairing a badly damaged brand?

We've talked about how the notion of brand has completely evolved in the past few years. Additionally, you now understand that every activity on social media counts. Anyone who claims *only* our books are our brand (and nothing more) doesn't understand the intrinsic changes human culture has experienced. Hopefully you now understand the importance of being mindful of what content you post. We need to be deliberate in our social media. Focusing on content no one sees will wear us out. Being thoughtless and creating negative somatic markers will hurt us long-term. It would be better to stay offline all together if we can't behave online (and maybe reconsider career choices). If we can craft our interactions to always create positive experiences, then we are investing in others and our author brands daily. Small actions, over time, add up to big rewards. Take shortcuts like mass automation, mass mailings and paying for "Likes" on a fan page are as effective for your brand as the All Cabbage Diet is for long-term fitness.

In this next section, though, I want to pan back and simply look at marketing books, because here's the truth; advertising and promotion alone doesn't sell books. It never has. Even literary mega-agent Donald Maass addresses this in his book *Writing the Breakout Novel.* "Word of mouth is the secret grease of publishing. It's the engine that drives the breakouts" (Maass 6). Word of mouth is the only thing that's *ever* sold books, but we humans like to control things (or at least possess the *illusion* of control). We believe our books aren't selling because there isn't a big enough marketing budget or there aren't enough ads or our publishers aren't working hard enough to promote us, but that is simply a self-delusion. Promotion, marketing, and advertising sells cars, mascara, panty liners, and trash bags. Why are these tactics so ineffective when it comes to selling books?

Good question. I'm not the type of person content with *Um, it just is.* I'm nosey and I want to know why, so I spent years reading and researching, and this is why I believe marketing has never been effective for selling books.

Chapter 5

MARKETING 101

PRODUCTS ARE OFTEN BROKEN DOWN into two types of purchases. There are **low-consideration** purchases and **high-consideration** purchases.

Low consideration purchases are of low social influence. If you buy a can of shaving cream, and your legs look like they were attacked by a hacksaw-wielding porcupine, you simply throw it away and select another brand (unless you're my mother). You're probably not going to get online and research the latest in jojoba shaving cream breakthroughs before you make a purchase. Additionally, you're not going to go around asking all your friends what their favorite kind of shaving cream is. You won't be looking for blogs to help you choose between *Berries and Cream Skintimate* versus good old *Barbasol*. When it comes to shaving cream, unless people are dying from shaving cream poisoning or crack heads are boiling it down to make a new kind of illegal amphetamine, we aren't going to hear much buzz about it. I can guarantee you that most of us won't need peer approval when it comes to this kind of product. And, if you do? That's, um, kinda weird.

High-consideration purchases are another story. Cars, vacations, flat-screen T.V.s, cell phones, fancy mattresses, and computers are all high-consideration purchases, thus peer review weighs heavily on the decision. If I'm about to drop twenty grand or more on a car, you can bet I'm asking for opinions and probably even surfing the web for honest reviews. You can even guarantee I'll take that car on a test drive before I buy. If we're purchasing a jet ski, a fancy vacation, or a new sound system, most of us will look to friends, peers, magazines, the web, and to consumer reports to make sure we are getting the best product for our money.

High-consideration purchases are heavily influenced by social definition and peer pressure. Sometimes facts are secondary to emotion and what that purchase means in a social context. Mac computers are one of the best examples I've witnessed. Their advertising made Apple a social definition, with Mac computers being synonymous with being young and hip and cool, while PC was the socially awkward butt of the joke. Whether you're a Mac fan or a PC fan, you have to admit that Apple's marketing worked.

How many consumers ran out and bought a Mac for the image it portrayed? Hey, I'd be lying if I claimed image wasn't a consideration when I bought my first Apple laptop. Oh sure the Mac was less prone to viruses and had better computing blah blah… but see how *cute* I look sitting at my local Starbucks with my Mac Book Pro? We humans aren't always rational creatures. We're also emotional. Apple appreciated the emotional aspect of human nature and they've cashed in big time.

Here's a news flash. **High-consideration purchases often require an emotional approach.** Corvette. Enough said. Nobody buys a Corvette for practical reasons.

Okay, but what about books?

Certainly most books don't cost much more than a can of shaving cream, and they certainly don't cost anywhere near as much as a bass boat. So are books high or low consideration purchases? Before we continue, I want you to forget the mythos of the die-hard voracious reader who devours books like candy. To these types of readers, books are a low-consideration purchase. These people *love* books and they don't need to be coaxed into forgoing other activities to read. They don't require peer review to guide their choices and will often finish books when they don't even like them (my dad, may he rest in peace). Readers like these don't need to be dragged away from competing activities like World of Warcraft, sports or television. These people want to read.

I want to point out something that should be obvious, yet isn't. Ravenous readers are not *most people*, and I feel this is where a lot of writers (and publishers) get tunnel-vision when it comes to social media. Many writers get on social media and quickly sign up for book chats and book review sites. They decide to blog book reviews and hold author interviews. They sign up for online book clubs and book-lover gatherings all in search of what I call *The White Stag*—the insatiable reader who has a gluttonous appetite for books. Yet, if we really look at those "reader" sites, most are comprised of writers who are all there for the same reason…The White Stag. They're forgoing a lot of brown deer in search of an anomaly. Wait too long on an outlier and we starve.

Unless some outside peer factor steps in, an author can be at the mercy of chance. Is your book well placed at a bookstore? Shelved at Walmart? Available in airport bookstores? Sadly, as we discussed earlier, this type of book placement is frequently fleeting and relegated to only a small fraction of writers. These days, with the new indie movement, many of those books will never see a CVS or a table at Costco, so how can they sell?

The Presto Change-O

WANA methods will teach you to become really good at making converts. Feel free to tap into book review sites and blogs and reader circles, but that isn't being creative. Those who really succeed learn to be original. The person who eats through a book a week is great to have as a fan, but in reality, how many books can you write? Who cares if someone only buys two books a year so long as one or both of those is *your book*?

The vast majority of Americans do not consider themselves to be readers. Of the percentage that buys books, I guarantee you most of them buy more books than they ever read. These consumers are most likely to purchase books on impulse while wandering a Barnes and Noble to kill time before a movie, or while standing in line at a drug store as the lady in front of them argues over an expired 50 cent coupon.

The largest part of the population is surfing YouTube and following American Idol. They're tossing plasma grenades at their buddies on Xbox Live or chatting with pals on Facebook. They're not likely to go to bookstores or sign up for author newsletters, because they're too busy shuttling kids to soccer and trying to make the 6:00 yoga class. I can with almost 100% certainty tell you that they aren't gathering on book review sites when they could be uploading the latest videos of their cats falling in toilet bowls. Trying to get their attention will feel like trying to connect with a toddler on a sugar high. Yet, how much of the current book marketing is targeting all those areas where we are least likely to find a majority of people?

Society has advanced to the point that humans crave and consume information and entertainment at unprecedented rates. This is great news, however, we need to remember that books are not like other information and entertainment media. Books take an average of *twelve hours of undivided attention*. Books take up what so many of us have so little of—time. Unlike a movie, we can't fold laundry at the same time we read the latest romance novel. We can't multi-task like we can with music or video. Thus, as authors, we are asking people to part with their most precious possession, their uninterrupted time. We are asking them to spend money and part with time they don't have to engage in an activity they do not believe they enjoy. Reading. The low-consideration purchase for one group (the avid reader) is, in reality, a high-consideration purchase for the average person.

This is why traditional marketing does not sell mega-loads of books. The only people that those ads likely influence are consumers who make up that super-small segment of the population of **individuals who were going to buy books anyway**. To the majority of humans in need of informing or entertaining, book marketing either never enters their realm or, if it does, it's white noise. Huge book sales that defy all imagination only happen when we mobilize that fat part of the bell curve—those who aren't avid readers but who will read one or two books per year— yet these people, by definition, are the toughest to impress.

Modern humans are tired, overworked, stressed and lazy. We're going to take the path of least resistance unless something convinces us to do things differently. Movies are easy. Music is easy. It's passive and requires little effort on our part. We can lie like a sponge and merely absorb. Reading, on the other hand, requires focus, time, effort and attention. *It also requires sacrifice.*

When trying to sell fiction, we have a tough job—we have the burden of getting people excited enough to rise above their natures. We also have to convince these individuals to part with money and time for and activity *they do not believe they enjoy.* Most Americans do not consider themselves "readers" and the word "reading" conjures of images of high school and gutting through *The Grapes of Wrath.*

Traditional marketing works for other products because the advertising targets a need the consumer knows she has. If you manufacture mascara, advertising in a woman's magazine is a wise use of money and time. Why? Because most women in Western culture don't have to be convinced to wear makeup. We gals love makeup and we love a good mascara that promises we can we have lashes like Gwen Stefani. Thus, the marketing and advertising makes sense and it will drive sales.

Books are different. Advertisements are virtually invisible because **most people don't believe they like to read**. Also, they are too busy checking out the mascara ad. Remember the brain, in the name of efficiency and sanity, filters out content it believes to be irrelevant. Unless we writers can change our approach to make our content germane to their lives of regular people, most of our efforts will pass by unnoticed.

Now it is time to look on the bright side.

Envision a massive boulder the size of a building perched above a chasm. Granted, it will take colossal effort to get that boulder to budge. Ah, but once it gets rolling, there is no stopping it. The average person who would not label himself a reader also represents the greatest amount of potential energy. He might be tough to mobilize, but once we him moving? This is when records are set. *Girl with the Dragon Tattoo*, *The DaVinci Code*, *Twilight*, *Harry Potter*, *The Hunger Games* are all mega-best-selling books because they motivated millions of people who didn't consider themselves avid readers.

One of the reasons I think J.K. Rowling, Lee Child, Stephenie Meyer, Dan Brown, and Suzanne Collins have been so successful is that they have been able to galvanize huge populations of people who ordinarily would not have defined themselves as "readers." **Like Mac computers, these authors harnessed peer pressure to make their books a social definition.** Whether they did so intentionally or by accident is irrelevant. They did it.

Once a book becomes a social definition, it then taps into our very human desire to join and be like the group. We long to fit in. I know for certain that, if left on my own, I would have never picked up *The DaVinci Code* or *Twilight*. Yet, there came a point that so many people were buzzing about these books, that I was an outlier for *having not read them*. Not a comfortable place for most humans. We are social and we enjoy sharing. I felt like I was some foreigner who couldn't connect because I didn't have the reference, so I bought and read the books. Trust me when I say there were many people who bought *Fifty Shades of Grey* who will never read another erotica novel, but they *had to see* what all the hooplah was about.

Ah, peer pressure. Not just for teenagers anymore.

Writers Are Not Apple

Granted, Apple launched a campaign that transformed their products into a social definition, but books can't be marketed like laptops. So what do we do? We generate word-of-mouth.

Many people believe that this type of word-of-mouth wildfire is like playing the slot machines. There is no rhyme or reason and it is some hoo-doo-voo-doo beyond any control. This is one of the reasons that so much book marketing is directed to hooking the avid reader. She's a sure thing. Those other folk? Who knows what gets them excited?

I do, but we'll get to that in a bit.

Too many writers, publishers, editors and book marketers are allowing fear to take the driver's seat. Fear is a noose for creativity. I'm not saying their fear is unjustified. I feel it, too. All of us have people depending on us. When our reputations are at stake, this can make us less likely to look at things in an unconventional way. If we take risks and go against the current train of thought, yet we fail, we take that failure full force. But, if we do what everyone else is doing and our idea flops, we have an out. We can say, "Well, everyone does blah blah blah." And then we have the luxury of chalking our failure up to the Fates, a bad day or a faulty alignment of the planets.

But nothing great was ever accomplished without risk. In fact, risk and reward are related. The fact that every writer and publisher gets the same bright ideas to market on "reader" sites makes sense. This is birthed from fear. We are afraid of failing, so we go to the sure thing. **The problem doesn't come from engaging on reader sites, the problem arises when we rely on them to the exclusion of everything else.**

When We Allow Fear to Control Our Marketing

Avid readers don't have a lot of inertia. I'm not saying that avid readers don't have discerning tastes, but I do feel it's fair to say that it's no monumental task to convince them to do what they already love. Read books. Yet, how much marketing is directed toward this very small sector of the overall population who could buy a book? Why is it directed there?

It's easier. It's safer.

For instance, blogging is one of the most powerful tools in a writer's social media arsenal, yet it is shocking how writers develop instant myopia the second they begin a blog. Since the invention of the written word, writers have been using symbols in various combinations to create entire worlds, to deliver the essence of the universe to other humans. Yet, when handed a tool with the potential to reach *millions*, most writers get tunnel-vision. We blog about...writing. We blog about the craft, the experience of writing a book, the changes in publishing and even the decline of the bookstore, but guess what?

Most people don't care.

Where Are All the Readers?

Ah, but then the big folk in publishing will often give a sly smirk and say, "We told you author blogs would never sell books." What everyone seems to be missing is that no one is connecting to the right people...the average person who doesn't generally read for pleasure. Writers flock to Facebook and Twitter and we befriend our friends, or friends of our writer friends who are also writers and we blog about writing and create nifty writing groups and then wonder why we aren't connecting with readers.

We never *talked* to them.

I've had writers email me and tell me how they plan on getting an author fan page so they can separate their writing friends from "regular" friends, family, work and school friends and casual acquaintances. Believing they are finally being "serious" about marketing, they write things like, "*My regular page is for my personal stuff and my fan page is for people who like books, namely my writer friends.*" Yet, these same people will later wonder where all the readers are? I can tell you where. They were dissected neatly out of the author's platform because she assumed only people in book clubs loved stories. Authors wear themselves out being part of twenty different online book-lover/writer communities and then wonder where to find readers?

Readers look a lot like the people we went to high school with. They look like our mail lady, our favorite checkers at the grocery store and the guy who built our fence. Readers don't all walk around with an *I Love Books* badge to make our job easy.

Writers can't find readers because we never tried to connect and create a relationship. We used social media to create one big writer party and forgot to invite anyone else. We grew so fixated on what we love and what we wanted to talk about that we forgot who really mattered. Regular people. Regular people in need of informing or entertaining.

I once had a best-selling author announce in front of a group of writers that Twitter was great for connecting with other writers, but that it was impossible to find readers there because only writers were on Twitter and only writers read blogs. Yet, I pointed out that this author blogged non-stop about publishing, ebooks, and the changing publishing paradigm. To me, it seemed crystal clear why he believed that Twitter and blogs were only good for connecting with writers. That's what he was baiting his traps to catch. If my goal is to nab a mountain lion, but I keep putting peanut butter in the traps, then who's the fool for complaining about catching mice?

Beware of Ego

One of the largest handicaps we have as writers is ego. We don't mean to, but we can unknowingly treat regular people condescendingly and assume that, since they aren't part of our book-lover cliques, they therefore aren't interested in reading. This phenomenon reminds me of another anecdote from Robert Greene's book *Mastery*. Greene relays the saga of the missionary

Daniel Everett and his journey to learn the language of a remote Amazonian tribe known as the Pirahã. In 1977, a Christian organization, the Summer Institute of Languages (SIL), sent Everett out into the field with his wife and two children to crack the maddeningly difficult Pirahã language so it could be translated into the Bible and then used to spread the Gospel to the people. Several missionaries had tried before and all had failed, believing the language was impossible to decode. Though Everett was a master of several languages, he seemed to be doomed to the same fate. After years living with this remote tribe, he still could not seem to decipher the language of the Pirahã people.

Like a good linguist/social scientist/missionary, Everett gradually pieced together a vocabulary and could grind through a handful of basic phrases. He took lots of notes and carried them on index cards and yet he made little headway. Later, Everett realized what had been holding him back. On some level, "perhaps unconsciously, Everett could not help but keep some distance and feel ever so slightly superior to the backward culture of the Pirahã" (Greene 345). This emotional distance kept him from the total immersion necessary to understand the very people he longed to "decode." It wasn't until Everett became aware of this bias that his experience began to change. Before, he'd stayed relatively close to the village. After his epiphany he began to venture deeper into the jungle with the men to gather supplies, fish, or hunt. Once out in the bush, he witnessed an entirely new side to the culture and this was when he made his first major strides in understanding the Pirahã language. He had to let go of *his* value systems. He had to stop judging the tribe members by his Western values. The Pirahã had no mythos, no legends, no words for the future or even the past, because this was a people who lived only in the present. The hard world they lived in demanded that they remain in the present if they wanted to be happy. Storms, disease, death and love meant very different things to the Pirahã, but an outsider would never see this looking through a Western lens.

Bridging the Culture Gap

Why do I mention the Amazonian Pirahã when talking about readers? Because as writers we hold a set of values that most of the world doesn't share. I hear writers complain that they post about their book and get one "Like" but post a picture of cute kittens and they get thirty "Likes." Why is this so shocking? When we post fun pictures or puppies or kittens we are connecting with others by what *they value*. This is how we begin a dialogue, as Everett did with the Pirahã.

Most writers can't envision a home not stuffed with books. We've all read Hemingway, Poe and Dickens. We love to post writerly quotes and jokes only other authors get. We brag about word count and fawn over writing blogs. We have a different vocabulary and an alien outlook in the eyes of most ordinary people. Most regular people can't fathom why anyone would sit still for twelve hours to read a book unless there was a gun to their heads or a test at the end.

If our goal is to grab the average person's attention, then it becomes incumbent upon us to meet him or her on common ground that has nothing to do with reading or writing or even selling books. When we section people out of our Facebook and Twitter followings because they "aren't avid book lovers," this is akin to staying in the safe village center, or even back home in the "civilized" world. We don't have to extend ourselves or do anything scary. The problem, however, is every writer is there in the same village with you talking to the same people and trying to sell them books. The great returns will come by braving the jungles of the unknown, and I know it's more than a little terrifying. Some of our self-segregation does come from our subconscious elitism, but a lot of it also comes from fear of rejection. We section out everyone but our writing friends because we feel safer with them. There is no one from college or work to mock us when we fail. No Aunt Gertrude to remind us that we should have gone to school to learn medical billing instead of trying to be a successful novelist.

Remember that a large part of social media is about *bridging cultures*. Yes, we can connect. Texans can hang out with fellow Texans, but they can also hang out with Australians and Canadians, with Scottish, Albanians, and Egyptians. We connect on common ground—family, food, recreation, movies, music—and that sets the stage to learn from one another, to come to value what our new friends value. In 1999, I did a brief stint of humanitarian work in a refugee camp outside of Damascus. How did we bond? Over Turkish coffee (*a lot of it*), food, music, and dancing. I didn't expect the refugees to meet me with *my language*. Instead, I toted around a dictionary and wrote endless notes in a notebook I carried with me so I could learn (and use) common phrases, greetings, and words. To my surprise, my willingness to learn their language flattered them, so, in turn they started keeping similar notebooks to learn *my language*. By the time I left, many of the refugees had a basic command of English and a taste for Jolly Ranchers. I had a decent grasp of conversational Arabic and an impressive collection of Middle Eastern pop music. Later, in 2004, I volunteered for a short mission trip in the jungles of Belize to rebuild a school. How did we establish a rapport with the locals? Again, food, music, and dancing. Before I boarded my plane, the villagers knew how to lay rebar and I had a new appreciation for the machete and its many practical uses. The key to real connection was the same, whether I was in Syria or Belize. The key was *respect*, for me to be interested *first* in them. Genuine interest, not fake interest to mask a selfish agenda. All humans want the same things, and we respond favorably to those generous enough to meet those primal needs.

Writers are a unique culture. I would almost wage money that most of you never felt you fit in until you decided to become a writer and you met other writers. Hey, I get you. Yes, I was *that kid*, too. I had no clue that toting around James Clavell's *Shogun* in the eighth grade negatively impacted my "coolness factor." I loved to read and books offered me solace from a family bent on destruction. In my world, we moved twice a year and I constantly changed schools, and books were always there. Books never said *goodbye*. When my father left, books remained. When my mom became ill, books were still by my side. In college, when I had barely enough money to keep the lights on, books offered me escape. But my intimate, personal love for books doesn't automatically mean the rest of the world has this same emotional connection. Yet, just because they don't currently have this relationship doesn't mean they can't *ever* have it. We as writers must extend ourselves and meet in areas of common interest, just like Everett had to extend himself—*all of himself*—to the Pirahã people. The Pirahã already had plenty of experience with missionaries trying to change them, trying to make them "fit" into a Western worldview. They had a wall of distrust because no one ever wanted to simply *know them*.

As writers, we run into a similar scenario with the typical "non-reader." We mock the spreaders of Grumpy Cat memes, and turn our noses up at Haz Cheeseburger. We have no idea why anyone would waste his time playing stupid games like Farmville. We poke fun at people who don't love books as if this makes us somehow superior to others who care more about Honey Boo-Boo than Hemingway. We are too busy to "Like" baby pictures or congratulate a follower for her twentieth wedding anniversary, because that is "wasting time" and "not real book marketing." Since we have no algorithm to monitor the joy we create when we take time to console the grieving, uplift the discouraged, or affirm those who struggle, that somehow doesn't count.

Just so you know.

It all counts.

Non-readers have the same wall as the Pirahã. Non-readers are marketed to non-stop 24 hours a day, 7 days a week, 365 days a year. They can't even go to the bathroom without an ad being shoved in their faces. When we fail to establish a dialogue and a relationship and only approach them with something to sell, the wall goes higher.

She doesn't care about me. She only wants to sell her books.

Have you ever done something new, something you never would have done in a million years, but you did it anyway because the recommendation came from someone you trusted? Have you ever become fascinated with a topic only because of someone you liked and respected? Back in college I briefly dated a guy attending school to become a chef. Before meeting him, I was a regular at Subway and Taco Bell and possessed zero interest in cooking. Yet, my boyfriend's passion soon became my passion. I saw his joy and wanted to experience it, too. I never understood my grandfather's love for golf, but because I loved him, I gave it a try. I wasn't any good, but I still had a lot of fun.

Relationships have a way of opening our world and giving us permission to love something new. This happens all the time, and frequently it goes unnoticed. But this is exactly how non-readers can become book lovers. Too many authors think too narrowly about their potential audience. We believe that if we write historical fiction, then we focus on self-professed lovers of history. Yes, that's a start. But social media gives us the ability to become *that friend*, that friend who made us care about the Roman Empire, the fall of Carthage, the women's suffrage movement. We've all had friends who inspired us to try something new—sushi, online dating, playing video games, getting our eyebrows waxed, scrapbooking, learning to knit or crochet, fishing, foreign films, traveling to a city we were previously terrified of, collecting coins, selling Scentsy, or even going camping. As writers, we need to learn to be *that* friend, the friend whose positive energy dares a non-reader to try sitting down with a book and take a chance on falling in love.

This is why we must appreciate the fact that we are bridging cultures on social media. Yes, there is a book-loving subculture, but they're being inundated with uncreative marketing. When we step out of our comfort zone and connect to real people, we have an opportunity to learn from them, to care for them, and then, in turn, help them understand why books are so wonderful. Just like I didn't understand why anyone would spend half a day chasing around a tiny ball with a stick, most "non-readers" don't understand why we'd spend days "doing homework."

It takes being vulnerable to really connect. It also requires that we never underestimate the simple things. One thing writers say to me constantly is, "Who would care what I had for lunch?" My answer? All of us. Food is universal. Food and eating are the grand ceremony that binds all of humanity. Want to connect to "non-readers" (code for "future readers")? Chat over food. Food is universal and has been creating alliances for tens of thousands of years. Food is something everyone can relate to. The "non-readers" have nothing to say about NaNoWriMo or Jungian archetypes used in fiction. They have even less to say about the advantages of Kobo or the pitfalls of iBooks. But, when it comes to grilling a steak or learning to juice kale and LIKE it? They finally have some common ground and can be part of the conversation. Fluffy kittens really do have the power to unite the world, and if you don't believe me, go look how many visits *Surprise Kitty* has had on YouTube.

The good news is that social media makes it simpler than ever to start a dialogue. The bad news is that nothing great happens in the comfort zone. *To become successful we must seek to bridge the culture of writers and regular folk who believe they don't like to read.* For some of you it might be easier if I asked you to join a tribe of cannibals in Papua, New Guinea, than to learn to talk to people who love football and celebrity gossip more than books. It will take time, but this is why we need our bellies in the boat. When we participate in ways that connect us with others, instead of looking for opportunities to "target our market," we will find countless occasions to connect. Later, we will talk more about an actual "plan" for social media, but for now I will just emphasize this point. Part of my everyday routine with Facebook and Twitter includes actively looking for ways to simply connect.

You cannot imagine the rewards.

I've been there for a woman who gave birth to a premature baby. The infant was little more than a pound and struggling to survive. My first encounter with this "Facebook friend" was her plea for prayers that her baby would survive. I was blessed to watch a preemie, who shouldn't have lived, grow bigger and get stronger. Every few days I looked for the woman (a photographer, *not* a writer) and posted words of encouragement and comment on any pictures. If she went too long without sharing a new baby picture, I would post on her wall, "Excuse me, um, more baby pics? You can't get us addicted then leave us hanging." I was privileged enough to watch this baby become strong enough to go home and now I can't tell you what a joy it is to see this fat-cheeked infant. Another Facebook friend (someone I didn't know) posted about being in the hospital. What began as me wishing her well became so much more. I learned why she was in the hospital, worrying her hand would be amputated. I was able to be there to give her comfort when the news was bad, and there to cheer when they saved her hand and reconstructed her thumb. Neither of these women were part of my "marketing plan" but they are forever in my heart. I am better for knowing them. There are people all around us who are lonely, hurting, or wanting to share something amazing. Go to them. Be a friend and then one day, perhaps, you will be *that friend* who opens their minds to something new.

Chapter 6

THE NEW AUTHOR PLATFORM:
Writers are the New Reality Stars

TEN YEARS AGO, no one cared what a fiction author looked like. No one cared if she had hobbies or was good with people. No one really cared if she was even likable. The only thing that mattered was whether or not this writer could write great stories. To a small extent this is still true. There are established authors who refuse to get on social media and they write fantastic stories that continue to sell, but this type of author is a dying breed.

Now entire generations are growing up on the Internet. Age groups that typically avoided computers are the fastest growing population on Facebook—the Silver Surfers (55+). I bought my sixty-one-year-old mother an iPhone for her birthday because she's addicted to text messaging and spends a lot of her free time on Facebook. Most people now have smart phones and computers, and we use this technology to connect with other people.

Also, we're spoiled. We've become accustomed to being able to talk to and interact with our favorite singers, musicians, athletes, actors, and authors in real time. We tweet and post to Facebook. We ogle the Osbornes and keep up with the Kardashians. We have been so indulged with intimacy that we expect it. No, we demand it.

No, we are addicted to it.

Who would have thought twelve years ago that millions of people would care about truck drivers carrying cargo to the Arctic? Who could have predicted that we'd care about fishing boats and their crews? Alligator trappers in Louisiana? Crazy people preparing for the apocalypse? Sad souls buried in a mountain of junk? Families staging drug interventions? Rich, spoiled housewives with four nannies to free up more time to throw each other under the bus? Who could have envisioned a world where television audiences would vote for the vocalists they wanted to hear? Or the models they wanted to grace magazine covers? We now exist in a world of ballroom dancing NFL players and Romani gypsies flaunting four-hundred-pound wedding dresses outfitted with disco lights. Modern audiences have tired of the canned sit-coms of the 20th century and long to be a fly on the wall of "real" life. We're a generation of voyeurs who are thrilled when given opportunity to be part of the pageantry.

Which woman do you think deserves a rose from our Bachelor? Text and vote!

Humans love to share, to klatsche, to give opinions, and to gossip. Why do you think all those networks and popular shows have hashtags? Do you love sharks and want to talk to other people who wait all year for the Discovery Channel's Shark Week? Hop onto Twitter and join the #sharkweek conversation. Get online and converse about #preppers, #hoarders, #NCIS, #mythbusters, #cakeboss, or even #Dexter. Today it is possible for a fan in Texas to chat with another fan in Australia about the latest episode of @GameofThrones on #asoif (*A Song of Ice and Fire*). If every other form of entertainment medium sees the value in generating community and conversation, why would audiences be interested in an author who never engages? If the best we have to offer Twitter is *Buy my book!* we deserve the frustration and dismal sales that follow.

I can't count the number of times I've had published authors tell me, "I just want to write, I don't want to *talk* to people." My response is this. We are asking people to part with money that is scarce in today's rough economy. We're also asking for time, which is even more precious. The very *least* we can do is talk to potential readers and have a good attitude about it.

The future is social media and writers who take advantage will reap tremendous rewards. Ah, but now we have to recalibrate what we think about as a platform and get rid of our myopia. We are no longer in the world of traditional marketing. In the past, marketing messages were static and fixed so as to avoid consumer confusion. In the 1990s most people were not online and social media was not yet a game changer. Nike was not counting on Carl Consumer seeing their magazine ads and then repackaging their messages to share with his friends, family and coworkers.

Traditional marketing is unidirectional. It talks AT people, not WITH them. Author platforms built solely on traditional marketing are rigid and FAKE. Social media, on the other hand, is dynamic. It's organic. It's conversational. It *engages*. The new author platform pulses with life and changes each day, renewing its cells. It has a human heartbeat. How? It has a HUMAN at its very center, the human author.

Ten years ago no one cared if a fiction author gardened, was a gourmet cook or a wine aficionado who loved Golden Retrievers. Today they still don't care and I want to ask why not? Because we writers haven't approached them as fellow humans. Why aren't we caring about what readers care about? Why aren't we using this common ground to connect? Why are we being so self-centered that we demand that readers find us via what *we* love? Books. Writing. Publishing.

As I see it, the fundamental problem is that we have failed to appreciate that authors now have the ability to become *personalities*. We are the new reality stars. Twitter, Facebook, and blogs are our "reality shows" that allow people to connect with us on common ground.

Traditional marketing was the cardboard cutout, a one-dimensional, soulless construct. Yet, now, social media has breathed life into that cut-out and offered writers the ability to be human again. When we approach social media with the old thinking, we seem strange, rigid and out of place. But, once we embrace our ability to be fully human, the results are nothing short of magic. The new author platform cannot be tightly controlled, measured with metrics, or enslaved by algorithms. It's a living organism, imbued with its Creator's very DNA. It changes as we change, grows with us and from us because it IS us—machine on the outside, human on the inside.

Consumers want authenticity. They long to connect on mutual ground. They get excited when they realize their favorite author also loves dogs and collects *My Little Ponies*. They will move mountains for those they like and consider a friend. What this means is that all those hobbies, passions, and idiosyncrasies that had no value before are now a priceless friendship chest. Real friends are those who will help you move your couch; real digital friends are the ones who will help you move books.

Chapter 7

REDEFINING WHAT "READER" MEANS

NOW YOU KNOW WHY traditional marketing, advertising, and promotion alone is a big fat time suck that's unlikely to impact sales. Sorry—I didn't make the rules. By now I hope I've made it clear why ads, commercials, trailers, mailers, bookmarks, blog tours, and free giveaways by themselves have minimal effect on your overall sales numbers.

Sometimes it seems that life would be easier if traditional tactics *could* sell books because then we could pay for a nice book trailer and program an automated platform to blitz out "commercials" on every social site. Yet, the fact remains that books are not tacos or car washes. What's a writer to do?

As we talked about on the last section, many of us spend far too much time marketing to a very small segment of the population that defines themselves as "readers." Additionally, too much book promotion is happening in places where we are least likely to find most people—bookstores, author blogs, book review sites, reader forums. And, you know who makes up the most of these "reader" groups?

Other writers.

Thus, not only are we marketing to one of the smallest sections of society—the self-professed avid reader—but we are also spending far too much time marketing to other writers. We get on Facebook and Twitter and hang out with each other, befriend each other, and talk to each other. Writers blog about writing and talk about writing...**at the expense of talking to potential readers.**

Make no mistake; writers are awesome. I spend most of my time talking to them. Yet, in fairness, you guys are my reading audience. Ah, but hold on. Calm down. Writers are incredible, kind and talented. We *should* befriend other writers. They are our professional core and our support network. The mistake is when fellow writers become our comfort zone. Do not mistake your professional network for your reader demographic. Will writers make up part of our fan base? Yes, of course. But fellow writers are only very a small fraction of our overall readership, and they're oversold and worn out.

We MUST reach out to fresh blood and bring new readers into the family. If we don't, our platform becomes inbred, then starts playing the banjo and firing a shotgun in the air and it's all downhill from there. Too many writers spend too much time talking to a small group at the expense of the big picture.

Another HUGE misconception many writers have is that, unless someone professes to love reading that he, therefore, does not read at all. Major fallacy. Avid readers simply need far less convincing because they already love to read.

Think of it this way. If I am from Thailand and I grew up eating peppers hot enough to melt flesh, then likely I will seek out Thai food restaurants. What if, however, I open a Thai food restaurant in Dallas? Dallas, happens to have a lot of people from Thailand. But the problem is that with a large population of Thai comes a larger number of Thai food restaurants. If all of them are catering to other Thais and offering all kinds of authentic cuisine, then there is very steep competition. How can my little Thai restaurant survive?

I have to think differently.

I can go after the same patrons as all of my competition (fellow Thais), OR I can seek to introduce an exotic food to outsiders who don't already believe they love Thai food. Maybe instead of strictly Thai food, I can create a fusion restaurant that adds in essences of Australian cuisine. Maybe I can use some imagination and make Thai food more appealing to an American palate. Whatever approach I choose, the goal is the same. If I can convince Joe American to try something different this once, then my food can make him a fan. Joe will see that *my* Thai restaurant has awesome food, and when he has a good experience he'll not only become a loyal patron (since he's still afraid other Thai restaurants will give him heartburn), but it's no stretch to assume that he might also tell all of his Joe American pals that my restaurant is *different* and worth a try.

Joe's opinion will carry more weight with this new population of potential patrons. Why? It's nothing shocking for a Thai person to love Thai food, but for Joe American who normally lives off hamburgers? His opinion is gold. Joe and his pals likely will still believe they hate Thai food, but THIS restaurant—MY restaurant—is different. My restaurant is that perfect choice for a date night or when you simply crave something out of the ordinary.

It just takes some creativity when defining our demographic.

Put another way, why was Julia Child so successful? She made fine French cuisine accessible to average people. The other French chefs of her time defined their demographic far too narrowly. They all targeted an elite group of foodies. Julia, however, saw her audience as anyone who could taste food and who wanted to enjoy the experience. If you liked to eat good food and maybe liked to cook? YOU were her demographic.

Guess what? That was a demographic of hundreds of millions.

The result? Julia Child became a legend. Unlike other chefs, she didn't look down her nose at regular people. She believed that just because average people hadn't grown up in high society, didn't mean they wouldn't embrace French cuisine and fall in love if given access.

Too many writers narrowly define their demographic as those

people who say they love to read books. By doing this, they exclude and underestimate "non-readers." Yet, as teachers and storytellers, what is our REAL demographic? Anyone desiring information or entertainment. THAT demographic is MASSIVE and when we writers mobilize THAT sector of society—the fat part of the bell curve—that is when literary history is made.

The Joy Luck Club, *The Divine Secrets of the Ya-Ya Sisterhood*, *Water for Elephants*, *The Help*, and *Killing Floor* all ignited a passion for stories in people who normally would not have defined themselves as avid readers.

"Non-reader" is really a highly inaccurate term. The fact that people don't list "reading" as a favorite hobby doesn't mean they don't read at all. In fact, this group that believes they don't enjoy reading can become some of THE most fiercely loyal fans. Why? Because they still believe they don't like reading unless those books are YOUR books. See that neat transition?

There are millions of people who claim they don't like reading, but they bought every last hardcover of the Harry Potter series. Many of them might not ever read another author because J.K. Rowling has their undying devotion.

How do we tap into this fat part of the bell curve? How do we convince people who'd rather watch *Duck Dynasty* or play *Call of Duty* that our books are worth spending their precious free time on? It's actually pretty simple. Get out of the comfort zone.

In the old paradigm, there was very little interaction between authors and readers, and this is why the books were the only way an author had of creating a platform. The only way an author could emotionally connect to readers was through characters and story. But note, novels aren't 80,000 words about writing and the craft and the changes in publishing. Novels are stories about people, about the human condition. They are about love, life, pain, disappointment, suffering, and triumph. The books created the dialogue that forged the emotional connection. In the old paradigm, books were the *only* way to do this.

Another thing I want you to do is to place content in *context*. I constantly hear marketing experts advising writers to blog about their books, the writing process, and their struggles as an artist. What these experts are failing to account for is that we live in a completely different world. In the 20th century, authors rarely interacted with audiences. Writers might have shaken some hands with readers at a book signing, done an interview for a paper or even scored a few minutes on television or radio, but that was pretty much it. Authors only emerged out of hiding a handful of times a year to "chat," so *of course* they needed to talk about writing, their books and their life as an artist. TV stations didn't give airtime to just anyone whenever they wanted. You had a five-minute spot. Talk about your book!

Five or ten years ago, websites were cost-prohibitive to own and build, and, for the fortunate writers who had them, managing the sites was time-intensive and expensive. Unless the author happened to know how to write code, changing a website involved hiring a webmaster. Due to these limitations, websites remained fairly static. Before 2004, no one noticed because they'd never known anything different. Audiences weren't yet integrated into a pulsing, living social media experience, thus had no basis for comparison. In a global village that engages in daily, real-time conversations, if all we do is talk about our books, our writing or ourselves we 1) run out of content pretty quickly and hit a wall. Face it, there are only so many times we can talk about our books before we want to punch *ourselves* in the face, or 2) we quickly bore others. We become that guy no one wants at the party because he can't stop talking about his glory days as a college running back.

If talking about ourselves non-stop isn't a good idea for the workplace, friendships, or dating, then why on Earth is this considered a good idea for social media? It isn't, and this is why we've spent so much time exploring how society as a whole has changed. If we don't understand our world and how we fit best within our modern culture, we'll wear ourselves out and have no time left for writing books.

What about Advertising, Marketing, Promotion and PR?

It is OK to use these traditional methods of attracting readers. What I want to make clear is that **advertising, marketing, promotion, and PR** *alone* **offer a lousy return on investment**. Marketing, promotions, ads, and PR firms are useful. The danger is in believing **we can solely rely on them.** Social media and the Internet have not only altered society, but technology has transformed the very structure of the human brain. As new machines invade our everyday lives, we crave human connection even more.

We can't write books, tuck our heads in the sand and hope some Facebook ads and contests will bring in the big book sales. If you'll engage in building your platform the WANA Way, then marketing and advertising work *better* and will have a far greater ROI because you've taken time to invest in relationships. When people have connected with you as a person, they're far more likely to *notice* your ad, your promotion, or that you have an interview on Sirius Radio because there is a wealth of positive somatic markers connected to your name.

All social media does is allow us, over time, to make our names meaningful and emotional and *that* is what will make any PR or advertising a valuable investment. PR people are great, but we have to give them something to work with. If we have a thriving community vested in our success, then the money we invest in advertising, marketing, promotions or PR expertise has better odds of yielding great returns.

PR and marketing people are wonderful, but don't task them with trying to spin gold from a void.

In the traditional model, we did a lot of our marketing and platform-building alone unless we were blessed to have the cash to hire professionals. Social media is a game-changer and, done the WANA Way, proves WE ARE NOT ALONE. This next section is to help you adjust your approach to social media. You don't have to be a social butterfly or a Chatty Cathy. You don't have to know a lot of people or be bold enough to regularly approach people you don't know. Why? Because you are part of a team, and we all can buttress each other's weaknesses. Additionally, we're going to explore the notion of "going viral." Who wouldn't want their content to spread across the globe? We all want to go viral. That's a noble *and achievable* goal, but we need to understand what content and behaviors can improve our odds of hitting the viral jackpot or we will wear ourselves out with ineffective activity.

Section 2
YOUR TEAM & TACTICS

Chapter 8

THE POWER OF GETTING "STICKY"

HOPEFULLY YOU NOW UNDERSTAND the word "non-reader" is a misnomer. "Non-readers" DO read. They just happen to be highly selective and tough to impress. The benefit, however, is that once one of these guys becomes a fan? He is the most loyal, devoted fan any writer can have. Often this guy is the best salesman a writer can have, too. He is the flint that creates the spark that can start the fire.

But how do we get his attention? Good question.

We Need to Get Sticky

British-Canadian journalist Malcolm Gladwell writes, "The Stickiness Factor says that there are specific ways of making a contagious message memorable; there are relatively simple changes in the presentation and structuring of information that can make a difference in how much of an impact it makes" (*The Tipping Point* 25).

The Stickiness Factor not only applies to our social media message, it applies to who we are as writer personalities. It also applies to our books. Nailing what I will call The Sticky Author Triumvirate is key to publishing success. We need to get sticky on all three to have the best odds of reaching the tipping point.

Let's take a look at The Sticky Author Triumvirate.

Get Sticky with Social Media Messages

One of the reasons that traditional marketing doesn't work when it comes to books is because the messages aren't sticky. In fact, we are so blitzed with marketing messages in modern society that most marketing messages become white noise and therefore invisible. Auto-tweets are ignored and are what marketing experts call clutter. Also, most of us hate being spammed, and we aren't exactly likely to share it.

Additionally, it isn't enough to have a million people "see" a message/pitch. There has to be a compulsion to **see,** then **act**. If a zillion people see my commercial for car insurance, but no one ever changes policies, then the campaign is a failure. It's a big waste of effort, time and money.

What can make people care enough to buy your books? You have to care about them first. Simply talking to people can go a long way toward making a sale. We buy from people we know and LIKE. Stand apart from all the takers and learn to give. Beyond that?

Yes, most of us love writing. Um, duh. But we love other things too. We need to extend ourselves and simply start talking to people. We have to learn to be unselfish. We must stop demanding that others connect with us via OUR interests—books, craft, writing—and take initiative. We need to locate our common ground then extend ourselves and connect where our potential **reader** feels comfortable.

Surely you have friends, family or coworkers on Facebook who are not writers. Who are they talking to? Go to their walls and join in the conversations and make new friends.

Just once a day make it a point to add non-writers who are active on social media to your network. Pay attention to them and start a dialogue. Be genuine and positive, and that will be STICKY. People crave attention and positive energy, so go be the light they need.

We Need to be Sticky Writer Personalities

The Stickiness Factor applies to who we are as writer personalities. Chit-chat on social media is actually very valuable. People who repost, compliment, question, serve, and are positive are also **memorable**. We're sticky. People like us. When they think "writer" we become the first person they think about.

This is one of the reasons it is beneficial to get out of the comfort zone and visit different social circles. As long as we are all hanging out with other writers, we blend into the din. But, if we start talking to other people who love sports, parenting, knitting, the military, politics, animals, cooking, racing, motorcycles, or celebrities, then we are injecting ourselves into groups that are not comprised of people just like us. We stand out, so we are a bit more sticky.

Pick a favorite channel on cable TV, a favorite show, or a video game, and I guarantee there is a Twitter # for it.

Start talking to people who love #PawnStars, #Pickers, #WestCoastChoppers, #BrideWars, #AI, #Glee, #ESPN, #Fox, #Fringe, #DrPhil, #Oprah, #Ellen, #MythBusters, #Hoarders, #Preppers, or #Taboo. Profile your potential reader. What does she like to do with her day? Maybe your reader is a #teacher or she plays #WOW. Maybe he is a #marine or likes #LordsofWar. Get creative and get out of that comfort zone.

Sure you can still hang out with writers, but we are your peers, not a substitute for a fan base. To be sticky, we must stick out. Go to the websites of your favorite channels and shows and find their Twitter # and then make a column for it (more about how to do this later). Chat with people. Every time I watch #MyStrangeAddiction, I can't help but *talk* about it.

OMG! That woman drinks BLEACH? How is she even ALIVE? #mystrangeaddiction

We can also use blogging to super increase this Sticky Factor. How? First, stop blogging about the same topics as every other writer. Blogging about writing is great, but not necessarily memorable. There are better things to blog about that can make you sticky like Super Glue. Author blogs, when written properly, are a fantastic way to increase our Sticky Factor exponentially. More on this later.

We Need to Write Sticky Books

This is why I teach social media for writers. We need to do social media in a way that is effective, that will eventually translate into sales, but—most importantly—we need an approach that leaves time to write great books. Great books are **sticky**. Sure, if I have a popular blog and a good social media presence, I will probably sell some books. Yet, the only way my book can break past that initial layer of contact is to write a sticky book. Turn politeness into passion. Though any sale is wonderful, it isn't enough for someone to buy your book. Readers must also *love* it so much that they *can't wait* to tell someone, recommend your book, or even buy a gift copy for a pal. Great sticky books are the best tools for igniting that word-of-mouth wildfire.

We all need to strive for that Sticky Author Triumvirate. It doesn't matter if your message reaches a hundred million people. If it doesn't translate into action, it's squandered time. Stickiness makes the difference, and we need to Be Sticky Authors, Be Sticky with Social Media, and Write Sticky Books. If we master one but not the other two, we'll do OK. Master two out of three? Better. True key to success? Mastery of all three.

This is one of the reasons it is so critical to write great books. Great books by nature are sticky, but alone they're no longer enough. Remember Mark Williams and Saffina Desforges? Their first book, *Sugar and Spice*, that sat at Amazon rank #123,456,790 was the same book that later rocketed to #1 and stuck like glue. Now that anyone can be published, relying on a great book alone is playing craps with your career. We have always been in control of writing great books and we had staggering failure rates to show for it. Mark and Saffina nearly failed, but then they learned to be *sticky* by using WANA methods. In the Digital Age, we finally can get sticky on all sides so there is no getting rid of us. We are gonna be triple-sided duct-tape. Yes, I invented a new duct tape dimension.

Ah…but this is when the panic creeps in.

What? *twitching eye* I need hobbies and friends outside of writers? How do I get some of those? Are they on eBay?

Yes, we need all the friends we can get, but don't be lured in by sites promising to deliver you a bazillion followers/friends. More is not always more. Don't assume that because an author has 30,000 followers, she is wields great social influence. In fact, it's been my experience that this kind of person is generally less effective because the network is not comprised of the right *kind* of people. These types of numbers, most of the time, are vanity stats. They make us look good, but, beyond that, this type of following is often inert.

Quality trumps quantity. Not all connections have the same weight. The cool news is you don't have to find a bazillion friends. You just need a handful of the "right" friends. It's the old adage, It's not what you know, it's WHO you know. That's truer now than ever in human history.

Who are the right kinds of friends?

Chapter 9

METCALF'S LAW & THE THREE FRIENDS WE **MUST** HAVE ON SOCIAL MEDIA

THERE ARE THREE KINDS of people who can make the difference between life and death for your message (book, idea, fashion trend, product, etc.) especially in the Digital Age, and we will talk about them more in a moment. First, though, I want to address some faulty beliefs and ineffective behaviors I witness daily online.

One of the reasons that the old blast out an automated message on social media approach doesn't work is that it separates the writer from the social media experience. To get connected to the right people, we need to be present so we can pay attention. But we need a large network for more reasons than selling books.

Say I am new to Twitter. My name is Nancy Newgirl and I have 10 followers and at least half of them are bots. The other five are members of my writing group and they are in the same situation. Our networks are almost insignificant. We are at the mercy of Metcalf's Law.

What Metcalf's Law Means to You

According to Seth Godin, Metcalf's Law states that, "the value of a network increases with the square of the number of people using it. So when there are 10 fax machines in the world, that is 25 times better value than when there were two" (*Unleashing the Ideavirus* 184-185). What this means is that any network is only as valuable as the number of people *actively* participating. For example, even though the very first fax machine cost $2000, it was pretty much worthless. Why? Who was the owner going to fax? There were no other fax machines. The machine only began to grow in value as more people bought fax machines capable of receiving, repackaging and then resending messages. "Communication products demand viral marketing because they're worthless without someone at the other end" (184). We can't sell books on Twitter if no one is at the other end *receiving, repackaging and then resending* the message.

Metcalf's Law also applies to social media networks. A person with 5 followers doesn't yet have a lot of value to her network. How can Nancy Newgirl increase the value of her network?

Three Friends We Must Have on Social Media

Malcolm Gladwell offers the perfect solution in his book, *The Tipping Point*. For Ms. Newgirl to increase the value of her network, she needs to connect to one of three kinds of people: a Connector, a Maven, or a Salesman. (I highly recommend you get a copy of *The Tipping Point*, because so many of Gladwell's observations about epidemiology translate brilliantly to writers and social media.)

These three types of people have always been responsible for word-of-mouth epidemics; we just didn't have the unprecedented access to meeting them that we do now. The awesome part about social media is that it's like a giant honey trap for these types of individuals. The Connector, the Maven, and the Salesman are intensely social people and they are drawn to social sites like mosquitoes to a bug light.

It's soooooo preeeetttyyyyyyyy…

If we pay attention on social media long enough, it's almost a guarantee we'll meet these sorts of people. If we can fold these personalities into our networks, we significantly increase the odds our messages will become epidemic. Nancy Newgirl might only have ten people in her network, but if Friend Number 11 is one of these three types of people, she's taken her social power to an entirely new level. Why? She's made a powerful ally who wields a lot of social influence.

Can you see how numbers lie when it comes to social media? There are publishers giving their writers a hard time because, Author Such and Such has 30,000 followers. Why don't you? You need to get on Twitter and follow more people!

This is part of what's making writers want to slam their heads in a door.

Sheer numbers are not enough. If we have thousands of Nancy Newgirls (or bots with no human behind them) in our network, then that is akin to being able to fax 10,000 other broken fax machines. They might be able to receive messages, but the message dies there.

WANAs work smarter, not harder. WANAs know we don't need to make ten thousand friends to influence ten thousand people. I actually have the potential to reach 10,000 people with just four friends (pssst...they hang out on #MyWANA a lot cuz they're social butterflies). Metcalf's Law shows why it's so critical for us to ignore the siren's song of tools and automation and to actually spend time on social media. Not a *lot* of time, but *meaningful* time. Pay attention. Who's active? Who's social? Who knows how to talk about something other than writing? These are the people who make the best friends to have in life and online.

If we disappear off Facebook for days and weeks or only tweet when we need something, we miss out on meeting these generous and wonderful people who can make the critical differences in our careers. We don't need to take our careers to the next level; we just need to meet the person who knows the person who gives us the opportunity.

What can you take away from this? Be kind. Be social. Be vested. The power of networking and authentic interaction cannot be properly measured. When we automate or fail to participate, we're likely to lose out on countless doors of opportunity disguised as relationships.

Any social media expert who sells you a bill of goods about how this or that program can tweet for you or post for you really isn't doing you a favor. This method is empty busywork that looks good on the surface, but has no real depth or effectiveness. It's all activity, no productivity. This approach will create vanity stats. Instead of being a hamster in a wheel tweeting into the abyss and "hoping" something sticks, take charge of your future and get involved. Talk to people. This will increase your odds that something will not only stick, but will set fire.

There are a number of approaches to being successful on social media, but I have a confession to make. I am lazy. Really. If I gave in to my nature, I'm so lazy I could easily slip into a coma. Don't let anyone sell you lies. Worker bees didn't create the wonders of modern society so don't go thank the industrious. Go thank the lazy and impatient.

See, the lazy man didn't want to get up out of his chair to turn the channel, so he invented the remote control. The lazy woman didn't want to spend each and every moment entertaining her child, so she invented toys that whistle, sing, and dance. It was lazy and impatient people who envisioned a world where we could drive a car—FAST— instead of having to bounce around in a carriage and hop several trains to go on vacation. The lazy and impatient invented cell phones so they didn't have to stay home and wait on return phone calls, and concocted drive-thru burger joints so they didn't have to cook.

Okay, maybe this is a little bit of tongue-in-cheek, but there's still some truth in it.

The Big Lie: Don't Drink the Kool-Aid

Here's the thing, society—especially American society—sells us a lie. We're told that the people who work 90 hours a week are more productive and valuable. Many of us take this lie hook, line, and sinker and then drag it into our writing lives. We believe that if we aren't spending hours and hours on social media, we aren't being productive. We need to be good little worker bees and everything will turn out dandy if we put in enough time.

Wrong.

Working until we're half dead doesn't mean we're productive; it means our approach is grossly inefficient. Lazy Kristen actually helps me be more efficient, crazy as that might sound. More on that in a moment.

The Writer's Two Main Social Media Fumbles

The Water Cooler Writer—Many writers fall into the Water Cooler category, especially when first starting out. This writer is on social media, but with no defined purpose and no real activity that will create a meaningful author platform. This writer often tweets using a cutesy moniker like @ProcratinatingWriter. She might blog about the writing experience or her daily struggles to be taken seriously, but her actual name is hard to find unless you work for Homeland Security.

None of the Water Cooler Writer's activities are focused or involve strategy. She's waiting until she has a finished book and an agent to worry about building her author platform.

This is an okay place for any writer to start, though not ideal. It's basically the social media training-wheels stage. But, if our goal is to race the Tour de France—be a professional published author who sells enough books to write full time—then the training wheels need to go.

The Automated Writer—This writer takes efficiency seriously. Too seriously. He automates everything he can. He has a webpage and a social media account on Facebook, LinkedIn, Tumblr, Goodreads, Google+, Instagram, and Twitter.

He is EVERYWHERE. Or is he?

No one has ever actually talked to this writer, so he never connects. This is one way to do social media, but the ROI (return on investment) is dismal. Every time I hear someone complain that Twitter doesn't sell books, I already know what their Twitter stream will look like—a perfect row of spam. This method will sell books eventually, sort of like if we spam 100,000 people with news of their inheritance from a relative they never knew they had living in Ghana some ~~sucker~~ person will eventually click the link and send cash. This is a game of mass numbers.

A lot of writers are wearing themselves out on social media because they are Water Cooler Writers—they are chatting with friends and don't have strategic content to build a brand OR because they are Automated Writers who rely on a tactic that takes MASSIVE volume for any return. This is worker bee behavior. Sure, if you do enough of this it might pay off, but it's an awful lot of work and time. I mean, we *do* have the option of cutting down trees with an ax, but a chainsaw might be more efficient, and leave us a tad less exhausted. I'm going to tell you guys the secret to being a **WANA Writer**. WANA Writers are smart, charming and known for being strangely good-looking. Wait… okay, yeah that's true but not part of what we are talking about in this section.

WANA Writers work as a team to create communities.

WANA writers work smarter, not harder. WANA Writers know that the only way to sell books is to 1) write a good book and 2) spark word of mouth. Thus, the WANA Writer, when she isn't absorbing every lesson she can about the craft and writing an awesome novel, knows that she needs to work on spreading word of mouth. WANA Writers know that being a worker bee is great, but knowing a social butterfly is better.

The Law of the Few

Why do we need to spot the Social Media Social Butterflies? Because of what Gladwell calls The Law of the Few. "People pass on all kinds of information to each other all the time. But it's only in the rare instance that such an exchange ignites a word-of-mouth epidemic…the success of any kind of social epidemic is heavily dependent on the involvement of people with a particular set of social gifts" (*The Tipping Point* 32).

See, the worker bees aren't the ones who change the world (well, not quickly at least). It's really up to the social butterflies. These are the people who pollinate the world with an idea. Without them, there is no genesis of new thought.

Three Kinds of Social Media Butterflies

At the beginning of this chapter, I mentioned Malcolm Gladwell's three kinds of social butterflies—the Connector, the Maven, and the Salesman. These are the people with the social gifts required to spread a message around the globe. Some people are only one type of social butterfly, but some can be two, and some rare people are actually all THREE.

Meet the Connector

The Connector is that person who seems to know everyone. Remember we talked about the importance of getting sticky in order to market books? As a WANA Writer, we understand that we might not be a Maven, a Connector, or a Salesman, but we can get to know people who ARE. *WANA Writers know how to get sticky by association.* WANA Writers don't waste time trying to change their personalities and be something they aren't. WANA Writers focus on working smarter, not harder so they learn to pay attention for signs of a Social Media Butterfly.

Signs of a Connector Butterfly

Connectors are authentically active on social media.

Just like real butterflies love flowers, social butterflies love people, and this includes Connector Butterflies. They can't help themselves. If you click on a profile and see nothing but automated messages, this is not a sign that this person loves people. In fact, this connection is almost worthless for the purposes of spreading the word about you or your books. These people might be good to learn from, or even a good source of information, but they aren't going to help us much when it comes to expanding our platform. True Connectors are present. Connectors know a lot of people, because they talk to a lot of different kinds of people.

Connectors like…connecting.

This seems a little obvious, but it's true. The Connector is the person at the cocktail party who is guaranteed to introduce you around and plug you into a group of people with like minds and interests. The Connector is a Social Media Match Maker. She pollinates flowers (people) and helps connections germinate into friendships. People thrive with a Connector in their midst.

Connectors are multi-dimensional.

Connectors might be fellow writers, but they are passionate in other areas as well. They aren't the All Writing All the Time Channel. They have friends in other walks of life and interests beyond craft and publishing, which makes them highly valuable for gaining access to new and different groups of people.

Many bloggers are Connectors.

Bloggers are the new way of spreading the word. People who blog and are good at blogging are the movers and shakers of the Digital Age. Get to know the good bloggers. Read their blogs, retweet for them, and comment on their posts. Connectors remember names and faces. Are they seeing yours?

Missing out on Connectors

One of the reasons "keeping our writing life totally and utterly separate" can seriously handicap our platform is that we will miss countless chances to meet Connectors. If we have a Facebook page for writers only, blog non-stop about writing, and tweet only with people in the publishing industry, then we miss opportunities to fold other worlds into ours. We miss out on possibly connecting with a Connector because our focus is too exclusive: Writers Only. All Others Keep Out.

Meet the Maven

According to Malcolm Gladwell, the word Maven comes from Yiddish, and means **one who accumulates knowledge**. "In recent years economists have spent a great deal of time studying Mavens, for the obvious reasons that if marketplaces depend on information, the people with the most information must be the most important" (*The Tipping Point* 60).

I recall the many times that Piper Bayard (a friend and a fellow author) called me The Social Media Maven. I thought she was just being sweet since the word "guru" makes me throw up a little in my mouth. Sorry. Being honest. I didn't care for "expert" either, since any yahoo with a Yahoo account and $20 to spend at Vista Print was an "expert." Ah, but Maven had a nice ring to it so I didn't stop her. At the time, I assumed that Maven was a synonym for guru, so I was down with that. I liked Social Media Maven, though I was really partial to Social Media Jedi (a nickname my friend Gene Lempp gave me).

I do a tremendous amount of research to back up my teaching and theories, so when I spotted this word Piper had used—Maven—and then uncovered the research surrounding Mavens, I was quite humbled and honored that she applied the term to me. But then, I thought back over my life and here are some conversations I'd like to share with you guys to help you recognize Mavens in your life.

Conversations with a Maven

Conversation #1: Man buying energy drink in local Exxon...

Me: Um, excuse me. You are the owner of the black truck out front?

Man: Yeah *gives me odd stare and holds his wallet tighter*

Me: I know I sound crazy, but I think you need to get your radiator checked.

Man: Huh? Why?

Me: As I walked past, I noted the smell of coolant superheated on your manifold.

Man: I didn't smell anything.

Me: Yes, I have a very sensitive nose, and I could definitely smell that you have a leak. I had the same thing happen once, so I recognize the scent. I would get that serviced right away. In fact, here's a business card of the guys that work on my car. They do great work and are fairly priced.

The guy took my advice (I heard this from the men at my service center) and the man actually did have a small crack in his radiator.

Conversation #2: Dark-Haired Woman at Walmart buying a box of hair dye (Blonde)...

Me: Are you going to use that for your hair?

Dark-Haired Woman: I was thinking about it.

Me: Well, I colored my own hair for years, and I know the box says it can make you blonde, but it really will turn you orange and make your hair melt. We used that same product on my college roommate, and it ended badly. Anyway, if you go across the parking lot, talk to Lydia at Sally's Beauty Supply and she can give you a professional product. Judging from what I can see, you'll want a color with blue undertones. That will keep you from turning orange. Also, make sure you invest in a good conditioner if you go down that many levels of color so your hair doesn't start breaking. If you want a good colorist, here's my colorist's business card. I finally gave up dying my own hair because she is so affordable.

Later, I heard from my hairdresser that the woman made an appointment to have her hair colored blonde. I also heard from Lydia at Sally's Beauty Supply that Dark-Haired Woman bought conditioner from her as well.

What Exactly is a Maven?

Mavens are pathologically helpful. We are collectors of data and brokers of information. Not only do we collect vast stores of information, but we also hold a rare ability to put that information in a useful context. We are unparalleled pattern filters and can spot trends and changes that others don't or can't yet see. Not only do we have all this information, but we also long to share it to make the lives of others better.

We Mavens cannot help ourselves. I often refer to myself as Helpful Hannah, and I've had to learn when it's best to just be quiet. Not everyone wants my two cents' worth. Yet, as much as I try to stop my nature, I can't help who I am. I honestly think I became a social media expert so that I could channel all my Maven energies in a productive way.

Mavens are the people who will stop you from buying steaks at one store because the grocery store across the street has better rib eyes and for half the price. We share coupons and tell you not to bother with the warranty from such-and-such because it's a big hassle. We keep business cards for great accountants, nail techs, housekeepers and massage therapists. We also keep the marketplace honest because we remember the prices of things. We are the people who can ignite word-of mouth outbreaks. We help new restaurants thrive, good hair stylists earn new clients, and honest mechanics gain more business.

We are flypaper for information, and we are the people who

write to magazines and offer corrections for misinformation. We are the people who write letters to the editor. We inspire accountability.

I remember about twelve years ago Vogue magazine had an article about a single mother starting her own successful home-based business after leaving her corporate job. Turns out the woman had left a six-figure job in Manhattan, came from a wealthy family and started her business from her home in Martha's Vineyard or the ritzy equivalent. Yes, she was a single mother...who had a *personal chef and a nanny!*

I wrote a long, disgusted letter to Vogue about how out of touch they were with much of their readership and the realities of being a start-up female entrepreneur, let alone a single parent. Vogue printed my letter with an apology.

Mavens make time for this stuff.

Why are Mavens Important in the Marketplace?

Mavens spell death for bad service, bad food, and bad products. If you screw up our hair, our nails, our car, or give us bad service, the world will hear of your misdeeds. We also spell death for bad books.

Why is It Great to Make Friends with a Maven?

Mavens are critical to have in your network because we love spreading news of a good thing, including good blogs, good people and good books. We are the people who will tell everyone we know about a really fantastic book we just read. We write reviews and often write letters of appreciation to the author. We stop people in bookstores and offer unsolicited recommendations. Since our only agenda is to be helpful, many people listen to us.

Mavens are critical for getting social media traction. Many Mavens are also Connectors. When I met *New York Times* Best-Selling Author Bob Mayer in early 2008 he'd never been on social media. I talked his ear off about a new platform called Twitter and how I knew it was going to be the new hot thing. I chatted on and on about Facebook and how social media was going to revolutionize publishing. (Remember, Mavens spot trends.) I could see the writing on the wall even though the agents and editors of the time thought I was a lunatic.

Facebook's only a fad.

People will always want paper books.

Right.

Anyway, the agents and editors may have thought I was crazy, but Bob was one of the few who listened to me. Long story short, I dragged Bob onto social media as my ~~experiment~~ eager student. I wanted to show him this amazing new tool and how it had the power to create a fan base and spread word like Spanish Flu. Authors could finally have control over their careers. I'm thrilled Bob had second thoughts about securing a restraining order and that he gave me a chance to prove my mettle by letting me help him, and then later publishing my first books. Considering that Bob is now making a healthy income doing what he loves, I think he might be a little bit happy, too.

Mavens help you work smarter, not harder. Mavens help you be yourself.

Here's where a Maven comes in handy...

In 2008 Bob started using Twitter, but there was a problem. Bob is an introvert. Don't get me wrong. He's an amazing teacher and speaker, but he wasn't the sort of person who naturally felt comfortable approaching random strangers to chat. Good thing I had no problem with that. I was happy to introduce Bob to everyone and tell them all about his books and workshops.

But this goes back to working smarter not harder. I'm not here to teach you how to change your personality. Bob didn't need to morph into a bubbly outgoing cheerleader. That would have been weird and kinda scary. Worse, it wouldn't have been authentic. Bob would have been trying to be someone he wasn't. But, he *could* be himself by merely allying with people like me. I could be me and introduce Bob so he could then feel comfortable being himself. Not only did I use my Connector powers, but I shamelessly spread recommendations for Bob's books and workshops, too. Still do.

Also, as a Maven I had an ability to spot certain trends. This helped Bob in that he could count on me to alert him of shifts and changes that were worth looking into. Bob's initial alliance with people like me helped him ramp up until he was a force on his own. Now Bob is one of the leaders in the new publishing paradigm, which is powered in large part by social media. I know I loved helping Bob not only because I like helping, but I also LOVE gathering information to help others. Bob Mayer was (and remains) a priceless resource to learn about writing and the industry. It was a great and fair trade. He could learn about social media and I could learn the best information about craft and publishing.

Some Ways to Spot a Maven

Mavens are eager helpers. I think a lot of bloggers and non-fiction people are Mavens. I know @PatThunstrom wrote an entire tutorial series teaching writers how to use TweetDeck. Did he write it for pay? Nope. He just wanted to help. He's the first to recommend a good computer program or information filter. Patrick is an invaluable Twitter Maven.

Mavens are a vast reservoir of information. All KINDS of information. We are natural teachers and helpers. @SusanSpann is a fantastic Maven to befriend. She's a publishing attorney with a passion for helping writers, and she even runs #publaw on Twitter to teach writers how to navigate contracts and legalese. @JennyHansenCA (Jenny Hansen) shares all kinds of helpful information from how to use Excel to how to deal with a high-risk pregnancy. When a writer is in trouble, she's Jenny-on-the-Spot with advice, a link, or a resource. @JamiGold is another

Maven. There's good reason I recruited all of these folks to teach for WANA International.

Mavens love to give advice, recommendations and reviews. We are compulsively helpful. @GeneLempp, @AmyShojai, @NatalieCMarkey, @Angela_Peart, @RoniLoren, @AngelaAckerman, @BeccaPuglisi, @RachelFunkHeller and @JayTechDad are a handful of people I would consider Mega-Mavens. They offer guidance, support, critique, and assistance because they love helping, not because they have an agenda. They have an underlying desire to serve.

If you want to befriend some Mavens, I highly recommend hanging out on #MyWANA. Why? I designed #MyWANA as a Maven Trap. The entire purpose of #MyWANA is NOT to blitz about blogs or books or pitch non-stop with no vested concern. #MyWANA is dedicated to HELP and to SERVE others. #MyWANA was created with the explicit purpose of creating community founded on service above self. This is irresistible to Mavens. #MyWANA attracts Mavens *because it was created by one.*

Many bloggers are Mavens. This is why bloggers are emerging as a new market driver in publishing. Publishing houses are now starting to court the powerhouse bloggers, because they know the bloggers hold tremendous sway over popular opinion and are almost unrivaled in their ability to spark contagious conversation. Many bloggers are unsponsored and unpaid. Many bloggers dedicate countless hours of research and work and write thousands of words a week for no pay. Their only agenda? To help others. Blogger Mavens are powerful allies.

Mavens are some of the most valuable people in our network. They will happily lend a hand wherever they can and they gain joy and purpose from helping and serving others. Maybe you are shy or an introvert. Maybe you're overwhelmed. It's okay.

Mavens dig underdogs.

Connectors might know everyone, and Mavens seem to know everything. Ah, but having a lot of connections (Connector) or a large treasure trove of information (Maven) doesn't automatically mean these talents will translate into sales.

Meet the Salesman

Since my social media lessons apply to selling books as an end goal, let's take a closer look at the third type of friend we all need on social media. Just because a Connector knows hundreds of people doesn't mean he can exert enough influence to break his network past their inertia. I think Bob Mayer might be a great example of this phenomenon. It isn't that Bob isn't charismatic, but he's a shy introvert. Selling doesn't come naturally. Bob has had almost thirty years in the publishing business and he knows a ton of people, but he's an artist, not a salesman. Back when Bob first started his Warrior Writer Workshops I remember having to kick him under the table to mention he had a workshop coming up. It wasn't part of his personality to "ask for the sale."

What about the Maven? Mavens have difficulties, too. True Mavens are not Salesmen. They are teachers and students. I know that, as a Maven myself, we are not always appreciated. We can be seen as busybodies, know-it-alls, or Helpful Hannahs sticking our nose in where it doesn't belong. Mavens mean well, but we can get ourselves into trouble, too.

Since Connectors and Mavens can be limited in their scope of influence, we need a third person capable of creating a tipping point—The Salesman. This person is naturally charismatic and highly persuasive. To start a social epidemic, people need to be connected (Connector), informed (Maven), and then persuaded (Salesman).

"Peer pressure is not always an automatic or unconscious process. It means, as often as not, that someone actually went up to one of his peers and pressured him. In social epidemics, Mavens are databanks. They provide the message. Connectors are social glue: they spread it. But there is also a select group of people—Salesmen—with the skills to persuade us when we are unconvinced of what we are hearing, and they are as critical to the tipping of word–of-mouth epidemics as the other two groups" (Gladwell, *The Tipping Point* 70).

Salesmen have an uncanny ability to ignite action. People listen to them when they make a suggestion. If they praise a book, people buy. If they recommend a workshop, people sign up. If they promote an event, people attend.

All three of these personalities are vital and work together. Sure there are rare people who happen to be all three, but they are few and far between. What social media allows us to do is to find and *connect* all three. If a person is a natural Salesman, but he doesn't know anyone, all he needs to do is connect to a Connector. She has the network and he has the skills of persuasion.

If a Maven wants to sell slots for her writing workshop, she doesn't have to. She can lean on her friend, the Salesman. In fact, since social media is social, it actually works *better* if someone else does our selling. It feels less like spam and more like community.

As we mentioned earlier, Bob Mayer has a lot of connections, and I would qualify him as a Connector. Yet, especially when he was new to social media, it simply wasn't in his nature to go up to random people and start talking. He also had a terrible time "closing the sale." The cool thing about social media was that Bob didn't have to be a Salesman to sell workshop slots. He just had to be friends with a Salesman or two or three. All of them knew Bob and had attended his amazing workshop and were more than happy to persuade on behalf of Bob.

On top of that, I happen to be a Connector and a Maven. I wrote blogs about Bob's workshops (ergo the *warriorwriters* in my blog's URL), and we used those first blogs as a hub of information to help the Salesmen sell Bob's workshops. Connectors, Mavens, and Salesmen all worked as a team to promote Bob, because we knew his teachings offered tremendous value to writers.

I called my first book We Are Not Alone for a very good reason. Too many social media experts try to change a writer's core personality. Why? Because their approach makes the writer do everything alone (until she can afford to outsource). Email lists, form letters, newsletters, vlogs, etc. give the writer the sole burden of being all things—Connector, Informer, and Persuader.

The reason this approach doesn't work well is that most of us *aren't* all things. Thus, we crack under the pressure of trying to operate outside of our natures. Even if we can wear all three hats, we still need time left to write books. This is why the WANA approach rests on the power of a team, which not only allows us to be ourselves, it's more effective so it frees up more time to *write*.

#MyWANA was established for the sole purpose of writers supporting other writers. It is a place of love and community. What has been interesting is that some people, when they first tripped and fell into Twitter, wouldn't have considered themselves to be a Connector, a Maven, or a Salesman. The beauty of creating a community is that we will be for others what we won't be for ourselves. For instance, we might be terrible Salesmen when it comes to our own book or blog, but we have no problem being the Salesman for one of our "twibe" members.

#MyWANA has helped all of us become Connectors. Blogging has helped us learn to tap into Maven energy. Love for our fellow #MyWANA tweeps has made each of us more of a Salesman than we ever thought we could be. Service, love and connection is what social media is really all about. Plant some love and wait. What blooms can surprise you.

Chapter 10

THE TRUTH ABOUT GOING VIRAL

WHY ARE WE ON SOCIAL MEDIA? To build a brand and a platform. Okay. But we could hand-sell books at flea markets or speak at Rotary clubs around the country to build brand and a platform. Again, why social media? Because it's easier, more time-effective, and there is this funny video with kittens. Okay, those are good answers, but I will tell you why we're all on social media. *We all want to go viral.*

It's okay to admit you want to go viral. It means you're smart. Face it, we can only build our brand and our platform so big on our own, and our friends can only help so much. There are only so many hours in a day and only so much content we can contribute. We all want that magic *bump* that makes our names, our books, our ideas spread faster than a cold during the holiday season.

Note: Connectors, Mavens and Salesmen can help with going viral because they're the most likely to spread your content on your behalf.

One of the biggest problems I see with writers is that they say they want to go viral, but then engage in activities that virtually ensure this will never occur. What is worse is that well-meaning social media "experts" teach tactics that will actually KILL most chances of a writer going viral. For us to create a brand that is effective in the Digital Age, we *must* consider its nature, and the content that we are using to create and buttress our brand. In order to maximize our time on social media, we need to make sure that our efforts are *focused* and *effective*.

There are no hard-and-fast rules to guarantee we will go viral, but there are some behaviors that will greatly improve our odds.

High Concept Content

Let me briefly introduce you to my method of blogging, what I call "High Concept Blogging." High concept is a tool employed by Hollywood to help increase their odds that a movie will become a blockbuster, which is code for "make lots of money." Can Hollywood *guarantee* that a movie will become another *Titanic* or *Star Wars*? Of course not, or they wouldn't put out stinkers like *The Watch* or *Green Lantern*. High concept is no guarantee that a movie will resonate on a large scale, but it's at least a solid bet.

High concept has three components: it is universal, emotional, and it gives the audience something to contribute and/or take away. We will discuss this more in the blogging section because, while it is simple, it certainly isn't easy. If it were easy, then every movie coming out of Hollywood would be a runaway success.

What does this high concept stuff have to do with writers and social media?

A lot, actually. I teach at conferences all over the country and part of my job is to listen to other experts in my industry. I love listening to new people teach social media because I don't know everything and I'm always learning. Yet, I will say that I hear a lot of misguided advice, especially when it comes to training fiction authors how to build a platform that will eventually drive book sales.

What works for non-fiction does not work for fiction, and a lot of marketing experts don't get this. Some believe that the same techniques for building a diet book platform can be used by thriller authors, too. Yeah, um. No.

Social Media/Blogging Advice That Will Guarantee You NEVER Go Viral ... Ever

A blog is one of the best tools for building a platform and a great way to eventually go viral, but author blogs require an entirely new way of writing. New York groans and says things like, "Author blogs don't sell books." I counter with, "Sucky author blogs won't sell anything." Blogging is a skill, but we can be very good writers who are choosing really BAD content for our blogs. This is an easy mistake to make since there is a lot of outdated advice floating around out there.

Bad Blogging Tip #1—You can do interviews on your blog.

When I attend writing conferences, I can wager that there will always be a marketing expert who will recommend for fiction writers to do interviews with other authors. Okay, aside from the fact that interviewing is a skill, why is this a really bad idea? Interviews take time we don't have. We have to get permission to conduct the interview, and then we have to research the person we are interviewing. Then we have to create questions, email the questions, wait for responses to the questions, edit the responses, and then finally post. Aside from this being a brutally time-intensive activity that leaves no time for writing, the main reason this is bad advice is this:

Author interviews never go viral (unless someone dies or behaves badly).

When was the last time you were at your day job and everyone in the office was buzzing about the same author interview? If an author interview has gone viral it is because the writer is dead or his career is. If an author writes a memoir and it is a total work of fiction and he apologizes on Oprah? Okay, THAT can go viral. Thing is, author interviews, by their very nature, are NOT going to travel that far beyond our own network. This activity is almost a total time suck that will do more to give you stress headaches than to drive book sales.

Non-Fiction Authors are Different

For the non-fiction authors out there, interviews can go viral for three reasons. First, your reading audience is *seeking information, not entertainment.* Secondly, unlike a fiction author interviewing another novelist, this information will not be *insanely niche.* We fiction writers go all fan-crazy when we hear that Dean Koontz is going to divulge his writing secrets. Most regular people? They don't care. On the other hand, if I write diet books and score an interview with Dr. Oz? Millions will care. The third reason that interviews work differently for the non-fiction author is that this author will likely be interviewing popular experts (who happen to be authors). These experts usually have very **large and active** followings. I can personally attest that many *New York Times* best-selling novelists don't even know how to work their own Face-book pages and they've been known to throw holy water at TweetDeck. I've interviewed huge authors on my blog and guess what? My hits *were actually lower.* All that time and effort for no real payoff. Why? The content only appeals to writers and that small population of self-professed book-lovers. Everyone else?

They'll wait until the movie.

Does this mean we can *never* do an interview on our blog? Of course not. But I do see a lot of writers working themselves to death to do interviews every week so they have blog content. There's a better way to have plenty of content that has greater odds of resonating with large numbers of readers.

Bad Blogging Tip #2—You could do book reviews.

Marketing experts love to recommend that writers do book reviews. Okie dokie. We need to read the book, analyze it, and then write a review. It takes 12 hours of undivided attention just to *read* a book, and, if we blog, we need to blog at least once a week to be effective. This means we need to read a book a week? When the heck will we have time to *write*? But all right. We'll bite. Let's say we can stretch the fabric of space-time and we manage to be able to read books then review them.

When was the last time a **book review** went viral?

You know, you were standing in line at Target and you heard people talking about the same book review as the people at the gym, then later at the park you overheard...NO.

Again, NEVER.

Not going to happen. If it does happen, it is a fluke and a weird confluence of events that probably can never be duplicated. Ever. There are better uses of your time, like figuring out how to stretch the fabric of space-time. Yes, you can still review books if the fancy strikes, but relying on this for a majority of your content will probably just make you want to throw yourself in front of traffic.

Bad Blogging Tip #3—You should write articles. Write about writing and be an expert.

Another bit of bad advice being given to writers is that they should write articles. Write about writing. This is why we have a bazillion newbie writers with writing blogs. Most blog hot and heavy for about two to six months, and then they burn out and dive face-first into a bowl of cookie dough. Writers have been condensing the whole of existence into symbols on a page for thousands of years, yet the second we get online we all write about...writing.

If your goal is to be a writing teacher or sell books about writing, go for it, but **fiction authors are storytellers, not experts.** Also, back to the notion of high concept—how many regular people care about the future of publishing, deep POV, proper use of a semi-colon, or the correct way to query an agent? Do readers care about this stuff? NO.

Remember, the first rule of high concept is to be universal. Are these topics universally interesting like love, pets, or family? No. Will readers (who are not also writers) feel emotional about these topics? No. Do these topics give a (non-writer) reader something to contribute or take away? NO. This is why articles are a big fat time-suck, too. They will do more to create burnout and frustration than they'll do to sell books. Fiction authors are creative people. They're storytellers, and they tend to swear and scream when we smear them in digital butter and stuff them into a "three-piece expert suit." It doesn't fit. It isn't natural, and it just doesn't work.

Setting all the high concept stuff aside, I will tell you why articles and interviews are almost useless for selling fiction. What side of the human brain is activated upon reading information and articles? The **left** side of the brain. What side of the brain is activated when we read fiction? The **right** side of the brain.

Why are you trying to sell a right-brain product with a left-brain blog?

When we're on social media, every post, every blog, every tweet, every image can connect emotionally. This is one of the keys to going viral. Content needs to be universal, emotional and offer people something to take away (compel them to share with their networks).

No matter our native tongue, *Surprise Kitty* makes us smile. The cat falling in the toilet bowl makes us laugh, and a dog dragging a toddler by the seat of his pants is cute no matter what nationality we happen to be. Science has proven that a water-skiing chipmunk is impressive to Americans and Asians alike. When a five-year-old girl clings to her soldier father just home from war, when an elderly couple holds hands, or a when a small boy with no legs wins a race, we are moved. These events are all snapshots of our humanity and we love to share them and *that is why they go viral.*

Social media is social. It is a place we talk, laugh and share. We love content that makes us feel emotion, and we love to share that kind of content with others. If enough people share our content, that is called *going viral.*

Yet, too many writers are trying to interview each other and post book reviews, and write deep, probing articles about the future of e-publishing, and then they can't figure out why their content doesn't resonate and why their platform is growing at glacial speed. **The reason is that the very nature of their content limits its reach. To go viral, we must be universal.** Last I checked *niche* is the opposite of *universal.*

If we can think of content in terms of food, this makes more sense. I don't want to make any sweeping generalizations, but I'd wager that most folks in the Western world don't say, "You know what? I'd love to go out to eat tonight and get some deep-fried grasshoppers. Ooh, or maybe some live squid. We can twirl it on a stick and see if we can swallow the little sucker before it expands and suffocates us."

I can almost 100% guarantee that conversation never happens. Granted, there are ~~weirdos~~ foodies who love strange exotic cuisine, grasshoppers and live squid included. There are entire shows on the Food Network and a guy named Zimmerman who will eat anything, but this guy is NOT the typical diner. If we want culinary success, then we should work to appeal to the regular person who doesn't eat live food. Burgers, pizza, and steak are better choices if we hope to have broad appeal.

Haggis has a fan following, but it is *much* smaller than the one for Buffalo wings. When we generate content, we need to ask if this content is something a large community would enjoy. If it is, then it's one step closer to going viral. Hot dogs took off way faster than the twirly-squid thing. Just sayin'.

To Go Viral, Get Rid of the Drag

The first place we need to look when we are creating viral content is to the content itself. Once we have great content that has universal appeal, is emotional and gives people something to take away, we're on our way to forging real and lasting connections with our audience. But, wait, we still aren't there quite yet. I see a lot of great content out there that is doomed to fail, simply because it has too much drag.

For any idea to go viral, it must be smooth. This means that people don't have to think much to "get" an idea. Something hooks them and won't let go. They don't need to do a lot of extra thinking.

Added Steps Create Drag

Added steps create friction and drag, and the more friction we add to our content, the less likely we are to have our content go viral. What am I talking about? Here is a quick example: have you ever wanted to buy something online, but you had to click to go to another page, then fill in a bunch of fields, then go to another page, then solve a CAPTCHA, then give a horoscope and a DNA profile? You know this experience? Did you buy or did you get ticked off at Hoop #3 and just go elsewhere? This merchant made a HUGE mistake. He made it too hard to close the sale. Anyone who has ever worked in sales will tell you that it is imperative that the sales process be seamless and easy. The same goes for social media.

How many times have you read a blog and wanted to comment, but you had to solve a CAPTCHA fourteen times, give your address, name, log into Google, leave five references, a home number and a urine sample? Did those steps make you want to subscribe to this blog? Or did they make you spout off a cloud of profanity that made the houseplants blush? Some writers have their blogs locked down tighter than the Pentagon and then they can't figure out why no one comments.

We are writers. None of us passed the Blogger background check. The breath analysis dinged most of us.

Writers don't have to be blogging to create a ton of friction with their brand. How many times have you been on social media and seen tweets by writers with names like these?

@FairyWriter   @ProcrastinatingMuse

@DragonLady   @ThrillerGuy

Let's say that @FairyWriter tweets about her latest book that is now available in bookstores. When I'm at Barnes & Noble looking for a new read, I think back to my fond memories of chatting with @FairyWriter. The problem is, though I want to buy her book, *I don't even know her name.* This means that, to purchase @FairyWriter's book, I need to:

1. Get on my iPhone.
2. Walk to an area where I can get more than a half a bar of signal.
3. Try to log into Twitter.
4. Have iPhone inform me I need to update that application.
5. Wait while new version of Twitter downloads.
6. Play Angry Birds.
7. Look at other books written by authors unashamed to tell me their NAMES.
8. Finally log into Twitter.
9. Scroll and hope to find one of @FairyWriter's tweets.
10. So I can click to view her profile.
11. So I can get her NAME.
12. So I can find her website.
13. So I can get the name of her BOOK.
14. So I can find the book in the bookstore.
15. So I can purchase the book.

Sorry, I was tired by step three. Look how many steps it takes for me to even locate this writer's book. This author added a minimum of eight layers of friction to her content. People these days don't have a lot of time, and they sure don't want to jump through a bunch of hoops to get what they need. They will default to purchasing books from authors who don't make them do a lot of extra thinking to buy their books.

When we use anything other than our names on social media, we're creating drag and friction that will hinder momentum. Adding this kind of friction will keep most avid readers from finding our books, let alone buying them. How can we expect people who don't believe they even like to read to look for our books when we make it such a hassle?

Your Name is Your Most Important Asset

Sandra Brown, Cormac McCarty, John Grisham, Clive Cussler, Anne Rice, J.K. Rowling, Dan Brown, Steve Berry, Amy Tan, Stephen King, and R.L. Stine all rely on *their names* to drive sales. So do C.J. Lyons, Amanda Hocking, John Locke, Joe Konrath, Aaron Patterson and Theresa Ragan. Every effort is channeled into the name as the brand. Brands are vital for success, especially in the Digital Age. Modern humans are so bombarded with options that we default to brands we can trust. Why? Because brands promise to deliver. It goes back to that "not wanting to do a lot of extra thinking" thing.

When I talk about the importance of brand in a sea of choices, I always think of the movie *Hurt Locker*. The protagonist is a member of the EOD (Explosive Ordnance Disposal) and there is a scene where he's home from Afghanistan and standing in the cereal aisle. The aisle is stocked with countless choices that seem to stretch on forever, and he's paralyzed by the volume of options, unable to make a decision. This is a very accurate portrayal of the modern consumer. In a sea of infinite variety, we will default to who and what we know. This is why proper branding is more critical today than ever before. Yet, too many authors are hiding behind cutesy names and engaging in behaviors that fracture, dilute or confuse their brands. Brands in the Digital Age are life and death. We should always use our NAMES.

ONE NAME ONLY, PLEASE.

When consumers buy Nike shoes, Coach purses, Levi's jeans, Apple computers, or Louis Vuitton luggage, they expect a certain quality and consistency. These companies don't slap their name on everything for no reason. As authors, our primary goal, aside from creating community, is to create a brand.

NAME + GREAT CONTENT + POSITIVE FEELINGS = BRAND

The point with social media is to create a brand readers trust. Once your brand is associated with consistent content people can count on to be a good experience, they won't care what you write. They'll want to buy your books because they trust your content and your brand. Having a consistent brand helps that smoothness factor that will eventually help your ideas (books) spread.

Yep. We are back to that whole "going viral" idea.

Cutsey Monikers KILL Viruses

The Internet is one of the few places that the word "viral" is desirable. Yet, few things have the killing power of a cutesy moniker. Want to almost guarantee your content will never spread? Bog it down with a moniker.

When we are hobbyists with no intention to sell books, we can use a cutesy moniker. Yet, **from the day you decide that you want to do this writer thing for real you need to start building your author brand.** Please don't think you can wait until you land an agent, score a publishing deal, or release a book to start building a brand/platform. These days, the competition is nothing short of a nightmare, and, if you hope to ~~play~~ survive in this glutted marketplace, you need to start building your author brand and platform yesterday. Platforms with the ability to fuel sales take time to build. You can't pull one out of the ether two weeks before the book comes out. I've lost count of how many authors have contacted me about "maximizing social media" because they have a book out in a month and haven't been doing any social media.

I'm an expert, not a magician.

Yes, in the olden days (before the Internet and social media) the author brand consisted of books. Well, of course it did. Books were the only building materials available. These days? We have new building materials to add to the platform called blogs, tweets, Facebook posts, fan pages, and Pinterest boards.

I get that we made houses out of mud and sticks at one point in human history, but guess what? There have been a few advances in construction materials, and, now that we have things like steel, sheetrock, Tyvek, siding, fiberglass insulation, and particleboard, we no longer need to live in a mud hut. Cool, right? Same thing with brands. If you want to rely on only your books to build your brand, I won't stop you. But, um, why would you?

Social Schizophrenia KILLS

There are a lot of writers who are worn out. They feel like they live on social media, but they never see any results. They whine that social media and blogging doesn't work. All right. Let's look closer, and we will pick on our friend @FairyGirl because she is a figment of my imagination and thus expects to be mocked. Yet, I will say that I run into more real-world @FairyGirls than I'd like. @FairyGirl is a prototypical example of *brand friction*.

My imaginary friend @FairyGirl is super active on social media. She tweets as @FairyGirl and has a blog, *Rainbow Kitten Fairy Dreams*. She has a regular Facebook page for friends and family under her real name, Jane Dough. Ah, but then she has a fan page for her erotic romance under her pen name Anastasia Hotflash and she has another fan page for her science fiction books under Penelope Fluffernutter. Jane has two websites for both identities and she tries to keep Hotflash and Fluffernutter separate lest it be a sticky situation. Jane uses Flickr, but has that account under her husband's name, John Dough. Jane is a busy girl, and on top of her *Rainbow Fairy Kitten Dreams* blog where she chronicles her struggles to make word count each day, she also contributes on a group blog with her writer friends. Jane writes a post a week for *The Inky Muse—Random Writer Ramblings* and talks about three-act structure and the trends with Smashwords. Oh, and then there is that other blog she started on Blogger when John made her a vegetable garden so she could post pictures of her tomato plants. But that blog shouldn't count since the plant died right about the time the cloud of black bugs ate all her tomatoes. Oh, and I forgot to mention that Jane also has three other Twitter identities—@DrakeDrako @VictoriaBlake @SirDurganWalsley—who are all characters in her various books (none of which are completed). She went to a writing conference and a social media expert told her to tweet from the perspectives of her characters and to interview them. She interviews Drake Drako on her blog every Wednesday even though she hasn't yet finished the book (and despite that it feels weird and creepy). The spam bots seem to like Drake, especially the male enhancement bots. Jane doesn't have the heart to delete their comments because then she will have no comments at all.

Yeah, blogging is totally useless.

Clearly you can see that social media just doesn't work, right? Or maybe Jane has developed what I like to call Social Schizophrenia. If we have more personalities than Sybil running around cyberspace unattended then, Houston, we have a problem. We have a mess and we have A LOT of friction. When we are this spread out, the odds that any of our content will gain traction, let alone go viral, is slim to none. This behavior also severely limits how much help our Connector, Maven, and Salesmen friends can offer. Not only will this approach virtually ensure we never go viral, but it will wear us out, leaving no creative energy to do the one activity that is most crucial to a successful writing career… writing more books. In this instance, Social Schizophrenia not only takes out our ability to go viral, but it has enough killing power to take our careers down, too.

The More You Sneeze, the Greater Your Chances of Spreading a Virus

In *Unleashing the Ideavirus*, Seth Godin calls people who spread content and ideas "sneezers." According to Godin, the more content we generate that is shared (sneezed), the more chances we have that our "bug" will jump onto others and then eventually infect a larger population. No one can promise your content will go viral. All I can do is help you increase odds that your ideas and content will catch on. Viral content behaves a lot like viruses in real life. If we are flattened with a bug and we stay home where we live alone, the chances are more than good that the virus we're carrying will die. The virus will live for a finite time until our immune system kicks in and kills it. Online we also have an immune system of sorts called *time*. If we post a blog but no one knows about it or cares enough to look at it, then eventually the content dies. We have to find ways to come in contact with new people to spread our virus. This is one of the main reasons that blogging once a month is all but worthless. We are popping up once a month and "sneezing" and hoping against hope that the right person is there at the right time to take our content and spread it. Does it happen? Sure. People win the lottery every week, but I wouldn't recommend scratch-off tickets as a retirement plan.

This has been one of the major hurdles for writers who read John Locke's book *How I Sold a Million Books in Five Months*. If you read his book, Locke repeatedly states that his book is not a How-To program, and that he isn't teaching writers the steps to guarantee success. He states over and over that *How I Sold a Mil-*

lion Books in Five Months is only an account of how HE sold books. That's it. Yet, time after time, I run into writers who use this book like a manual for success. They argue with me that, "Locke says it's only necessary to blog once a month. Why are you wanting me to blog three times a week?"

I want writers to blog a minimum of three times a week for a number of reasons, but the biggest reason is that it will drastically improve the odds of going viral. Yes, Locke blogged once a month and when it came to blogging, he hit the equivalent of the Internet jackpot because his blogs that went viral were *high concept*. Locke pulled the ~~lever~~ blog and ~~coins~~ readers spilled all over the floor. Does this mean that every writer who bellies up to the Internet slot machine once a month will hit the viral jackpot? No.

Please understand, Locke did a lot of stuff correctly and he has a lot of great wisdom to offer, namely he had *a lot of titles for sale*. But we have to be smart enough to discern which tactics worked because they were sound business strategies and which ones worked simply because of blind luck. Blind luck is awesome. I would love some myself, but blind luck is a bad bet to rest our careers on. Writers like Locke did a lot of other things right that maximized the effect when fortune shone down upon them, and those are what we will spend time focusing on. If we streamline your time on social media, you have time to do what matters most to *sell a million books in five months*. Write more books.

The more we are present on social media the better chances we have of our content going viral. The more we talk to people, engage in conversations, tweet, and blog, the more potential energy we are adding to our virus once it does catch on.

SHARE BUTTONS: Make Sure You Give Readers a Way to Sneeze

When you do blog, make sure you include share buttons (widgets) to make it easy for people to share your content on their favorite networks. People like sharing cool stuff they find, and we need to encourage this behavior. Make sharing *easy* for us to share on *our* favorite sites. No need to panic, we'll talk about widgets in the next section.

Time to start building.

Section 3
WANNA RELOADED:
Putting Together a Plan

Chapter 11

GETTING FAMILIAR WITH
SOCIAL MEDIA TERMS

BY THIS POINT, I hope you have a clear understanding of where you fit in the greater scheme of things. We have to grasp where we sit on the larger timeline of human history to ensure we are using the correct approach and the most effective tools. The structure of the human brain has changed to keep pace with changes in our global culture, thus we need to make sure we are choosing content that people will see, like and *want to share*. We've also discussed how being present helps us team up with others, and how this greatly increases the fun factor and our chances at being successful. You also now have an idea about what "going viral" means and how to better approach trying to hit that Internet jackpot.

Now that you're aware of the big picture, it's time to talk about you. Where do you start? What are the necessary steps? That's coming, but first we need to understand some basics.

Social media is a world of its own and it has a unique vocabulary. Some phrases have been used so much they've been integrated into the common language. "Can I *friend* you?" Others might not be as familiar, so we'll go over some of the major terms you'll need to understand.

Search Engine Optimization (SEO)—is the process of making it easier for search engines to *find* us and our content. There are some simple changes we can make that will help us dominate a Google search for our names, and even appear in searches related to our content. If you write a diet book, then SEO can help people find YOU when they google *Ways to lose weight safely.*

Social Media Optimization (SMO)—Basically, SMO makes your content linkable, easier to tag and bookmark, helps to reward inbound links, increases the reach of your content, and encourages the mash-up (a webpage or application that presents a hodgepodge selection of the best of the best, which will increase your influence). SMO helps your content travel. It's great you have a blog, but do you have easy ways for us to tweet your blog or "Like" it on Facebook?

Tag—metadata (data about data). Tags help search engines locate content on the Internet.

Keyword—a word that describes content or subject matter. Google uses this information to tune your search results to ensure they are as relevant as possible and to promote the most relevant pages in their search engine. Used properly, keywords can help your content stand out.

Bookmarking—a method by which users can share, organize, search, and manage content.

Stream—a continuous live update that lets you know what others are doing—new pictures posted, new video, blogs, "Likes," etc.

Blog—a term that came into existence in the late 90s. Blog is a combination of two words *web* and *log* to form *blog.* All blogs are websites, but not all websites are blogs. The difference is in presentation. Blogs—which may consist of diary entries, text, stories, articles, video, or images—are updated regularly and frequently. By contrast, a static website normally serves as a resource of information that doesn't change often. My recommendation is that authors should blog from their author websites. By blogging regularly, search engines will favor your site and this can keep your author webpage at the top of any search.

Vlog—a video blog.

Hyperlink—a digital breadcrumb. This is when the address of a post is embedded in text posted on the web. For instance, when I blog on certain topics, I'll hyperlink to other blogs that reinforce, refute, or even expound upon my chosen topic. When readers click these hyperlinks (which are often underlined and/or in color) my readers are redirected to the other material. On WordPress, when you include a hyperlink, there is an option to "open on a new page." Always check that box so that if readers choose to look at the other sites, they aren't directed away from your site.

Pingbacks/Trackbacks—These notify an author or owner of a website that someone has linked back to their site. Your website dashboard should notify you when there are sites linking to yours and you have the choice of whether or not to approve. Trackbacks are great for a number of reasons. First, trackbacks extend our digital reach and can direct new people to our content. It is a major way most of us to discover new people and new bloggers. Secondly, trackbacks provide us with an opportunity to thank the person who linked to our content. I make an effort to visit all the sites that are thoughtful enough to mention my blogs. This is a great way to network and create a relationship with other bloggers. Thirdly, trackbacks afford us an opportunity to make certain our content is being used appropriately. It can provide us a chance for rebuttal if the need arises. For instance, a couple of years ago I blogged about why writers shouldn't create writing blogs and this created a flurry of panic in authors who mistakenly believed I'd said that they couldn't blog about writing. That wasn't the case at all. Writers can blog about writing, but creating a *writing blog* is a different pursuit altogether. When those blog posts linked back to me, it gave me a chance to comment and clarify my position.

Status Update—Facebook, Twitter, Google+, and others all have a format for *microblogging* known as the *status update*. Basically, this is a small window where we answer very simple questions.

What are you doing?
How are you feeling?
What's going on?

The status update is crucial for connecting with others, creating community and getting our content out on the web (more on that later).

Tweet—a post on Twitter, which is a social platform that focuses solely on one aspect of the social media experience—the status update.

Retweet (RT)/Repost—Social media is most effective when it's exponential, not linear. Our reach is only so far, but when others decide our content is worthy of *sharing* we increase our influence logarithmically. Twitter is our *force multiplier.* This is one of the reasons spamming is ineffective. Most people will tune it out, thus never share that content. Writers who choose to spam go it alone. They can expect little to no help from Connectors, Mavens, and Salesmen because the burden for influence rests solely on the shoulders of the person posting. There is no vested community to help transport (sneeze) the content and give it greater reach. Most of us detest being spammed, so why would we share it?

Domain Name—your "address" on the Internet. Ideally, it should be your name or a form of your name. www.authorkristenlamb.com

Widgets—are portable chunks of code that can be embedded in a larger HTML image. Think of widgets as refrigerator magnets that serve a specific purpose stuck to your fridge. The magnet might be a calendar, a bottle opener, a chip clip, or an easy reference for Poison Control. They all hang out on your fridge for the purpose of making some task easier, yet their presence doesn't alter the purpose of your refrigerator.

CAPTCHAs—used to distinguish between humans and computers to keep spammers off your page. **Don't use them.**

CAPTCHAs might keep spammers away, but they also create drag and make it extremely difficult for real humans, too. Remember, in the Digital Age, we like stuff to be *easy.* Anything that makes us jump through extra hoops is annoying, so we go elsewhere. I recommend authors invest in a paid WordPress.org website, because you don't need a degree in IT to manage one. The free WordPress.com automatically includes Akismet, which is extremely effective in filtering out most spammers. For those of you who take my advice and invest in an author site, you might need to add a spam filter plug-in to your WordPress site. If you don't, the bots will drive you nutso.

Plug-In—a form of widget. A plug-in is a piece of portable code that can enhance the function of your blog or website. In this instance, think of plug-ins like "extras" one might add to a stock production car to enhance performance. A Honda Accord comes as a stock car, but a spoiler would be an extra that's designed to use aerodynamic principles to give the car better control on the road, which one might need—especially if the intent is to race that Honda. Your website (or blog) comes to you in a standard form, but you can use plug-ins to give your website additional functions and abilities.

Content—this is what brands are made of. Every post, blog, tweet, video, vlog, or status update falls under the banner of "content." The more quality content we can provide, the better. Content creates community and generates dialogue with others. If we don't have good content, that's like a cocktail party where no one wants to be the first to speak. We all just stand around staring at each other.

Critical Mass—the number of individuals in your network where interaction becomes meaningful. One of the main advantages of social media is that we have access to "the hive mind" and we don't have to have all the answers. We can rely on our network. When I was having the WANA International website built, I had a certain image in my mind, but not the terminology.

This made it extremely difficult to communicate what I wanted to my website designer. Instead of spending hours on the web trying to find the right word, I turned to my Twitter network. "What was the period of art right at the turn of the 18th and 19th century? Very Moulin Rouge." Within less than five minutes, I had ten responses with *Belle Epoque,* which was exactly the term I was looking for. If I'd only had three followers, I might not have heard anything back. Yet, because my platform had surpassed the point of critical mass, it suddenly became a precious reservoir of information. Remember Metcalf's Law.

Application Software (App)—a fancy name for a *tool.* My favorites are TweetDeck and HootSuite (better for Macs) because these applications allow us to organize a large body of followers into something manageable. If we can't manage our social interaction, then it is next to impossible to make our interactions *meaningful.* **Tools are a way to manage our social media, but they should *never* be a substitute for being present.** It's unfair to expect from others (time and attention) what we are not willing to give. No one likes to be the *friend with benefits.*

I use apps to program my blog to post automatically on certain platforms. For instance, my WordPress automatically tweets (once) that my newest post is now live. This isn't the kind of automation that annoys people. The major gripe is with those who seek to "fool" us into believing a real person is present.

Tools like Social Oomph, Triberr, TweetDeck, and HootSuite are wonderful, but I've seen them terribly abused. If a writer pre-programs a tweet to read, "Hey, guys! How is everyone doing this afternoon?" and no one answers back when we reply, we catch on quickly no one's there. It might be shocking to some, but we generally don't like people who insult our intelligence.

Hashtags—are those #s you've likely seen all over the place and they're essentially a word filter. What a # does is offer a way for us to instantly increase our critical mass and connect to others based on similar interests. There are millions of tweets every day, but how do we make sense of it? How do we connect? Hashtags help make that happen. If I love watching *Wives with Knives* and want to chat with other fans about the show, I can use the #IDAddict. We can talk about *Game of Thrones* at #ASOIF (*A Song of Ice and Fire*). We can chat about #SVU, #CakeBoss, #gypsies or our picks for #AmericanIdol. If we like to cook, we can connect with other #cooks or chat about #IronChef. We could talk about #yoga, #pets, #Discovery, #History, or #fitness. We can trade notes at #BiggestLoser or horror stories at #hoarders. Hashtags will help you connect with other writers at #My-WANA, keep on top of industry news at #pubtip, or even find a team of support and accountability at #amwriting. Hashtags are a great way for our content to have a further reach. If I write a post about *Star Wars*, then when I tweet about it, it's probably a good idea to add #starwars at the end. Adding the hashtag will make my tweet not only appear to people who *are directly following me on Twitter* but it will also make this tweet visible to anyone following the #starwars. This broadens my influence exponentially and helps me earn new followers. I happen to be a military wife, so I follow #airforce, #military and #USMC. This helps connect me to people on Twitter who aren't also writers with a book to sell. Hashtags are a valuable tool for connecting to that fat part of the bell curve in need of informing or entertaining.

NOTE OF CAUTION: NEVER automate Tweets with hashtags. I am against pretty much all author automation, but I get that some of you will want to do it anyway. If you do preprogram tweets, then please DO NOT include a hashtag. If I follow someone on Twitter and then realize no one's there, just some social tool pumping out links, I can unfollow the person. When it comes to the hashtag, however, the only option is leaving that hashtag. We talked about this earlier in the book. An author coach with four identities nearly ended #MyWANA. She set up her stuff to tweet automatically every day and every few hours which wouldn't have been much of a problem, except that she included #MyWANA in those tweets. Since she wasn't present, she didn't see what havoc she was creating with her tweets. Because she used #MyWANA we couldn't escape her non-stop infomercial, so our only recourse was to either abandon the community we loved or report her as spam (since she wasn't responding to any tweets or messages).

NOTE OF CAUTION ABOUT *ANY* AUTOMATED TWEETS: Our modern world can change in a heartbeat, and when tragedy strikes and people are grieving, a chatty auto-tweet to buy our books can make followers seethe. The day of the Boston Marathon bombing, a lot of writers landed in hot water because they didn't shut down their automated tweets quickly enough. This "time-saving" device created a brand nightmare and cost these authors far more time to do damage control than they ever "saved" with automation.

Memes—powerful tools for spreading influence and engaging an audience. A **meme** (pron.: /'m m/; *meem*) is an idea or element of behavior that passes through a culture usually by imitation. Grumpy Cat and Haz Cheezburger are two viral memes. People laugh at Grumpy Cat then go create their own meme, which is why we see so many different versions floating around Facebook. All those funny captioned pictures we share? Famous inspirational quotes? Memes.

Chapter 12

AN EASY WAY TO
UNDERSTAND SEARCH ENGINES

MY GOAL IS TO HELP you build an effective platform, but you need to understand how search engines work before we start. If you don't, then we waste a lot of time and energy. This description will be very basic, but the whole point of WANA is that it's perfect for technophobes.

All the technology stuff aside, think of search engines as a codependent genie. Anything we ask for, Google the Codependent Genie is there to grant us our wish as quickly as possible. Google wants to make us happy, so it wants to not only give us what we want instantly, but it also wants to deliver quality goods.

Envision the Internet as a giant warehouse filled with anything you could ever need. There are hundreds of millions of miles of shelves filled with boxes containing information. When we search for *anything* on the Internet, the search engine's job is to find what we want out of all those billions and trillions of boxes.

In the list of terms, I mentioned tags. Tags are how we label our content to make Google favor our content over someone else's. If you had a job to search through a closet or a garage for something specific, what would you search through first? The boxes neatly labeled, or the unlabeled boxes where you'd have to rummage through the contents? I'd pick the labeled boxes. Turns out, Google is not very different than we are. Google or Yahoo or Bing all want to find great content at light speed, and the way they do this is by first looking for tags.

Properly tagged content (websites, bios, blogs, videos, images) will win out every time and will make the first page of a search. And who bothers with page two, right? If Google the Codependent Genie finds *no tagged content*, it will then go to Plan B. Plan B is when Google searches the *body of the content* for the key search words. What this means is that I could create a premium blog post about how to write a synopsis for a novel, but if I fail to tag it, a lesser-quality post could outrank mine because that person took the time to tag when I didn't.

Tags Work Together with Keywords

Our keywords and tags can often be the same. In fact, it is a good idea when you blog to use as many of the tags as keywords in the first paragraph as possible (without looking weird and obvious). Search engines know that spammers and bots misuse tags and try to mislead the search engines. To combat this, Google will give due diligence and check to see if the label on the box matches what's inside.

Thus, if a box has the tags *novel, synopsis, writing synopsis,* **Google will expect to see those keywords in the body of the content, ideally at the beginning.** Spam bots will try to lure us with a post that promises *synopsis* and opens to *sex.* The way search engines keep us happy and safe is to do this kind of double-checking between tags and keywords.

Ways to Make Search Engines Happy

Google the Codependent Genie is highly motivated to make us happy, lest he be banned to the Dark Realms of AOL. Search engines make money when people use them, thus the plan is to offer the best content the fastest. We can help search engines favor our content by taking a few simple steps that makes them look good.

1. Tag your content. This puts you on the search engine's radar.

2. Use keywords in the body of your content, ideally toward the beginning. This makes it easy for search engines to suggest your content. The search engine knows that the tags match what's in the content, so it "feels better" about recommending you.

3. Post regularly and frequently. This is one of the main reasons I encourage authors to blog from their author websites. Search engines prefer to recommend the "happening places," and if your content is updated regularly you will win favor. Static sites that only get updated sporadically, such as when an author has a new book, will not get a lot of attention. This is simple to fix by blogging off your author site.

4. Use images. Search engines (and Facebook) give a lot of weight to images. Use this in your favor.

5. Harness the power of link love. Hyperlink to other content as much as you can. When I blog on a topic, I hyperlink to any of my previous posts that might also be relevant. Not only does this make life easier for my followers, since they don't have to go digging through my archives, but using links also scores major brownie points with search engines. Search engines dig content that makes the Internet a community. Additionally, I hyperlink to bigger bloggers. I might hyperlink to an online article by the *New York Times* or *Huffington Post*. Look for the big blogs in topics that interest you and then link to them. Hyperlinks help you, they help the sources you link to, and they help those browsing the web to have a better experience. Hyperlinks are also a WANA way that we can help each other, especially the new kids. Very often, I use the power of my platform to jumpstart new platforms. If I mention a new blogger in a post and hyper-link, odds are my following will click because I've demonstrated that they can trust me to steer them to great content. This makes my followers happy and also gives a boost to a newbie. When writers work together and link to one another, we help each other's SEO, and this makes it easier for readers to find new content and bloggers they love. Everyone wins. Search engines like it when we link to others, but they *love* it when those others link back. Spam bots are notorious for abusing hyperlinks, so search engines are doing their duty by checking to make sure that the link love is going both ways. If someone is posting a lot of content with out-going links, but no one ever links back? This is a clue to Google that the content is spam or something harmful.

When you understand some of the basics, it will help you keep your energies focused and increase your ROI (return on investment).

Chapter 13

PLAN YOUR WORK
THEN WORK YOUR PLAN

WHEN I WAS IN SALES, we had a mantra: *Plan your work, then work your plan.* When we fail to plan, we get distracted, and our energies are easily diffused. Most of us, when we begin our journey towards becoming professional authors, don't have the luxury of doing this job full-time so we need to make sure what we do *counts*. This doesn't change. Once you successfully publish, you will be *even busier* so you need to create a platform that supports your author brand, not a monster that eats up all your free time and joy and makes you want to dive into a wood chipper.

One of the most common mistakes writers make is getting on social media with no plan, no prepared content, and little to no understanding of the big picture.

Creating a brand is like building any other structure. You wouldn't try to build your dream home with no blueprints or supplies, so why is that a good idea for your author brand? It isn't.

1. We need a clear idea of exactly *what* we are building.

2. We need a blueprint to give us guidelines and direction.

3. We need materials.

4. We need a team of helpers. Large structures would take forever to build alone.

5. We need to build something that can be easily maintained and added onto at a later time. We need an organic structure that is fluid and yet resilient.

What are You Building?

Everything revolves around you. YOU are the brand. Thus, your *name* is the single greatest asset you possess. One of the reasons writers get worn out on social media is they spread themselves too thinly. They have three different pen names and a separate fan page for each, and fan pages for each book. Maybe they tweet from the perspective of characters and all of this is like running in a hamster wheel. A LOT of effort, and very little payoff.

The way I teach you to build your brand has every action funneling into the same place—your name. Think of your actions on social media as energy. If energy is dispersed it's merely light, but energy focused becomes a *laser*.

Goals are important because they help us maintain focus. Also, goals give us a clearer idea *what kind* of platform we are going to build. If you're a traditionally published author, you need a platform. Yet, because you currently enjoy greater distribution and may have some support from the publisher, your platform doesn't necessarily have to be as big. Those of you who self-publish or go indie? It's all on you. To publish a book with no platform is playing Russian Roulette with your future and, last I checked, that's a game that ends badly for most who play.

Goals

When anyone takes my blogging class, the very first assignment is to write out a list of goals. Goals must be attainable, actionable, and have accountability (deadlines). Now, when I say *attainable,* this isn't permission to sell yourself short. If you long to be as big as J.K. Rowling, then write that down. This is an attainable goal for any writer willing to put in the work. What isn't attainable would be me wanting to be a super model. At a fluffy 5' 3" and almost 40, *it's not going to happen.* I can't possibly meet the physical standard of the fashion industry. Yet, as a writer, I could write, take classes, study, write, and work for the rest of my days *in the pursuit of becoming as popular an author as J.K. Rowling.*

One of the reasons I ask students to set goals first is that often the goals will offer a clearer picture of what kind of platform we need, what size, and what social sites should be included. For instance, if your goal is to be a mega-successful self-published non-fiction author, then LinkedIn is a *must*. LinkedIn will help you build a speaking platform to compliment your social platform. This type of author frequently gains sales traction by selling books "at the back of the room" and by offering training and consulting that pair well with their books.

On the other hand, if you write category romance novels, LinkedIn might not be a big priority. It still has some value, and we will talk about that later, but other sites are a better use of time. For the romance author, Pinterest is extremely valuable to you because most romance readers and *potential* romance readers are women. Pinterest is a social site dominated by those of the fairer sex who love to spend time looking at clothes, shoes, and other sparkly things.

To be clear, any social site done well can give us advantages. A Pinterest site can be beneficial to the self-published non-fiction author just as LinkedIn can help the romance author. What I want to clarify in these examples is *where we place our priorities and our time* is important to maintaining sanity and having time left over to do the most important part of our business—writing more books. You can't be everywhere equally and with the same passion, thus you need to structure your platform in a way that works the best for your goals. I would rather have you do a couple things really well than spread yourself so thinly you get discouraged and give up. Remember, WANA methods work on *any* social platform, so feel free to select only the ones that work for *you*.

Also, we live in an age where *all writers' dreams can come true.* There are those who only want to write a memoir and maybe sell enough copies to have extra spending money. Others might want to write books that help the profession they love and have no intention of leaving. One of my blogging students is married to a pediatrician. He noticed the parents of his patients asked a lot of the same questions. Even though he took time to explain his answers in detail, the parents were only able to retain so much (probably because they were exhausted and worried about their children). To help the parents, he's decided to write small ebooks the parents can download and refer to when needed. Also, since many of the parents might have language barriers or reading comprehension problems, he's looking to make these instructional books into audio books and ways to offer them in several languages. He has no desire to be the next Michael Crichton. Rather, he wants to use his writing skills to be a better *doctor.* Our goals directly affect the type and size of platform we need, therefore goals are a crucial starting point.

Building Blueprint

Once we figure out *what* we want to build, we need a plan, an overall idea of what our platform will look like. Think in terms of architecture. Will we build a corporate skyscraper of metal and glass? An adobe home? A colonial-style two-story house? We will use a combination of social platforms, but one will be your foundation —ideally it will be your blog. Others will be load-bearing walls (e.g., Facebook). Still others? Sparkle and fluff (Pinterest). What is load-bearing versus what's decoration will vary from author to author. WANA is not a Social Media Snuggy. You guys are special and unique and your platforms should reflect that. WANA is a process, not an assembly line churning out identical writer-marketing bots.

The largest component of your author brand will be your books. Your social platform is a close second, so you need to be deliberate when you build. Platforms are constructed from social sites + content + authentic interaction.

Chapter 14

THE MAIN PLATFORMS

THERE ARE A LOT of social platforms out there and, by the time you read this book, I guarantee there will be more. I can't go over all of them because, frankly, I don't know or understand all of them. That was the largest reason I created WANA International. It would've been foolish of me to teach all authors to have the same exact social sites and be little clones of me. It would have been equally foolish to try and understand every last social site and then teach all of them poorly. This is why I recruited top talent and people smarter than me to teach classes. In this book, I'm not going to teach you much about how to use the social platforms. There are no walk-throughs. Why? The technology changes too quickly. But I will go over the major points of what you should accomplish. If you want to master a particular platform, I recommend a WANA International class or browsing YouTube for free walk-throughs.

Facebook is notorious for randomly deciding to change its entire layout, so why waste pages of this book with instructions that likely won't last? In fact, *as I write this* Facebook is completely reworking the fan page to be more like the mobile version. Technology is a moving target, so I won't waste your valuable reading time.

This book focuses on purpose and content. Tens of thousands of people start blogs only to fail. Why? They didn't understand that blogging is a unique form of writing birthed from a digital, multi-media society that expects connection and conversation. A pretty blog is useless without content that connects and inspires. Thousands of people sign up for Twitter and get nowhere. Why? Because they don't know what to say, how to connect, or how to encourage others to *care*. All the social sites are like that. Easy to sign up, and follow the prompts.

It's the rest that's the hard part.

An Author Blog

Your blog is your most valuable social media asset. Blogs cater to our strengths. Writers *write*. We might not all be social butterflies but we should be good with words. Blogging makes us better, faster, and cleaner writers. Blogging can sharpen and hone our writing voices and connect to people the same way as our books. I won't walk you through all the ins and outs of creating a Word-Press site, but I will teach you how to *write* a killer author blog.

Blogs are resilient. Facebook could implode and Twitter could flitter away, but as long as we have the Internet, your blog will remain (and if the Internet goes away we have bigger problems than book sales). Search engines will deliver new fans to you daily. It's statistically unlikely that some random person querying Google will stumble across your tweets, your Facebook posts, or your Pinterest board, but they *can easily* discover your blog. I have blogs I posted *years ago* that are still getting comments and earning me new fans. Google "Falcor" and see whose blog pops up. I wrote a post *What Went Wrong With the Star Wars Prequels?* and, over 220 comments and a year later, people *still show up* to offer an opinion and debate.

We control our blogs. If Facebook goes down, our entire platform goes poof along with it. In my first book, *We Are Not Alone—The Writer's Guide to Social Media* I mentioned using MySpace (namely because I felt it could serve as a temporary free website until authors could afford to have one built). Even then,

I knew MySpace was faltering. It went from being *the happening place* to a digital ghost town almost overnight. I had a very strong platform on MySpace that simply evaporated.

A blog is different. Ideally, a blog should be written from your author website. You control your website and, so long as you pay your webhost on time, your site and content are *yours*. Your blog will be your point of solidarity. In the beginning of this book I told the story of the Micronesian navigators and how they viewed their vessels as static points and envisioned everything else moving around them. Your blog is the digital core of your author brand. It's a fixed point in an ever-changing sea of uncertainty.

Facebook

Yes, you need to be on Facebook. Why? Facebook has over a *billion* active users. Remember, we fish where the fish are, and most fish are schooling on Facebook. Facebook will help you activate and recruit those intimate connections and loose ties that are critical for success. People buy from the people they know and like. Fellow students who barely acknowledged you in high school can become some of your biggest fans and loudest cheerleaders because they can say *they knew you when*. Never underestimate family and weak ties. Daily I am stunned by who reads my blog. I've gotten fan mail from second and *third* cousins or people from high school who constantly recommend my books and blogs. Who knew?

Twitter

Twitter is one of the most valuable social sites a writer can be part of. First of all, there is #MyWANA. This means that you can go from knowing no one to suddenly having a group of peers and friends. We talked about this before when we explored what the heck that # thingy actually did.

Twitter will help you grow your platform exponentially, recruit support, locate experts, and make friends. Twitter is one of the most effective ways to tap into that fat part of the bell curve responsible for making novels into legends. Twitter is also one of the best ways for our content to go viral.

Flickr

Flickr is a social site dedicated to sharing images. It's a useful tool for creative professionals whose primary art is visual—photographers, models, sculptors, etc. For writers, Flickr is of interest to you for one main reason. WANA Commons.

Our world is changing and so is the notion of what constitutes copyright infringement. "Fair Use" isn't as cut and dried as it used to be. In the old days of marketing, I didn't want to give my content away. I wanted to charge as much as possible. These days, if we don't create content for the sole purpose of freely sharing, we're rendering ourselves invisible. The problem is that on the Internet, it's hard to know who wants to share and who will sue your tail off if you do. A dear writer friend of mine found a random image on the Internet and used it in a blog post. The photographer tracked her down, took her to court, and it cost my friend a couple thousand dollars and a lot of heartache. She didn't post the picture *knowingly* infringing on copyright. She did it out of ignorance and even took the image down. The photographer drove the matter into court and won. It was a sad situation all around.

I can appreciate the position photographers are in, but WANA Commons is one way we can all work together for the betterment of everyone.

Writers need images. Blogs with images are favored in search engines. I created WANA Commons so writers could have a safe haven. Any image posted to WANA Commons is yours to use without fear of being sued. All we ask is attribution.

Photographers? You need people to see and love your work enough to pay you for your art. Many of you have thousands of images sitting in your hard drive that are doing nothing for your platform or sales. We have quite a few photographers who contribute images to WANA Commons and guess what? We *know* them and *like* them. Who do we do business with? People we know and like.

Many of us will eventually need a professional author photo, or images for book covers. Creative people all *need* each other. I constantly get emails requesting information about using WANA Commons images for magazines, e-zines and book covers. WANA Commons is a great place to generate business if you make your money taking pictures.

Flickr will give you access to images you need and you can post your unused pictures there and let them help other writers. This can increase how many people *see* your name and it helps your SEO. Win-win.

Pinterest

Pinterest is very useful and I ask all of you who do my WANA Plan to join Pinterest. Why? Pinterest is an excellent place to store your WANA Commons images (or your own) for later use. Instead of hunting around WANA Commons for the best images at the last minute, take a weekend and browse, take time to collect your favorites. Pin (save) the best ones onto a Pinterest board folder. This way:

1. When you need an image for your blog, you can get to it quickly, saving time.
2. If people like and "repin" your images, that helps your platform and your SEO.
3. Your pictures are working for your brand. You might never actively participate in Pinterest, but your pictures are still helping your brand instead of sitting in your hard drive where they hang out with the spam bots, take up smoking, and join gangs.

WANATribe

Yes, I'm partial because I started this site, but WANATribe offers a LOT of advantages, namely *tribes*. If you are new and want to learn more about self-publishing? Join a Self-Publishing Tribe. Make friends, and ask questions. Everyone on WANATribe is a WANA and WANAs are a helpful bunch. Many are Mavens, Connectors, and Salespeople.

Part of why I created WANATribe is that most of us hop on Facebook or Twitter and then say, "Okay. What now?" It's tough making friends once we grow up. When we were kids, it was easy. Look for the kids like you, right? If you loved sports, you sought out the kids shooting hoops or playing catch. If you loved gymnastics, you took off for the bunch at the monkey bars. If you were a sadist or a masochist, you located the closest game of dodgeball. Kidding! Yes, I was *always* the kid taken out first. I still have dodgeball PTSD.

The point is it's easier to make friends with mutual interests, and writers are interested in a lot of stuff *other than writing*. Rather than making lists or dragging people into circles, we can join tribes. Hang out in the Zombie Apocalypse Tribe to talk about B movies then hop over the Nerdfighter Tribe to talk about Mythbusters, and then go back to your Amazon Tribe to do writerly things. No one feels excluded because they were left off a list or not dragged into a circle. For erotica authors, you can join an Erotica Author Tribe and talk about men and handcuffs all you want without Mom or your boss being privy to the conversation.

Yes, employers are on Facebook doing witch-hunts, but they are not likely to be on WANATribe. At WANATribe, we are ruthless with spammers and bots and have zero tolerance for form letters or any other spammy behavior. The best part is that WANATribe is a massive support network for writers, and we need all the help we can get. This is not a platform that generally appeals to the corporate folk. It's a big family of creative misfits who finally have a place—other than ComicCon—where we feel at home. Aunt Edna isn't there and neither is the manager from your day job. We are the artist salon of the Digital Age. Come be inspired. Join a tribe or better yet? Create one. Live in an area with no critique groups? Form your own. Create a tribe!

LinkedIn

Non-fiction authors can get a lot of value from LinkedIn. You can connect and even build a speaking platform to go along with your social platform. Also, a lot of us need to make money to supplement our income, especially in the beginning before our books are selling well. LinkedIn can help you land freelance work if you possess that skill set. Even fiction authors can benefit from LinkedIn. A lot of the traditional publishing professionals are there so this is a place to connect and learn from them. If you desire to go indie, it's a great place to check out potential publishers and find where your work might fit. For those who self-publish, you are the publisher so unless you learn to do *everything*, you will probably have to *hire people*. I don't have the time or patience to learn to build my own website, format my own books, or design my own covers. That's a lot of time I could be using to write more books. More books make more money, so it's clear to me where my time is best spent. LinkedIn can help you locate professionals who have a reputation for quality work. You're going to need a website designer, a cover designer, a formatter, a content editor, a line editor, etc. so why not choose a team of professionals who've been endorsed?

YouTube

YouTube is a social site dedicated to video sharing. If you happen to be good in front of a camera, vlogging (video-blogging) could be a fantastic idea. YouTube will be essential later when we talk about blogging. For now? Just know it's a lot of fun. Probably too much fun. But YouTube is actually going to help you get more time to write.

Trust me.

For most of you, YouTube, Flickr, and Pinterest will fall into the "supplies" category more than the "blueprint" category.

I'm not going to talk about any other sites because then this book would be too long, and we have more important things to do. If you want to harness the power of Squidoo, Goodreads, Tumblr, Technorati, Digg, Instagram, or Google+, then come to WANA International for a class, or browse YouTube for tutorials.

But *tempus fugit*. Let's sally forth…

Chapter 15

WHAT KIND OF AUTHOR ARE YOU?

LET'S TAKE A LOOK at the Authors of the Digital Age, because they look far different than any authors in human history. Time to talk a little about you—special, unique, one-of-a-kind *you*.

Let's return to the basics and focus on the author and all her seasons of life. How does her identity affect her career, her choices, and her destiny?

I meet all kinds of writers who are out of balance; they either see only advantages or only disadvantages. Take a moment to pan back and gain a clearer vantage point. This will allow us to create a platform that is tailor-made.

WANA begins with *you*. Yes, it is important to have goals, but we need to begin with an honest starting point—ourselves. There is no good, bad, or best time to become a writer. There is only the here and the now, yet where we are in life will dictate a lot of how we build our platform.

The Spring Writer

First, let's talk about what I like to call the Spring Writer. Maybe you're in your late teens or early twenties, and you believe that you're far too young for anyone to take you seriously. You're probably right. Hey, us older wiser folk know that you're still young and forging your identity. Maybe you want to be a writer, but you could just as easily wake up and decide website design, the Army, or becoming a tattoo artist is more your style. But you also have a *huge advantage of perspective*. Young Adult and New Adult are two thriving genres, and who better to write them than a Spring Writer?

You're in your formative years, and probably unsure what the future holds. That's okay. Enjoy life. You *shouldn't* have all the answers yet.

Do you need to wait another ten years to publish your writing? You could, but there are new avenues to publish and even sell your initial works. You could get an early start, laying the bricks that will form your larger body of works over a career. Why not? This is the time of your life to do some exploring. As a Spring Writer you don't have a mortgage, a 401K, a house full of kids and a husband to feed. You are in the best season of your life to take risks.

Most Spring Writers are experts with social media. Many of you already have huge followings on Facebook, Tumblr, and/or YouTube. You grew up in the Digital Age. Computers have always been a part of your life, and social networking is like breathing. This book will add some focus to your existing social platform and start shaping it into an author platform.

The Summer Writer

As a Summer Writer, you're mature enough to know what you want to do, but too often, out of fear, you make the decision only *after* you've already committed yourself up to your eyeballs with other obligations. Many of you are balancing day jobs, family, and babies while you write. Risk is very scary because failure has a steeper price.

Summer Writers have some advantages. You are more mature, more stable, and generally have a source of income. You've also had some life experience, and experience is a vital ingredient for great writing. Ah, but Summer Writers can have a lot of disadvantages as well. Many of you didn't discover you wanted to write for a living until later in life. Or perhaps you knew it all along, but denied it.

Maybe you have always known you wanted to write, but that ranked right up there with telling your wife that you were selling everything you own to join a cult of moon-worshipping vegans in New Mexico. Perhaps out of fear, or a lack of self-confidence, you settled for the day job. Maybe you have a mortgage and kiddos who need braces and a wife with a Honey-Do list longer than your arm. Because of this, maybe you believe you missed your shot. Perhaps you think you no longer have the luxury of pursuing your dream, or that maybe you should wait until the kids are grown or you retire.

No time like the present.

You are at a wonderful point in life. You're still young. You've lived enough life to add depth to your fiction or authority to your non-fiction. Odds are, you're computer savvy and you're likely already familiar with social media.

As Summer Writers, you probably have a heavy load of responsibility. Any free time is usually grabbed while hiding in the bathroom. Well, until your spawn learn to turn doorknobs, that is (I tell you, once the little buggers get free will it's all downhill from there).

Many of you write to keep sane, but yearn to do more. You need to be able to demonstrate results to family and friends who might not be initially supportive. You need to connect with other industry professionals, but do this while under house arrest (code for "no babysitter" or "too poor for a full-time nanny").

Most Summer Writers have a day job, and writing is your second job. Building a platform shouldn't be a third full-time job. There are only so many hours in the day. Any career plan that ends with you curled in the fetal position with a bottle of vodka is a bad plan. I'm here to help your transition to career author be seamless and fun.

The Autumn Writer

Autumn Writers are at a tremendous advantage if you can embrace technology. Your children are grown and can fend for themselves. Maybe you still work during the day, but your free time is now yours, so it's time to do more with your life. Maybe you were like the Summer Writer and you chose your profession because it paid the bills, but finally you're at a point in life that you can begin thinking of what you *want* to do, instead of what you *must* do.

Autumn Writers are ripe and ready for harvest. Fifty-five is younger than it's ever been and it's getting younger every day. The fastest growing demographic on Facebook is the fifty-five and older category (the Silver Surfers). Autumn Writers have many advantages. You've lived a lot of life, so you bring experience and maturity to the table. Since you already finished school, tended a family and had a career, often you are better at time-management and are more patient.

Unlike Spring and Summer Writers, your main disadvantage will be that you didn't cut your baby teeth on a computer keyboard. Yet, in my experience, Autumn Writers are one of the best types of writers to work with as long as you are willing to face your fear of technology (if you have one). Technology is becoming far more affordable and much more user-friendly.

The Winter Writer

What about the Winter Writer? Is being an author a foolish dream? Is it too late?

Many people dismiss the Winter Writer, but I've worked with this type for over a decade and can attest that this group is often highly underestimated. Of all seasons of writers, they're probably the most technology challenged, but the good news is that anyone with the spunk to start writing at this time in life has true grit. Since Winter Writers know that they don't have indefinite time to get published, they're frequently better at self-imposed deadlines. They're often harder workers and more dependable. They no longer have time for the hobbies of youth. The Winter Writer's "hobby" is actually her new career, and this writer can be counted on to throw everything she has into this final stretch.

Historically, human society has been very labor intensive. As people grew older and no longer had the strength and endurance they had in younger years, they found that their usefulness shrank accordingly, even though their minds were as sharp, if not sharper, than their younger counterparts. In the Digital Age, the mind is most important, and age and infirmity are not the obstacles they used to be. If you are over seventy, the digital world that might be driving you nuts is the same digital world that can help you realize your writing dream. There's never been a better time to be a Winter Writer.

As we move through the coming sections, it's vital to overlay my teachings with your season of life, your strengths and weaknesses, your advantages and disadvantages. A twenty-two-year-old writer's platform is *very different* than a sixty-two-year-old writer's platform, and, frankly, it should be.

Your author brand begins with *you*.

Chapter 16

TEN SIMPLE STEPS TO BUILD AN AMAZING AUTHOR PLATFORM

ONLY TEN STEPS? Yes. I like to keep things simple.

Step 1: Goal-Setting for Max Advantage

The first thing I want you to do is to write your goals. Write them in present-tense and narrative form. Use your skills as an author to make the experience as visceral as possible. When you truly begin to *see* yourself a certain way, your inner compass shifts and points you in that direction.

1. Write Your LIFETIME Goals
2. Ten Year Goals
3. Five Years
4. Three Years
5. One Year
6. Six Months

Depending on where you are in life, you can do all of these or only a few. Remember, this approach is uniquely *yours*. On the following page, let's look at an example from a real WANA brave enough to share. Appendix A has more examples for further inspiration:

Example A: KAREN HUBER
Lifetime Goal
20 years from today (2032; I will be 80)

In 2032, my life insurance policy matures and is invested in the Second Chance Sanctuary Foundation, a retirement and permanent home for elderly and chronically ill animals, first established in 2022. The sanctuary is prominent in my mainstream novels that feature aging and chronic illness in animal and human populations.

The belief system of the novels is based upon my short but pithy nonfiction book on consciousness that makes the *New York Times* Best Seller list in 2017, the same year Oprah Winfrey and I have an online Super Soul Sunday conversation on consciousness. The exposure from both those events leads to the development of an online course on consciousness.

My weekly blog, A Boomer Being, is a regular Sunday online feature with 150,000+ subscribers. Infrequently, Deepak Chopra, Oprah Winfrey, and Michael Singer write guest posts on aging, chronic illness, ayurveda, and quantum healing. Annually, there is an online consciousness conference that also offers a social media component.

10 years from today (2022)

My blog has 50,000+ subscribers. I have just traditionally published my second novel, which has the animal sanctuary as its setting. As a promotion, my publisher is bringing out a special edition of my nonfiction bestseller with an introduction written by Deepak Chopra; the majority of the proceeds are sent to the Second Chance Sanctuary. The promotion is so successful that the sanctuary is able to establish its own foundation.

Five years from today (2017)

My nonfiction book on consciousness is traditionally published;

it boosts the sales of my first novel that was quietly and independently published in 2014. The complementary nature of the two books leads to significant sales.

I contact Dr. Mac of the Second Chance Sanctuary; together, we draft a business plan. Dr. Mac and her husband will continue in their roles as 24/7 veterinarians—the young family continues to live onsite—but now with significant financial support. Everyone seems excited.

My blog subscribers reach 25,000+. I get a call from the Oprah Winfrey Super Soul Sunday producer.

Two years from today (2014)

I publish my first novel independently; my blog has reached 8,000 subscribers. Traditionally published Florida author Adrian Fogelin writes a blurb; additionally, her positive review widens my sales circles. I attract the attention of a small press that is interested in my nonfiction manuscript. I send the first three chapters; I receive a contract.

I am able to donate monthly to the Second Chance Sanctuary.

One year from today

I am ready to learn the self-publishing process as I await the final line editing of my first novel from a professional editor. I reach 1000+ regular blog subscribers. I continue to assist the sanctuary with grant/technical writing.

Now that you have an example, you can start. Dream big or small, just be brave. This is *your dream* and no one can live it but you. There are no right or wrong dreams. A dream to be a *New York Times* best-selling author is just as valid as a goal to publish love-letters from your grandparents. Never let anyone belittle your dreams. Sometimes it takes far more courage to dream small, so don't feel bad if you don't have a goal to write books that are made into movies. Just make certain all of your goals are actionable and positive.

A goal to "not hate social media" is counterproductive because it offers no target to focus your energy. Now you see why we took time to talk about the seasons of a writer's life. Your age, what you want, what you seek to achieve are all deeply integrated into who you are and at what point your journey begins.

As you can see, Karen dreams big and her goals are all positive, specific and actionable. Refer to Appendix A for more examples.

Step 2: Get Signed Up

The next step is for you to open accounts on all the major social sites, and use *the name that will be printed on your books*. Even if you don't use a certain social site, it is wise to at least claim the digital real estate by having an account in your name. If you can't get precisely *your name* then feel free to be creative, but maintain the integrity of your brand by somehow securing your name.

For instance, there are lots of Kristen Lambs, so on Twitter I am @KristenLambTX. I could have been @AuthorKristenLamb @WriterKristenLamb @KristenLamb_author @KristenLamb007. There are all kinds of variations that can preserve the integrity of your author name. My website (domain) is www.authorkristen-lamb.com. In the Digital Age, people are overworked and this makes us a bit impatient. We don't want to have to go through fourteen steps to find your real name. Unless you plan to change your name to @TragicMuse or @WriterGal then those Twitter handles are doing you little good and they make it difficult for followers to remember your name when they go looking for books. Most of us struggle to recall *one* name, so please don't make us have to remember more. Also, cutesy monikers will score little favor with search engines. Remember, the key to power is *focus*.

It's unrealistic to believe we will use all of the social media sites we sign up for, but part of the reason I want you at least having an active account is because we can't predict the future. Spammers and bots can quickly ruin a social site we currently love, and if we already have an active account, we can then deftly shift to another platform. For instance, back in 2010, it was easy to defect from MySpace because I already had a Facebook account established. Also, we never know what will be the next huge deal. I started using Twitter back in 2008 when few people even knew what it was. Now, every major television show, event, and business uses Twitter. Because I already had an active account, it was easier to enjoy the advantages as the trend gained momentum.

Eventually, your goal is to have search engines favor you above others who might have the same name. Social sites rank very favorably, so it's a good plan to have a profile on at least the major sites. If you google my name, I take up most of the front page, and most of the entries are social sites, even ones I rarely use like LinkedIn and Goodreads. Just to be clear, it isn't that Goodreads and LinkedIn aren't great sites, but I can't be equally passionate everywhere. I have to pick and choose, and so will you if you want to remain authentic.

At this point, especially if you're a beginner, your profile will be very sparse. We are going to flesh it out in a little bit.

To earn the favor of search engines, we need to have information that is redundant across the platforms. This means the same author picture, same information, and similar bios filled with identical tags and keywords.

Step 3: An Author Picture

Use a picture that shows your face and that is inviting. Smiling faces will connect and attract more attention than an avatar of a cat or even a hunk's six-pack abs. No one expects us to be supermodels. We're writers. A profile that has a face connects to others emotionally and we are much quicker to feel we *know* a person. Remember, we buy from people we like and people we *know*.

You can spend money on author headshots; that's up to you. But these days we have the ability to create wonderful images that might not be as good as a professional photographer's but are more than good enough for our purposes.

One of my favorite sites is Pic Monkey (www.picmonkey.com). This site gives us amateurs the ability to get some of the Photoshop results without having to buy a program and learn how to use it. We can airbrush, change the lighting, brighten teeth, get rid of red-eye, cut out extra background, and use different filters for fun effects, all for free. All of us have a wonderful picture but there are too many shrubs in the background or we had salad in our teeth. That great picture can now be cleaned up with ease and made into an author picture you can be proud of. Then, once you've met a certain sales goal later down the road, feel free to treat yourself to a photo shoot. Meanwhile, use as many free or nearly free tools as possible.

Once you have a picture of your face that is friendly and inviting, go through all the social sites where you created a profile and add it.

Step 4: Getting to Know You - A Word Cloud

We are going to do a simple exercise that will be vitally important as we go along. Since your bio is *you,* we need to know all about you. If we could put an ingredient label on you, what would we see? A word cloud will give us the lion's share of the materials we will later need to create your author brand. We're going to use your word cloud to make your brand as multi-dimensional as *you are.* The paper dolls of the 20th century no longer interest audiences of the Digital Age.

You are more than just a writer. I want you to focus on emotional words. What makes you *feel?* Names of songs, fragments of thought, images, movies, moments of power, hobbies, television shows you love or hate, etc. I'd recommend you ask friends and loved ones to add to your cloud as well. Outsiders often see things about us we don't. Their input can be priceless.

I've included an example from a former student who was kind

enough to share her word cloud, but we will only share part of her word cloud. Why? The bigger the word cloud the better, and hers is *massive* (which is perfect!). This is essentially a free-writing exercise that will let your right brain have some fun. Please refer to Appendix B for the remainder of Jennifer's word cloud and for more examples.

Example: Jennifer Fischetto
Mother, daughter, friend, sister, girlfriend, introvert, author, writer, stubborn, procrastinator, Sims 3, fat, eating disorder, feminist, fun, funny, goofy, talks in baby voice to cats, talks for inanimate objects, sings, TV addict, French fries, chocolate, shrimp, Chinese food lover, over-eater, binge eater, in recovery, dislikes activity, walking is okay, Criminal Minds, loves rain, smell of coffee and fresh-baked bread, cooks from scratch, food, anti-bullying, magic, witchcraft, ghosts, supernatural, mysteries, amateur sleuth, Grey's Anatomy, green, purple, nose ring, purple hair, short, pink, black, bi-racial, diversity, plants, hates bugs of all kind, cemeteries, love being scared, Dean Koontz, Whispers, Intensity, Before I Fall, women are people and more than bodies, fat acceptance, intuitive eating, health at any size, hates diet mentality, honesty, Scandal, Pink, Kelly Clarkson, women who use their minds and not their bodies, celebrities with talent, dislike media and their decisions in how we should feel about ourselves, reincarnation, the Universe, family, self-esteem, confidence, self-worth, psychology, organized, insecure, General Hospital, romantic elements, horror, suspense, thrillers, YA, Hide and Seek, Solstice, The Uninvited, Shutter Island, Perfect Stranger, Once Upon a Time, murder, serial killers, Kiss the Girls, Alex Cross, psychological thrillers, being unique, dislike sheep and mob mentality, protect our girls, raising respectful and gentle boys, hates cigarette smoke, dancing, race, main character of color, whitewashing, sarcastic, dry-wit, sass, cats, fright, This is Not a Test, books, book covers without faces, ice cream, brownies, pizza, veggies, avocado, nighttime, midnight,

full moon, tarot cards, sensitive, nail art, lip gloss, mixed race, romantic suspense, twist endings.

I hope this is an eye-opener. Didn't you get a real sense of who Jennifer is as a person? We are more than our books. If all we talk about on social media is our books and our writing, we quickly bore others and ourselves. Once you're satisfied with your word cloud, print it out. Then take a highlighter and highlight key words and phrases that would describe you and your writing. These are words that will be consistently used to tag your content.

For instance, no matter what I post, when I tag, I always use: Author Kristen Lamb, WANA, We Are Not Alone, author social media platforms Kristen Lamb. We Are Not Alone has been a huge phrase for UFO believers and was also a Breaking Benjamin song, yet google it and my book will be at least on the first page. Also notice I put *author social media platforms*. I don't want to give Ike's Plumbing Supply help with social media. My specialty happens to be writers and building *author platforms*. Tags help writers find me when their agents tell them they need to build a platform. It also keeps Hamed's Car Wash from trying to hire me to tweet for them.

Using tags is one of the ways we differentiate ourselves from other people who share our name. I frequently run into writers who want to endure the time-suck of a pen name all because some florist in Pennsylvania has the same name. Well, unless this florist is an active blogger (which likely she isn't) it's no tough task to crowd her into at least page two of the search.

Your word cloud should be a living document. Keep adding to it.

The word cloud gives us a better perspective of ourselves and makes it much easier to see where we can connect with potential readers. We will use your word cloud to build your brand, help write your bios, help your SEO and we will even harvest it for blog content.

Step 5: Interesting Bios

Bios are important. They tell people who we are, and that's an opportunity to hook potential readers. Additionally, if we can saturate our bios with certain keywords, then we can become identifiable to search engines (look to your word clouds). Yet, it is a big mistake to believe that all authors should have the same kind of a bio.

The Non-Fiction Expert

When it comes to non-fiction, this is a realm dominated by *the expert*. It's great that you have an opinion or an idea. Now, we need you to convince us why we should value your information, opinions, or analyses over others.

There are actually two types of non-fiction experts, and your bios can reflect this. There is the Professional Expert and the Experiential Expert. Some experts go to schools or acquire various licenses to gain their titles as experts, but don't let this intimidate you or keep you from writing your non-fiction works. A mother of an autistic child is just as much of an expert as a practicing child psychologist. Yes, they are different kinds of experts, but it doesn't mean a doctor and a mother can't tackle the same topics from different perspectives.

The Professional Expert

If you happen to be a Professional Expert, then your bio is the place to list your credentials. You earned them! We want to know where you went to school, and any professional licenses you happen to hold. If you were a guest on Dr. Phil or an expert on a local news show, then put that in there. Your bio should reflect what makes you the right person to inform us or teach us. We want to feel secure that you are the person we want to listen to.

The Experiential Expert

Don't get discouraged if you don't have a string of letters after your name. You've been there, done that, and got the t-shirt, and the bio can make us (and Google) care about your opinions. Jenny McCarthy didn't have to go to medical school to make us care about autism. She's been rearing her son, Ewan, who has autism and she has an intimate perspective readers care about.

Did you fight in a war? Survive a disaster? Lose weight? Get your debt under control? Run a marathon? Were you abducted by aliens ~~too~~? We want to see how your experiences can help us learn to heal, cope or succeed.

You don't need to get your PhD in American History to make people care about your passion. Your bio just needs to reflect your love for the subject. Are you part of certain historical societies? Do you speak on your topic? Are you a part of a reenactment group? This is all vital information we want to know and they **are all words that should be in your word cloud.**

Whether you are a professional expert or an experiential expert, you need to make certain that your bio is full of keywords people would use when searching for you, your topic, or your content.

Refer to your word cloud. Print off a copy, and then highlight keywords that reflect you as a non-fiction expert. Those words need to be in your bio, because this is how search engines will discover you *and recommend* you.

Fiction Authors

One thing that cracks me up about fiction authors is you guys *lie for a living*, yet when it comes to writing a bio, you feel you need to tell the truth, the whole truth, and nothing but the truth.

Nothing could be further *from the truth*.

No one searches for a good book to read by googling authors who earned their MFAs at the University of North Texas. The same information that can serve a non-fiction author well does *nothing* for the novelist. Your bio needs to be an opportunity to *hook* readers that you are a great storyteller.

Here is an example from one of my favorite students (okay, they're all my favorites), Diana Beebe.

> Diana is a proud native Texan with no drawl—unless she gets upset. She's been an avid reader and writer of science fiction and fantasy even before there were categories called "middle grade" and "young adult" fiction. It was in those worlds that she found escape while vacuuming (one area of the carpet was really clean). She wrote her first novel during a college course and got an A for the semester. Even though her universities didn't offer degrees in science fiction and fantasy literature, she took more SF lit classes than anyone thought possible and wrote her master's thesis about the Grand Dame of SF literature, Andre Norton.

> She is a wife, mother, and dog owner of two semi-human dogs. This accidental technical writer and organic gardener is neither a perfect housekeeper nor a mermaid.

When it comes to fiction bios, apply the rule of *show, don't tell*. Diana is a science fiction and fantasy writer, but she spends a lot of time talking about subjects that 1) no one will search or, 2) if they do search, she doesn't want to be tied to those words. Notice she uses the word **technical writer**. Diana doesn't want to promote herself as a technical writer, so putting those words in her bio takes up valuable space that could help her fiction.

Granted, Diana's bio is cuter than the average, but let's take a look at her bio after a WANA Makeover:

> Diana Beebe woke up one morning only to realize her parents had been replaced by Pod People who

couldn't appreciate that Diana was really a mermaid, and that mermaids don't do windows. As a kid, her parents were less than supportive of her request for a unicorn and refused to pay for her pet dragon to have obedience training. Now grown, Diana has a very well-trained dragon. Okay, potty training is still a challenge, but he at least no longer incinerates the furniture. And then there is the demonic squirrel in her yard, but that's another story.

Diana can be counted on to randomly shout "INCONCEIVABLE!" and she always makes sure to pick up her Holocaust Cloak from the cleaners. She writes stories filled with all the adventure and magic that Pod People hate. Caution: If you are a Boring Pod Person, Diana's science fiction and fantasy novels are NOT for you. But for the misfits, dreamers and mermaids-in-human-form? Welcome home.

Now *this* looks like the bio of someone who can tell a story and it's loaded with keywords that will work in Diana's favor. Let's look and see:

Diana Beebe woke up one morning only to realize her parents had been replaced by **Pod People** who couldn't see that Diana was really a **mermaid**, and **mermaids don't do windows** (this is the log line for Diana's blog—more on that later). As a kid, her parents were less than supportive of her request for a **unicorn** and refused to pay for her pet **dragon** to have obedience training. Now grown, Diana has a very well-trained **dragon**. Okay, potty training is still a challenge, but he at least no longer incinerates the furniture. And then there is the **demonic** squirrel in her yard, but that's another story.

Diana can be counted on to randomly shout "**IN-CONCEIVABLE!**" and she always makes sure to pick up her **Holocaust Cloak** from the cleaners (high concept element from *Princess Bride*). She **writes stories** filled with all the **adventure** and **magic** that **Pod People** hate. Caution: If you are a Boring **Pod Person**, Diana's **science fiction** and **fantasy novels** are NOT for you. But for the **misfits, dreamers** and **mermaids-in-human-form**? Welcome home.

Your bio can do more than take up space. Put that sucker to work. Not only can it help readers find you via search engines, but if you can make people love reading your bio, it's no great leap for them to believe they'd love your books, too. Notice how in Diana's bio there are phrases that connect to the cult-like following of *The Princess Bride*. Diana's bio connects her in a personal way to her audience. Additionally, it is likely that someone using Google to look up stuff about *The Princess Bride* will discover Diana, just as many people who've searched for *Falcor the Luck Dragon* have discovered my blog.

Step 6: Adjusting Bio Length

When you create your bio, ideally you want to have four lengths—long, short, shorter and Twitter short. On our author websites we have time and space for 500 words or longer, but Twitter gives us only a sentence. On Facebook, you might want something middle of the road in length.

If you prepare your bios ahead of time, then all you do is go back through all those social sites and cut and paste the appropriate length. That way, you will have consistent profiles across multiple sites all using the same keywords in conjunction with your name. See how we are doing more with less?

What I recommend is that you write your long bio, then progressively shorten from there.

Example: Jolene Navarro

Jolene Navarro is from one of my blogging classes and she was kind enough to let me share her bios as examples. These bios were all created by using keywords we highlighted in her word cloud, and I've taken the liberty of bolding them for you to see.

Long version:

Jolene Navarro was born from a sunrise over **Texas Hill Country** and raised by the Indian Paintbrushes. They taught her how colors of **life** weave together to create **magic** most people miss. Thus Jolene promised her flower **family** that she would recreate this **wonder** in **books**. Her **stories** would capture the **beautiful**, **powerful**, weak, and **wonderful** like a damselfly in amber.

Jolene knows that, as much as the world changes, **people** stay the same. **Good and evil. Power and secrets. Lonely hearts**. Vow-keepers and **heart-breakers**. Jolene **married** a **vow-keeper** who showed her that long slow **kisses** and **dancing in the rain** never gets old. A dark bowl of **night sky** dotted in **stars**. The velvet softness of a **horse's** muzzle. **Stream of consciousness.** Pushing the edges. Something new from something old. **Modern fairy tales** and **super heroes**. The **weak overcoming**, rising to be righteous.

These days, Jolene **writes love stories** for **Harlequin**. Her life, much like her **novels**, are filled with **faith, family, football, art, laughter, dirty dishes**, and all of **life's wonderful messiness**. When she's not chauffeuring and refereeing her four **kids**, she loves to **dance** in the **rain** and commune with the **wildflowers** who taught her so much.

Short version:

Jolene Navarro was born from a sunrise over Texas Hill Country and raised by Indian Paintbrushes. They taught her how colors of life weave together to create magic most people miss. Thus, Jolene promised her flower family that she would recreate this wonder in books.

To fulfill her vow, Jolene writes love stories for Harlequin. Her life, much like her novels, are filled with faith, family, football, art, laughter, dirty dishes, and all of life's wonderful messiness. When she's not chauffeuring and refereeing her four kids, she loves to dance in the rain and commune with the wildflowers that taught her so much.

Shorter Version:

Jolene Navarro was born from a sunrise over Texas Hill Country and raised by Indian Paintbrushes. They taught her how colors of life weave together to create magic most people miss. They handed her a pen and the power of story. Now, years later, Jolene writes love stories for Harlequin so that everyone can experience a little wonder, to know that love really does win in the end, and to always listen to what the flowers tell you.

Twitter Short:

Jolene Navarro was born from a Texas sunrise and raised by Indian Paintbrushes, who handed her the power of story. Now she writes love stories for Harlequin.

Look in Appendix C for another great example from author Cole Vassiliou.

At this point, you should have open accounts on all the major platforms. Each account should have a nice, smiling picture of you and a bio of the appropriate length loaded with keywords. **Make certain that you include a way for people to contact you.** No one demands your cell phone number, but it is nice if we can email you.

Step 7: Beginning Your Blog

This step is about securing your blogging real estate. We will talk about *how to blog* in the next section. Earlier I mentioned that it is ideal for you to have your own author website. You will have far more flexibility (e.g., you can include a shopping cart for book purchases) and you will have greater control over your content. At the very least, try to secure your domain. Yes, you can do the free option, but I strongly recommend investing in an author website and blogging from there. Even if you can only afford something very basic, it's an investment in your future success and it will save a lot of headaches down the road. Trust me. I did all the dumb stuff so you don't have to.

WANA uses TechSurgeons for all of our web services. After two disasters with other major webhosts, I finally was fortunate enough to switch to TechSurgeons. Jay (the owner @JayTechDad) offers special discount rates on the WANA International website. He offers a lot of personal attention and backs up all of your content. I was a victim of a hacker who managed to not only take over my page, but he also planted a giant laughing skull smack dab in the center. I wasn't laughing. I was crying. At the time, I was with another webhost who did nothing to help. Jay stepped in and evicted the hacker and his skull, restored my content and beefed up my security, which is why I am Jay's most loyal fan.

If you don't have the money yet for a website, you can at least secure your name as a domain. You might have to get creative and add *writer* or *author*, but make sure *your name* is part of the domain name.

Should you choose to get a free blog, I recommend Word-

Press.com because it is very user-friendly, has excellent spam filters, makes it simple for others to follow, comment, and subscribe. It's also easier to upgrade it to the paid site when you have the money. Yet, if at all humanly possible, go ahead and get your author website. You'll thank me later.

I DO NOT recommend Blogger. Now, I know some of you might have been blogging for years off Blogger and have no troubles. If you don't want to switch, that's your call. My pet peeve with Blogger is that it is a *nightmare* for others to leave a comment. I have to jump through all kinds of Google hoops, leave a blood sample, three letters of recommendation and do a background criminal check *just to leave a comment*. (Hopefully this will change over time.) All these extra barriers create friction that will stall how quickly your platform can grow. There are times I will see a tweet with a blog that looks interesting. If I click and see it's a Blogger site, I no longer even bother reading. I know I will want to leave a comment, and I don't have that kind of time or patience. Also, Blogger isn't as easy to upgrade into a full website (as of this writing).

Step 8: Sign up for Flickr

By this point you should have a Flickr account, and I hope you will contribute images to WANA Commons (remember to tag them appropriately). *Your* images, the ones that have been doing *nothing* for your brand sitting in your hard drive, can now help your SEO simply by being posted on Flickr or in WANA Commons. When other WANAs use your images, this raises your ranking. Just make sure to change the licensing on any images you contribute to WANA Commons to "Attribution License." This means we can use your images if we promise to give you credit.

Take some time exploring WANA Commons. You can also explore the Flickr Creative Commons and look for images that catch your eye. We want blogging to be simple, easy and effective. Few things can eat up time like hunting around for an image that's not only appropriate for your post, but that's also safe to use.

Step 9: Sign up for Pinterest

Open your Pinterest account and create a folder for your images. You can label them *Inspiration* or *Fun Stuff* or *Kristen Made Me Do This*. Take some time to save images you loved from WANA Commons into that Pinterest folder. This will do a couple of things for you. First, because your images are on Pinterest, this helps your SEO. Secondly, because they are in a neat folder, it's now super easy to access an image you need almost instantly. Even if you never actively participate on Pinterest, those images are now working for you and your brand.

Step 10: Hang Out on YouTube

Your next assignment is to open a Word document, then spend some time on YouTube. YouTube? Yes. This will be important later when we delve deeper into blogging. Blogging is more than writing article after article and video is highly favored by search engines.

Spend some time having fun. Look for videos that make you laugh or cry. Videos that inspire you. Search for favorite songs. Many of the current vocalists have their "official" page where they have their videos posted. They uploaded them there for a reason. In the new marketplace, if people don't share our stuff, we might as well be invisible.

Some of my favorite videos are *Cows with Guns*, *Spiders on Drugs*, and *Jedi Kittens*. Yes, I'm warped. Invite spouses or teenage kids to help you. Teens are masters when it comes to finding the coolest stuff on YouTube. This is a great way to let your family be part of your success and even free up more writing time.

Every video on YouTube has a tab that says SHARE. You want to copy and paste the "embed code" (which looks like a block of symbols and gibberish) into your Word document then label what video the embed code is for. We don't have to *write* every blog. Our blogs are simply a way for us to create community. Videos are great for Friday posts because most of us are fried. We don't want to read about how to query an agent; we want to watch kittens fighting with light sabers.

Do the *Mayhem* commercials crack you up, too? Post them. Give people a laugh. Trust me, Allstate Insurance knows we are all using our DVR powers to scream past commercials. They know if we don't share their content with our audience, fewer people will see their advertising, thus they're *counting on us* to share or they wouldn't be loading their content on YouTube. And yes, Allstate has officially shared the Mayhem commercials.

We aren't the only ones hoping to go viral.

In the new economy, we all help each other. Allstate gives us content that makes us and our followers laugh, and we give them 30 seconds of our valuable time to hear what they have to say.

You can also add one more step, if you choose. WANATribe is a great place to connect with other writers and gain invaluable peer support.

I know this feels like a lot, and some days it will be, but few things can help us maintain enthusiasm like a great network of friends in the trenches with us.

Now that you have been through this section, you should have:

1. A basic understanding of social media terms.

2. A fundamental grasp of how search engines work.

3. A clear understanding of why tags and keywords are vital.

4. A list of goals.

5. An idea of what social sites will fit with your platform/brand.

6. Accounts on at least the main social sites.

7. An author photo.

8. A detailed word cloud.

9. Bios of four lengths—long, short, super short and twitter short, all loaded with keywords.

10. Your accounts on all the main sites have your image, the appropriate bio, and contact information.

11. A place to blog; either your author web site or a free Word-Press site.

12. A Flickr account with any images you've uploaded (tagged accordingly).

13. A Pinterest account with a folder of your favorite images.

14. A word document with embed code for minimum of fifteen YouTube videos.

15. A membership on WANATribe (optional).

If you have all of this, you have a solid foundation for your author platform. You have tagged and *consistent* content across all major platforms and you have a home base to begin blogging. When I help authors create a platform, my ideal combination is a blog, Twitter, and Facebook—and, of course, WANATribe.

Our blogs do us no good if they passively sit and wait for Prince Charming. Twitter and Facebook are powerful allies. I'm not going into much detail, because WANA has classes for the most current uses for those platforms or you can probably find tutorials on YouTube that are current and free. But, as I said earlier, the signing up is the easy part. Most of us can follow prompts. Where most people get stumped is in the *What now?* Or the *Why is this relevant?*

In the next section, after we've talked about Twitter and Face-book, I'll teach you how to write a killer blog that will appeal to that fat part of the bell curve that has been largely left untapped. I teach blogging in a very unique way that channels your creative energy and connects to your readers the same way as your books, through your writing *voice*. Yet, no matter how great your blogs happen to be, you will need to learn how to use at least one of the next two platforms we'll explore—Twitter and Facebook. How else will readers find you?

Chapter 17

UNDERSTANDING TWITTER

ONE OF THE BEST WAYS to drive traffic to your blog is by using Twitter. It's is a wonderful place to connect and make friends. It's also one of the best ways for any content to go viral. This section will help you gain a better understanding and thus open your mind to a powerful tool for writing success.

Beware of "Regular Twitter"

I believe most writers who hate Twitter are trying to use "Regular Twitter." Regular Twitter has one main feed and if you have more than three followers, it's easy to get lost. This is why I recommend two applications—TweetDeck and HootSuite. I prefer TweetDeck, but now that I use mostly Apple products, Tweet-Deck makes my computer try to cough up a hairball. At this point, it seems that HootSuite plays nicer with Mac. Also, Twitter is shutting down mobile use of TweetDeck and focusing on building applications for Web browsers and a Chrome App. So, no TweetDeck for your phone, which is fine because it never worked that great anyway. There is nothing we really *need* to do on Twitter that requires us to be plugged into our cell phone 24/7. Desktop is plenty.

Regardless, both applications work virtually the same way. Regular Twitter is for regular people who don't need platforms and who will be following less than a hundred people. Authors are not regular people, so Regular Twitter won't work. TweetDeck and HootSuite will help you be able to effectively manage and interact with thousands or even tens of thousands of people.

A Word of Caution

TweetDeck and HootSuite will offer you the ability to pre-program tweets and to tweet from multiple identities. *Resist the temptation*. Automatically generated content is largely ignored or resented. I would rather you tweet less and be genuine. We don't have to tweet fifty times a day to make a meaningful impact. In fact, if we're tweeting too much, others will start to wonder why we aren't writing. Checking in one to three times a day a few days a week is plenty. If we automate content, we become white noise. If when we do show up we're present and vested, people notice. Twitter doesn't close, so don't worry what time of day you're tweeting. I actually made a dear friend in the UK during a bout of insomnia. I happened to be on Twitter at four in the morning. Donna Newton and I crossed paths and now she comes to visit me in Texas at least once a year. Additionally, my UK following suddenly exploded. Somebody somewhere is awake and on Twitter, so there are better things to fret about than what time we tweet.

We only need one identity, because a strong brand is about focus. Everything goes under our names—the *names* that will be printed on the front of our books. People love authenticity, so anything that damages trust damages the brand. This is why pre-programming tweets to make it seem we are present is bad juju. It doesn't take long for others to realize we're bots and it ticks them off. This is also a *huge* reason it is a bad, bad, bad idea to tweet from the perspectives of characters. There is no good reason an author needs multiple identities on Twitter. It fractures your time, energy, focus and eventually, your platform.

Why Shouldn't I Tweet As My Characters

First of all, the goal of much of your social media is to convert *new* readers. The only people who will know or care about our characters *already bought the book*. To everyone else, this tactic will seem weird, lame, and even insulting.

Also, sometimes it isn't clear that a Twitter profile isn't a real person. There was a popular author who used this tactic and I fell for it. This author kept having conversations with some person who supposedly worked for the CIA. The profile looked like a real person and the image was blacked out like someone who required a protected identity. Being naïve, I assumed someone from the CIA was tweeting and using a front to give his opinions. Since the author wrote political thrillers, it was no stretch to believe he had people in the CIA he talked to and used as information resources (*New York Times* Best-Selling Author Barry Eisler does this all the time). I even followed and *talked* to this CIA person. When I finally *did* go to buy this author's book and read the book jacket I realized, to my horror, I'd been talking to one of his characters. I was mortified. I felt like an idiot and unfollowed both of them (and didn't buy the book). I didn't like being duped, and I can assure you I'm not alone in this.

Tweeting from the perspective of characters is a gimmicky time waste.

Twitter gimmicks remind me of that scene from *A Christmas Story* when Ralphie finally gets his Little Orphan Annie spy decoder ring and the "secret message" is "Drink More Ovaltine."

Gimmicks don't work and they're irritating. Most of us don't have a lot of free time, so when we realize we've been talking to an author's imaginary friends we feel duped. Tweeting as anyone but *you* is a gimmick. Don't tweet as your latest book. We can't connect emotionally to an inanimate object, and, if we're already following your author identity, then we're likely getting buried under duplicate content. Save yourself time and don't go there.

How to Organize Twitter

Once you've resisted the temptation to program tweets or tweet as a character, you can move on to the important stuff, namely, organizing all the people you're following. TweetDeck and Hoot-Suite offer us the ability to filter by giving us a way to make lists and create columns. By default, when you sign up for one of these applications, you will have some columns generated for you, usually:

Home Feed—this is the column where *everybody* you are following goes into by default. I am currently following over 4,200 people. There is *no way* I could hope to keep up with over *four thousand people*. Truth is? I don't. I do, however, scan the Home Feed periodically to see if anything catches my eye, and that's how many friendships have begun.

Mentions—this column shows any time someone mentions your name. Any time there is a tweet to or about @Kristen-LambTX, I see it appear in my Mentions column. This column is important to keep. It's how we can respond to others who are engaging us.

Direct Messages—this allows us a place to send and receive messages privately. Maybe someone needs your email address, flight number or cell phone number. You wouldn't want to tweet this information publicly, so you can reply via DM (direct message).

Unless something has changed, TweetDeck or HootSuite might give you extra columns like News or Sports. I would delete all extra columns but the three mentioned above. You will want to see everyone you're following because certain tweets (and people) might jump out and you can chat and connect. You obviously want the Mentions column because you need to respond when people talk to you or about you, and it should be clear why the Direct Messages column is important to have as well.

Beyond these three, hashtags (#) are important. You can click the icon that looks like a magnifying glass and type in words to filter all the tweets that are floating through the Twitterverse. Go back to your word clouds. What words jump out? Where are some places you could meet and befriend people of mutual interests? If you write cowboy romances with lots of stories about horses and rodeos, then #horses and #rodeos are a good place to start. Ideally, you will connect with people who share that same passion, and people who are part of the horse world are a fine market for stories set at the rodeo.

Not all hashtag searches will be productive. I love the show *The Big Bang Theory* and was certain that a #TBBT would be filled with geeks all talking about the show. Nope. It was stuffed with spammers trying to sell merchandise. No problem. Hit the X, delete the column and try again. Turns out #TheBigBangTheory, though long, happens to be the official place to talk about the show.

TweetDeck and HootSuite will also allow us to search for keywords, but I strongly advise against this tactic. People who are tweeting and using #s understand that other people are following that #. Thus, if I strike up a conversation with someone talking about #preppers, they aren't freaked out when I tweet to them and engage in chit-chat. Searching hashtags is different than searching keywords. One has a # in front, and the other does not. People actually have to type in the hashtag symbol at the end of a tweet, whereas **keywords are searching the body of the text for certain words.**

Spammers search for keywords so they can follow us and then spam us. Thus, if I tweet:

It sure was hot mowing my yard today.

It's not uncommon to suddenly realize that Frank's Landscaping is now following me. This tactic is just plain white-panel-van-creepy. Also, if you use that search function to find readers and then tell them about your book? Twitter can delete your profile.

For example, if someone tweets: *Had so much fun riding our newest horse today.*

If you have a search for *horse* then follow this person and tweet, "Wow, if you love horses, then my cowboy romance is perfect for you," it will seriously weird the person out and that behavior will endanger your account. Instead, I recommend avoiding the search function unless you're looking for information or trying to find a specific person. Stick to engaging with people in the hashtags, because then they won't feel like we're pouncing down on them from the ether. If a person is using a #, she's not shocked when someone tweets a response.

Hashtags allow you to connect to people around the globe who you couldn't meet any other way. Donna and I met on the #amwriting. If people are on Twitter, we can talk to them. Using hashtags can help us build community with others who share our passions and who *are not writers.*

This said, it is still very valuable to connect with other writers and people in our industry. My point is that our professional peers should not take the place of our potential reading audience. There are too many writers all talking to each other and we all have books for sale.

There is a brilliant quote from the introduction of Stephen Harrod Buhner's book *Ensouling Language* that fits perfectly.

"I think that they (writers) must, of necessity live in the crucial but commonly overlooked transition zone that lies between human habitat and the wilderness of the world, the place where wild plants exchange genome with their more domesticated cousins" (xi).

We are stronger when we step out into the wilderness and exchange ideas, talk, and build community. We need platforms that are a diverse, rich, vibrant ecosystem capable of reproducing and growing stronger with each generation. When we all hang out with more of the same, we are sad, sterile crops, indeed. Our platforms are sickly, inbred, and unproductive.

How Do I Get Started?

After you download TweetDeck or HootSuite, I would create columns for #MyWANA, #pubtip and #amwriting. You might even add #selfpub and #indie. Yes, these are places writers hang out, but it's good to have a solid network of peer support. #MyWANA is generally very active and we are ruthless with spammers. Thus, it's an easy place to meet people, watch, and learn. #Pubtip is used by agents, publishers and authors, so it's a precious resource for tips on craft, publishing, querying, etc. Agents are very valuable, even if we don't publish traditionally. There are foreign rights, movie rights, audio rights and all kinds of contractual issues that an agent can help you navigate so you can sign a contract that is most favorable to you and your career.

Twitter Helps Us Learn the Industry and Connect with Professionals

Before social media, it was far tougher for writers to keep up with industry standards. The print paradigm was so slow one couldn't always rely on the resources purchased at the bookstore. Many years ago, I bought a *Writer's Market* and out of twelve queries I sent, six were returned because that agent was no longer working at that agency. These days, because of the Internet, that is no longer an issue.

Ten years ago most readers assumed if a book was in a bookstore, it had been vetted. We had no way of knowing whether or not a book was self-published. I recall purchasing a book about how to get published, and there were all kinds of recommendations that I now know were far more likely to get a writer tarred and feathered than a book deal. The author of this book advised using colored stationary and being creative in approaching agents, like sending the query in a pizza box.

No, I'm not kidding.

To this day, I wonder how many agent horror stories this book spawned. Writers didn't have the benefit of social media so we were left to trust that the $20 book we purchased was giving industry-standard advice. Even back in 2007, it was rare to find an agent or editor who used email. Agents and editors weren't as Internet friendly as they are now. This is why it rocks to be a writer these days. With social sites like Twitter, we can be more educated and empowered than ever before. We have no excuse for not understanding our business and industry expectations.

Twitter can help us keep a finger on the pulse of publishing. What are publishers looking for? What is a certain agent looking to represent? What are the trends? Changes? Who are the scammers?

Twitter is also a great way for you to follow agents and pay attention to how they act. I hate saying it, but some of the worst Twitter behavior I've witnessed (other than young men between fourteen and twenty-two) has come from literary agents. Sometimes I wonder if I'm on Twitter or I've stepped into a nest of vipers. I've seen agents tweeting lines out of query letters, making fun of writers openly and posting content that is simply inappropriate. What I find interesting is that agents all want writers who act like professionals. The same can be said of agents. We want adults representing our content, not high school mean girls. Writers, pay attention. How does your dream agent treat authors? Is he or she kind, professional, courteous? Or is she a bully? Would you want this person representing you?

Agents will google you and see how you act online, and what's good for the goose is good for the gander in my book. Google agents before querying. Twitter is a wonderful place to get a sense of the person you want to query. Yes, there are some agents out there who act like jerks on Twitter, but there are also a lot of kind, generous and thoughtful ones, too. There are agents who genuinely love helping authors and finding great homes for good books, thus they are far worthier of your time and art.

Writing is a business, and who we partner with is crucial. Don't take these decisions lightly. As I said, agents are valuable allies even if we go indie or self-publish, and Twitter can help us choose wisely. Twitter can even help us locate agents who are in touch with the trends and changes in the paradigm, who are open to new and innovative methods of publishing; agents like Laurie McLean (@agentsavant) of *Foreword Literary* and Dawn Frederick of *Red Sofa Literary* (@RedSofaLiterary) are two lovely and talented agents who come to mind. Look them up on Twitter. They're not only generous with advice, but they're also crazy-fun.

Also, and I cannot state this enough, **the Brave New World of publishing is rife with predators, both on the indie and traditional side**. Twitter can alert us to danger and can keep our careers from being destroyed. A big New York publisher was forced to redo its predatory boilerplate contracts with its new digital imprints largely because bloggers spread the blaze of outrage using platforms like Twitter. Twitter keeps us informed, thus keeps us safer.

Twitter Maximizes the Six Degrees of Separation

Make friendships and connections. You never know who you might one day call "friend." I am a HUGE fan of *New York Times* Best-Selling Author James Rollins and so I ~~stalked~~ followed him on Twitter. Whenever I saw his name appear, I said hello and asked questions. When it came time to search for people to blurb my second book, I wrote a list of Hail Mary letters to those authors I dreamed about reviewing it. When Jim received my email, he recognized me, so it wasn't like a cold call. Not only did he blurb my book, but we're also now friends. Twitter is a wonderful tool for building some of the most important relationships in your writing life.

Make sure you get out of your comfort zone and follow other hashtags that might be more dynamic. But, just because we create a column doesn't mean we need to keep it. If it's inactive or spammy, delete and try again. Remember, look to your word cloud for hashtags to try. What television shows do you like? What keywords are in that word cloud that could connect you to your audience? If you write thrillers, #military people *love* thrillers, especially military thrillers. Write mysteries? People who watch #downtownabbey and #CriminalMinds probably like mysteries. Even if "regular people" on Twitter wouldn't define themselves as readers, it doesn't mean we can't connect, form relationships and convert them to loving books (our books). Remember we are missionaries of a different sort, and we have the power to connect with others in their comfort zones in hopes that one day they will love books as much as we do.

Tapping into the Hive Mind

Twitter is really excellent for finding resources quickly. Have a question? A problem? Need help? Tweet it. I mentioned this in an earlier section, but it is worth revisiting. If you're writing a crime thriller, follow hashtags frequented by law enforcement. Tweet your questions. Twitter is full of Connectors and Mavens eager to chime in. Ask for resources. Many humans are pathologically helpful, so use that to your advantage.

I once contemplated writing a book with a female bounty hunter as the protagonist. I didn't want to waste time with dead end research, so I tweeted for help. Within less than ten minutes, I had twenty leads, many of them from people in the profession.

There are certain professionals who are using that search function for keywords. If they respond to a *question*, it's no longer creepy. There will be legitimate recovery agents running searches for people who tweet using "bounty hunter," and many of these professionals are eager to help writers get the information *right*. I read a lot of books where writers made big blunders that could have been avoided by simply asking someone who knows. I once put a book down because an author had her protagonist putting "the safety" on a revolver. That showed me this author not only knew nothing about guns, but she didn't bother taking the time to get that simple but important detail correct. Had this author followed hashtags frequented by the police, military, or gun community, this mistake could have been easily avoided. If you have medical questions, military questions, history questions, etc., Twitter is a tremendous resource. I've had writers from the other side of the world who wanted to set their stories in Texas, but had no idea of the terrain. I could step in and offer information and even images. Twitter can make research easier, faster and far more accurate.

It is Better to be Interested than Interesting

We don't need to spend all day on Twitter to be effective. Pop in 1-3 times a day a few times a week and scan for questions you can answer, encouragement you can offer, or chime in on a conversation. Start a conversation. Ask questions that other people want to answer. If you just finished watching the #Oscars, tweet about it. Ask people if they agreed with who won. Who should have won? What movies should have been nominated yet weren't? Twitter is a giant cocktail party, so either join a conversation or start one. Ask people about *them*. Make Twitter about others. If you've ever read the timeless book by Dale Carnegie *How to Win Friends and Influence People*, then you know that we humans are inherently self-interested. Our favorite subject is US. We are accustomed to being overlooked and ignored, so when someone is **genuinely** interested in us, our ideas, opinions or accomplishments, *we remember them and like them*. People remember those they have *engaged with* much better than auto-tweets scrolling by with free ebooks.

If we take the time to learn about others and talk to them we become richer as human beings AND our platforms benefit.

Some Twittequette

1. Do NOT automate to appear you are present. We don't like being "tricked."

2. If you automate, use VERY sparingly.

3. If you automate, DO NOT include hashtags.

4. No auto Direct Messages. This abuses the privilege of being able to privately message and IT IS SPAM.

5. No Zombie Tweeters. Zombie Tweeters are those whose accounts have been all but dead until the writer needs something. They rise from the grave to sell a book or ask us to read their blogs. It's bad manners, and if we do this, we'll be about as welcome as family members who only call when they need a personal loan.

6. No begging. Don't *ask* people to retweet. Provide content they *want* to retweet of their own volition.

7. DO NOT retweet with the same hashtags. Change the hashtags when you retweet so you don't clog up a column. This also gives those you are retweeting better reach. Just delete the hashtags they used and insert ones that might apply.

8. No "True Twit Validation." When you "verify" others, those services redirect the person trying to follow you to another site. This is not only annoying, but it opens them up to being phished. Giving a potential fan a "social media disease" when you first meet is bad form and as unwelcome as head lice. It is NOT that big of a deal to report, block and unfollow spammers.

9. Tweet about your blog no more than three times a day. If you post a blog, tweet once in the morning, once at lunch and once in the evening MAXIMUM. If you are doing Twitter properly, then others should want to retweet your content. Twitter moves faster than Facebook so posting more than once a day is okay…just don't get crazy.

10. No rants, fights or unprofessional behavior. This should be common sense, but yeah. Here it is in black and white. Twitter makes it easy to go viral, so it should ALWAYS be handled with care. A woman made an offhanded nasty remark about actor/rapper Ice-T's wife, and the backlash was so bad the poor woman practically needed to move and change her name. Think before tweeting. Tweets can easily get out of control and become a Tweetenstein Monster.

11. Stop selling your book. We're tired of it. Really.

12. Don't be a Hashtag Hog. Use one to three—no more. Some #people #use #so #many #hashtags, #the #tweet #is #no #longer #even #legible. Connect with others and provide content they will want to share. Then let *them* change and add the other hashtags to the tweet.

13. Praise in public and criticize in private. If someone follows you and you are grateful, don't send a direct message. Just tweet back a "Nice to meet you!" When people see they have direct messages, that's a hint they need to discuss something in private. When people fill our DM columns with "Thanks for the follow!" it's annoying. If you find yourself having to correct someone, try to do it in a DM. For instance, we can tell them their link is broken or their account has been hacked. When I spot authors spamming #MyWANA, my first action is to try to DM and offer gentle correction.

14. Never unfollow for inactivity. Feel free to unfollow obvious bots, but unless someone is being obnoxious, just leave it. Someone might be new or in the middle of a family emergency or health problem. We don't know why that person is inactive, so unless it presents a problem, leave it be. For all we know, she could read this book and become one of the best connections you have once she knows how to actually *use* Twitter.

15. Never manipulate others with Twitter. No, "I retweet you and you never retweet me." We are professionals, not third-graders.

16. Never tweet or retweet content you haven't first vetted. Everything is part of your brand, so be careful where you put your stamp of approval.

17. Avoid inflammatory subjects unless they are part of your platform or brand. Bill Maher and Ann Coulter can rant on Twitter about politics. It goes with their books and is part of their brands. They also have rhino skin and a legion of interns to deal with trolls. We have better uses for our time.

18. No using Twitter as personal, free ad space. Keep promotion to a minimum. It is okay to have contests and give free stuff and tell people we have a book, but that should make up less than 10% of our overall activity.

19. Never follow people, then offer your book out of the blue. It's weird. It's like someone chatting with you in the grocery store and suddenly trying to sell you a water filter or vitamins. We feel awkward and manipulated so avoid it.

20. Never badmouth anyone. Bad news travels faster than good, and publishing is a small world. We can disagree and still be respectful and kind.

Chapter 18

UNDERSTANDING FACEBOOK

DO YOU NEED TO USE FACEBOOK? Yes. First of all, Facebook has over a *billion* active users, thus sheer numbers give us an advantage. Beyond this, Facebook helps us take advantage of *weak ties.* In Malcolm Gladwell's *The Tipping Point*, he details a 1974 study by sociologist Mark Granovetter, "who studied hundreds of professional and technical workers from a Boston suburb, asking them in detail about their employment history. He found that 56 percent had found their job through a personal connection" (53-54). When Granovetter looked closer at what constituted a "personal connection" he found that a majority of those connections were weak ties. His conclusion was that most people weren't landing new jobs through their friends; they were getting them through their *acquaintances.*

My first real speaking break came from Facebook. Indie romance author DeeDee Scott happened to be friends with one of the panel organizers for the Romantic Times Booklovers Conference (a *massive* conference with thousands of attendees). When that friend asked for suggestions for the social media panel, DeeDee connected her to me (notice DeeDee is a Connector). At this point, DeeDee and I had chatted a few times, traded cutesy pictures, and were in a wide orbit around one other. We weren't hanging out every weekend braiding each other's hair. We were acquaintances, but it was enough to land me the reference and the conference that changed everything. That year I was on a plane to LA and was even quoted in the *Los Angeles Times*. My foot was in the door and word of mouth ignited and spread. The next year, invitations rolled in to speak. Last year? I traveled to so many cities, I gave up resetting my watch, and this year looks like more of the same. Hooray DeeDee! Had it not been for a weak tie friendship, who knows how long it would have taken me to hit the tipping point?

Why did DeeDee recommend me over *all the other* social media experts? I can only guess, but it may have been because I was real. I talked to people. I asked questions. I shared fun stuff. I wasn't an all-marketing-all-the-time bot, so perhaps I stood out. On some level my actions must have connected to her *personally*. People default to who they know and who they like. I cannot stress this enough. This is likely how people are going to discover you and your books. It will be people one or more degrees of separation away who make the crucial difference.

Do You Need a Personal Profile or Fan Page?

The straight answer is you need both. My recommendation is all writers should start with a personal profile. Those weak ties—people we went to school with, those we've worked with, family—are going to one day be your best customers and salespeople. Sure, they might laugh at you for wanting to be a writer, but once you have a finished book for sale? Their attitudes will change. Those weak ties are *priceless*.

A personal profile will allow you a lot of two-way interaction you can't get on a fan page. It gives you time to build your following. I wouldn't even contemplate a fan page until you hit 500 friends. The reason? We writers already suffer from severe insecurity, and there are few things that can make us want to cut our wrists like starting a fan page and having three "Likes"…and two are from our mother. If we don't yet have a book for sale, the fan page really isn't a pressing matter.

The downside of a Facebook personal profile is it has lousy SEO. What does that mean? It means that the Author Kristen Lamb Fan Page will show up in a Google search faster than my Kristen Lamb profile page, even though I am most active (currently) on my profile page. Also, when it comes to a regular profile page, we can't sell goods or services or hold contests, lest Facebook banish us to Facebook Jail. We can get our accounts suspended or deleted. Thus, when I have a book for sale, new classes open, or we're holding a WANACon, we do all the promotional stuff on the WANA International fan page to make sure we're not getting on Facebook's bad side.

When it comes to a regular profile page, there can be another disadvantage. People have to know us to friend us, and that can get awkward. Facebook assumes most of us aren't pals with John Grisham or Pink. Also, profiles are limited to 5,000 friends, but anyone can "Like" a fan page and the "Likes" are unlimited.

I prefer socializing on the profile page because it affords far better two-way interaction that's crucial for building relationships. I held out from creating a fan page as long as I could. When I passed 3,000 followers, I finally gave in. Yet, though I have a fan page, most of my interaction is still off my profile.

Once I max out my 5,000 friends, I then have a choice. I can let new followers merely "subscribe" to my posts. This is a way of getting around that 5,000 friends limit. Or, I can tell my 5,000 followers that I will be interacting more on my fan page and to please follow me there. If I have been working hard on relationships and posting content people love, then many will eagerly follow wherever I go.

Fan Pages ARE NOT to Separate Our Lives or Identities

I know I will get a lot of disagreement on this, but it's my book so you get my opinion. We can't neatly separate our personal and authorial lives and, frankly, that's a flawed plan anyway.

Privacy Concerns

We're in the Digital Age. No such thing as privacy. Unless we live off the grid, pay cash for everything and never use a computer, we have no privacy. Yes, there are ways we can make lists so that certain people see only certain content, but I have a couple of warnings about that.

First of all, never trust technology. We can post stuff we think will be private, and all it takes is an *oops* on our part or a glitch on Facebook for that content to be open to the world. I post pictures of my son all the time, but I refer to him as The Spawn. I don't use his name or give any specifics. That is my choice. If you're uncomfortable with a stranger seeing certain content, don't post it. I never post stuff my mother can't see. This is just my rule, because I love my mother, but also because she scares me. Everything I post is open, and I don't bother with privacy settings because I believe the illusion of privacy can lure us into a dangerous sense of false security.

We are the Brand

Writers are the new reality stars. Potential readers will connect far more with pictures of your garden, your dog, or your homemade cakes than they will a non-stop infomercial about your books. A lot of writers believe the profile is the place to act like a human and socialize, and the fan page is for business, then they can't figure out why no one goes to their fan page. Well, um, nothing is happening. There's no party. Why would people show up? We must give others a reason to visit other than to bow to our awesomeness, buy stuff, or sign up for a newsletter.

A lot of people were in an uproar when Facebook offered fan page users the ability to pay to promote their content. Why pay to promote content? Because fan page content wasn't showing up in the newsfeeds of those who'd "Liked" the page. If people can't see the content, then what good is it? What many fan page users failed to understand is that this wasn't a nefarious plot by Facebook to squeeze users for money. Rather, those with fan pages weren't using their posts to engage their audiences. There was no reason for followers to seek out the pages. Facebook tries to give us the best experience possible, thus it will only add to our newsfeeds the sites we are *actively* interacting with. When writers use fan pages for "business only" it's really just more of the advertising that we're scrambling to avoid. Most of us aren't going to deviate from socializing to seek out a fan page offering us a new book, a way to sign up for a newsletter or a schedule of book signings.

Snooze fest.

We will, however, interact with pages where a live person is present asking and answering questions, starting conversations, seeking opinions, and posting content *other than books and all things writerly*. When we take the same behavior we use on our personal profiles to the realm of the fan page, we give reasons for others to interact. This means more people see and respond to our pages, thus we have no need to pay to promote. Since users are interacting, sharing and talking, our fan pages will show up in their newsfeeds and we will enjoy far greater reach. The WANA International Fan Page regularly hits as high as 86% engagement, and we don't pay to promote. Lisa Hall-Wilson (our WANA Facebook instructor) and I regularly pop in, post, chat, and start discussions.

Humans are social creatures. We need community. We love to talk, offer opinions and chat. Fan pages are more than monuments to our egos and digital bookstores. They are simply ways of taking those communities we started on our profiles to the next level and interacting beyond the 5,000 friends limit. Horror Author Clive Barker is one of the best examples of this I've seen. He regularly asks questions, posts artwork and fun stuff. He is present and *talks to people*. He asks their opinions and ideas and *even responds.* This makes Clive feel like a *real* friend. James Rollins is another wonderful fan page role model. Jim is there, vested and real. Never underestimate your ability to create meaningful emotional attachment using social media.

Fan Pages: Rethinking Product Placement

Our fan pages are more than a storefront to showcase books and announce book signings. To highlight my point, I'll refer back to Martin Lindstrom's *Buyology*. We are all familiar with product placement. Many of us remember being kids and seeing the Stephen Spielberg movie, *E.T.*, where a frightened kid, Elliot, led a strange being into his home and into a relationship by using a trail of an (at the time) unknown candy, Reeses Pieces. After *E.T.*, sales of Reeses Pieces exploded. Product placement paid off big.

In the late 1970s and early 80s, Ray-Ban, a U.S. based manufacturer of sunglasses, was struggling to stay alive until it brokered a deal with Paul Brickman, director of the 1983 hit movie *Risky Business* featuring a young, sexy Tom Cruise sporting Wayfarer shades. Sales skyrocketed. The movie *Top Gun* catapulted the sales of leather aviator jackets and Ninja motorcycles. Bolstered by these successes, suddenly Hollywood went crazy with product placement, only to fail dismally.

"When *Die Another Day*, a 2002 installment in the James Bond franchise, managed to display 23 brands over the course of 123 minutes, audiences were royally peeved. Most critics questioned the movie's integrity, some even dubbing it *Buy Another Day*. But this was nothing compared to Sylvester Stallone's 2001 *Driven*, which managed to jam in 103 brands in 117 minutes—almost a brand every sixty seconds. More recently, the movie *Transformers* had unannounced cameos from AAA, Apple, Aquafina, AT&T, and Austin-Healy—and those were just the *As*. All in all 68 companies made utterly forgettable, face-in-the-crowd appearances in the 2007 film" (Lindstrom, *Buyology*, 46).

Do any of us remember the Apple computers, Omega watches, or Louis Vuitton purses we see in the movies? Do we *see* the Pepsi or Doritos? No. We have what Lindstrom refers to as "snow-blindness."

What Does This Have to Do with Facebook?

Let's look back at Hollywood and *successful* product placement. Reeses Pieces were an integral part of the overall narrative. Same with Ray-Ban glasses in *Risky Business*. What would *Top Gun* have been without Tom Cruise racing around on a crotch rocket wearing a leather aviator jacket? Rather than this ham-fisted shoving a product in our face because they could, the products became part of the greater story.

This is one of the reasons that being personal on Facebook generates better results. When we share about our lives, talk about fun stuff, ask questions, we're creating an overarching narrative of us-as-authors. No one can follow me long on Facebook without hearing about zombies, *Star Wars* or *The Big Bang Theory*. I talk about laundry, family, and struggling to keep up with life. I talk about The Spawn painting my living room with Mac and Cheese and share stories about my grandmother (who's suffering with dementia) playing Bubble Guppies with my son. Facebook isn't a storefront, rather it's a narrative of who I am, and my books aren't the sole centerpieces. My books aren't the convenient can of Coke thrust into view in an awkward attempt to sell. My books become part of a bigger narrative of me, the author. Those who engage with me become part of the story, and the story of Author Kristen Lamb *happens to include my books*.

My "product placement" is now natural and others pay attention because Kristen Lamb would be a different story is she didn't happen to also be an author. This is *the exact same effect* as socializing in person. When I was a Rotarian, I did business with a lot of other Rotarians. Did they sell non-stop? Did they hand me coupons and mailers? No. They hung out with me, had lunch, talked about family, and over time these individuals became the *friends* who *happened* to be accountants, dentists, veterinarians or authors. Their professions became part of a friendship narrative, so I automatically sought their services *first*.

Also, when it comes to Facebook, because I am not the all-books-all-the-time channel, I appeal outside of the realm of writers and "readers." Regular people can relate to having so much dirty laundry they are tempted to just buy all new clothes. Regular people know about dirty diapers, piles of dishes, yard work and unfinished projects. They can join the conversation and bond.

I can't count the number of people who've emailed me asking for recommendations about books. These folks aren't "readers" per se, but they happened to get a new Kindle for Christmas and wanted direction. These followers came to me because I made Facebook about *them*, and engaged in a mutual comfort zone— Monty Python, *The Princess Bride, Star Wars,* science, kittens, funny videos, etc. Because they felt comfortable and connected, they considered me a friend and I, of course, am always eager to help. Many of these "non-readers" also happened to have friends or family who were writers, and guess who they referred when those writers needed social media help?

Engaging in Facebook this way is not only far more effective, it's a lot more *fun*. Marketing, even if it did work, feels weird to most artist personalities. Since it feels icky to us, others sense our unease and then our efforts fail to resonate. When we can relax and just act human, Facebook (and all social media) becomes more effective, more enjoyable, and the results are longer lasting.

Facebook shouldn't be all about writing and selling books. Every day I see so many new groups for authors to cross-promote to each other, but most lack a core of community and service and quickly devolve to non-stop spam. It's all writers trying to sell books to each other, taking and not giving. That is an unrewarding approach that leads to burnout and failure more times than not.

More about Facebook

I know there are a lot of nifty tools on Facebook—groups, invites, and so on, but I'm not going to talk about any of those, simply because I don't use them. I focus on blogs and books. If we are motivated, Facebook (and all the other sites) have added advantages, and if you want to learn those, take a WANA class or go to YouTube. I will say that simply doing the basics, talking to people a couple times a day, is more than enough. I almost never talk about my books. Posts on Facebook stay up longer, so posting four times or fewer a few days a week is plenty. Scan your news feed. Share something funny or inspirational. Comment on someone else's post. *WOW! Cute Baby! What a beautiful dress. Happy anniversary! LOL, my dog does that, too. Oh no! Tornadoes? Stay safe.* These little moments add up. They are small investments in people and relationships that will grow over time. We are all human and we remember kind people who take the time to be authentically interested in *us* with no strings attached.

Since Facebook moves far slower than Twitter, only post a link to your blog *once*. Otherwise you can drift into the dangerous Land of Spam. Beyond that? Have fun. Start conversations. Join conversations. Enjoy being social. No, this isn't an approach that can be measured in algorithms or fancy reports. It isn't a get-rich-quick approach. WANA is a long-term investment in our fellow human beings that is guided by the simple trust that we reap what we sow. If we plant seeds of love, kindness and support, over time we will see the fruits of those labors.

Favor with Facebook

Like search engines, Facebook gives a lot of weight to images. Images are the most likely content to appear in the newsfeed of our followers and they are also the most likely content to be shared. All those funny memes? Share them. Make some of your own. If you see memes you like, look and see what site was used to generate it and create one. If you haven't yet figured it out, I love Grumpy Cat. She cracks me up. I used a meme generator to create Grumpy Cat content that writers would find funny and want to share. I also made regular memes that non-writers would love sharing as well.

Want to generate discussion? Instead of typing in a status update (which ranks lowest on the Facebook priority list), put the question, observation, or thought in an image. You now have access to WANA Commons and have Pic Monkey, so there are all kinds of images at your disposal that can add power to your posts. I've put some of the more popular quotes from my blogs on images (with my website at the bottom) and they travel faster and farther than any other kind of content. See how I am advertising *without* advertising? This is content that makes others laugh or feel inspired and so they connect and want to share. This tactic is *very helpful* for the non-fiction author especially.

They are not called "growing fluffy kitten touches." They are called "growing PAINS!"

~ Kristen Lamb

Photo courtesy of M.G. Edwards

This is a simulated image our Facebook expert Lisa Hall-Wilson created using one of my quotes, and it quickly went viral:

"Art isn't always supposed to be pretty. It's to challenge us, make us think, shove us out of our comfort zones and challenge what we believe."
~ Kristen Lamb ~

Photo courtesy of Dana Mason

Marcy Kennedy (our WANA Twitter expert) posted a question on Facebook.

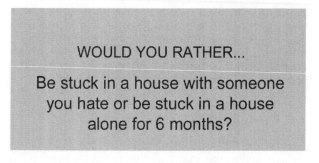

WOULD YOU RATHER...

Be stuck in a house with someone you hate or be stuck in a house alone for 6 months?

Instead of posting this as a status update, Marcy made her conversation-starter into an image. Not only did this image get a lot of discussion, it was something that others wanted to share on their own walls. As an image, Facebook gave this far higher priority, thus Marcy is working smarter, not harder, which is a huge part of the WANA Way.

Images will get the most weight. Links? Not so much. Status updates get the least Facebook love, so this is part of the reason I urge you to embrace images and use them in your favor.

Facebook Etiquette and Pointers

1. Don't sell your book. Facebook isn't our personal free ad space.

2. Don't send form letters. They are rude, and they're spam.

3. Do NOT post ads on other people's walls. I've had writers who haven't taken two seconds to say hello, believe (VERY mistakenly) that it is okay to post an ad on my wall. This is akin to putting up signs for your business in other people's front lawns without asking.

4. Do NOT add people to groups without their permission. Again, I've had writers who couldn't be bothered to actually talk to me suddenly add me to their *Fans of The Dragon Brotherhood Book Group.* Let me get this straight, this writer is too busy to be a human being with me, but I am supposed to drop everything to support and help sell his/her books? Yeah, um. NO.

5. Do NOT separate regular friends from writer/reader friends. Everyone can be a potential reader. Just sit in a doctor's office with no magazines for an hour. Trust me. Instant reader. When we separate people based on what *we believe* they are interested in, we're pigeonholing them. We aren't omniscient so we can't be certain what people would be interested in. Also, when we use a scalpel to dissect our followings, we lose out on those powerful loose ties because we have amputated them from our platform.

6. Don't use Twitter to post on Facebook. Twitter moves much faster and we can quickly overwhelm our Facebook followers. Also, since there is a little Twitter icon to tattle on us that we aren't even present on Facebook, it's insulting. What it tells others is we are "friends with benefits." The person wants the benefits of Facebook without actually having to give and interact.

7. No ranting. We all have beliefs and a faith. We can support our beliefs in a positive way that doesn't alienate others and make them avoid or block us.

8. Be present. A little Facebook goes a long way. Engaging a couple of times a day is more than enough. Let us know you're alive. Few things will irritate others like a person who's never present until he wants something (i.e., to sell books).

9. Never underestimate the little things. Small kind actions add up over time.

10. Don't rely on algorithms. Those change every time Facebook rearranges the digital furniture and can be a fast ticket to Crazy Town.

11. Don't send mass emails, especially to people you don't know. It makes our messages blow up and it's annoying. No, I won't post what color my bra is in my status. I support breast cancer research by donating *money*.

12. Don't mass tag people in photos. Again, it's irritating. I've had people post a picture of their book cover then tag fifty people. It's rude and doesn't make us want to buy the book. Rather, it makes us notify Facebook that this post is spam and can land the offender in Facebook Jail.

Section 4
LEARNING TO BLOG

Chapter 19

BLOGGING TO CONNECT
WITH READERS **AND** BUILD A BRAND

BLOGGING IS A GREAT WAY to change the odds in our favor. Why? Because, first off, writers write, and blogs give others a sample of our writing voice. But, even this isn't enough. If it were enough, then we could slap up some writing samples and be done with it.

I've spent the past few years studying all kinds of blogs. What made them popular? Which blogs generated triple-digit comments? Which blogs had loyal followings? Which blogs generated the most hits? Which blogs created the most subscriptions? After years of studying and testing using my own blog and the blogs of my ~~guinea pigs~~ other writers, I finally have the answer. I give you The Golden Key. This is a gift for you from your WANA Mama. This approach is highly effective for fiction authors, but it can also help the non-fiction expert as well.

The Golden Key to Successful Blogging
For a blog to really become popular
it needs to be high concept.

This is where we take a lesson from Hollywood. High concept sells, and sells BIG. But what is high concept? High concept is one of those terms that are tough to define, but people know it when they see it. We've already touched on high concept, but it's time to dig deeper. What can it do for your platform and your blog?

Publishers also crave writing that is "high concept." But what on earth does it mean? The best explanation I've found? Screenwriter/producer Terry Rossio refers to *high concept* as "mental real estate" (Rossio, *Wordplay Columns*, Screenwriting Column 42).

High Concept → Mental real estate that is owned by the most people.

Huh?

Bear with me.

If I wanted to write a book about what it was like to live with Geraldine Fitzgerald, most of you would go, "Okay. Um…why should I care? This means nothing to me."

Most other people in the world do not know Geraldine Fitzgerald and she holds no mental real estate in the minds of others. She is my made-up character for my story. I know her. I care deeply and passionately. Do you? No.

Ah, but what if I said I was going to write about living with an emotionally absent perfectionist who never gave her daughter a hint of praise, thereby leaving her daughter an emotional, drug-addicted wreck?

Oh, now I might have your attention. Most of us have dealt with someone—a boss, a parent, a grandparent, or maybe a lover—who always kept praise and love just beyond our reach. This concept holds some territory in the emotional database of your mind. It makes you *feel* something. This layer has helped a fuzzy idea gain greater focus, and is a vast improvement over my first try at pitching my idea.

Now, what if I took that idea another step? What if I told you that I am going to write about an emotionally absent perfectionist who is abusive to her daughter? My story is *Mommy Dearest* for the 21st century.

Wow! Now almost anyone familiar with American culture has an even MORE vivid picture of my story. The picture is crystal clear with razor-sharp detail. We now envision wire hangers and scrub brushes to go along with that abuse. This pitch is far more visceral, and we can relate even if we, personally, have never suffered serious mental and physical abuse. This mental image is universal, emotional, and we walk away from stories like these with strong opinions. These are the novels we remember, the ones that stay in our minds and that even form pop culture.

This is high concept.

One of the reasons that the *Harry Potter* series has been so insanely popular is that J.K.Rowling was able to elevate a fantasy story to high concept. How did she do this? According to Rossio, Rowling took an experience that is almost universally shared—going to school—and made it exciting. Everyone can relate to attending school. Memories of school are emotive, for better or worse. Rowling capitalized on this universally emotional experience and made it magical.

So how does this apply to blogging?

The same tool we use to write great novels and screenplays also works for blogging. In order to gain a large following, our blogs should follow my Holy Trinity of High Concept.

High Concept Rule #1

Our blogs must have broad appeal—Our blog topics will, ideally, hold interest for as large an audience as possible. When we spend every post talking about antagonists, the challenges of life as an indie author, and the ins and outs of designing book covers, we must realize these topics only appeal to a very, very small section of the overall population. If a non-writer wanders onto this blog, those posts will hold zero interest. It's no wonder that many agents don't get very excited about author blogs. Most writers are blogging to each other.

This is one of the reasons I recommend that writers do not

start a writing blog. Then your blog merely devolves into a hub of information. It lacks the broader appeal that can make a blog resonate with non-writer readers. It also has a ton of competition, all clamoring for a small section of the population's attention. But, most importantly, it lacks this next component.

High Concept Rule #2

Our blogs must be emotional—When I mentioned *Mommy Dearest* earlier, I imagine a few of you might have winced internally. Why? The title alone evokes an emotion. Yet, when I mentioned designing book covers? Eh, not so much.

When you step away from a blog post, ask, "What emotion would my reader feel? Is that coming across in my writing? Is the emotion generated powerful enough to resonate?"

Emotions connect us and compel us.

Blogs that elicit emotional responses will gain more hits and enjoy larger, more loyal followings. Humans connect via shared emotions and shared experiences. By writing emotive blogs with questions designed to compel readers to contribute, we are taking the first steps at building a loyal community that transcends all boundaries.

Emotive topics will generate more comments and will also make readers naturally feel more loyal to us and our blogs (and eventually, our books).

Why? Because we didn't talk AT readers, we shared WITH them. We connected on a shared concept/emotion and now we're peeps. Haven't you ever noticed that there are bloggers you love from the get-go? You don't care what they blog about, you just want to hear their opinions? And if you don't have time to leave a comment you feel guilty? Often this is birthed from that blogger's ability to connect with her readership. We feel a part of that person's team, and we feel an innate urge to support our "friend." Is this so strange? Why are we loyal to novelists? It's because of how their stories made us *feel*, and, by connecting on experience and emotion, we become loyal. All a blog does is keep the emotional fires burning between books. Blog loyalty, book loyalty and author loyalty, when we get down to basics, are all birthed by the same process.

This is one of the reasons that blogs that are essentially online journals do very little to inspire loyalty and build a brand. If we merely blog about our word count, another query rejection, a nice conference, then we are emotionally closed. We're having a party with ourselves.

High Concept Rule #3

Your blog needs to give the reader something to contribute or take away—If you write posts that emotionally connect, chances are, the reader will want to share this pleasant experience. This is how you generate word of mouth for your blog. You always need to ask, "Does my blog give more to others than it takes from others?"

People are already giving up their most precious possessions— their time and attention. So, when they walk away, are they in the black or in the red? Are we taking more than we're giving? Too many writers talk non-stop about their writing experiences. Okay, not to be a jerk, but who cares? Until we're a mega-author like Stephen King, only a handful of people care about our writing journey. And even then, how much could Stephen King talk about writing before he bored himself to death? Then bury himself in a Writer Sematary so he could come back as a far more interesting zombie alien.

I constantly see writers on Twitter announcing:

My thoughts on such-and-such
My struggles with la la la
My opinion about thus and such
My musings on this and that

And when I see tweets like these, my brain instantly chirps, "Why do I care?" My brain can be kind of insensitive, but it still makes a valid point. We aren't born with the divine right of people caring what we have to say. We have to earn that. At the end of the day, why should others care? They don't. Our blogs can't be about us. They need to be about the reader. We have to meet others on common turf.

Follow my Holy Trinity of High Concept and what happens? Our names will gain mental real estate. Earlier I mentioned mental real estate. Why will blogging help you sell more books? Simple. It will help you use existing mental real estate to gain your own mental real estate. Every post is a connection. Every blog can generate discussions that eventually become friendships. Our blog contributes to that emotional Coca Cola experience we talked about earlier. No one can connect with just our names (early on), but *they can connect* on topics of universal and emotional interest. When we talk about *Star Wars*, pets, kids, killing our houseplants, our laundry, or wanting to toss our printer out the window, we are using concepts people are already familiar with and using them to gain more mental real estate in the readers' minds. On Facebook, I constantly have followers share posts about zombies, *Star Wars*, *The Big Bang Theory*, Febreze, all because I have talked about this stuff in my blogs. All these broad concepts become linked long enough to my name and eventually that coalesces together into what we call "author brand."

We can use the same tactic Hollywood uses to make great movies to create our author brand.

If we blog regularly in ways that connect with others on high concept, eventually people will recognize us and our names will become linked with existing mental real estate. Our names are front and center multiple times a week and become tethered to concepts that are emotive and universally shared.

Tether those together long enough and that is called an Author Brand.

High Concept Content → Mental Real Estate → AUTHOR BRAND

All an author brand really means is that your name has become high concept.

1. Your name becomes recognized by larger and larger groups.
2. Your name becomes emotive.
3. Your name alone promises people that they will take something positive/valuable away.

Name recognition is good, but it isn't a brand. All brands have name recognition, but name recognition alone does not make a brand. Name recognition alone cannot compel people to part with their hard-earned money.

What's the difference? A brand comes attached to emotion and content. This is why getting on Facebook and Twitter and spamming everyone in sight is a bad idea. People might recognize our names, but our names will come tethered to the wrong emotions. At worst, people will hate us because we're spammers crapping up their Facebook walls and email. At best, our names will be familiar, but, because they hold no emotional or mental real estate, people won't feel compelled to part with their money to buy our books.

Here's a quick demonstration:

Angelina Jolie, Princess Diana, Mother Theresa, Robin Williams, Steve Jobs, Paula Dean, Chef Ramsay, Stephen King, Bill Clinton, Jerry Springer, Donald Trump, Johnny Cochran, OJ Simpson, Paris Hilton, Lance Armstrong, Snookie, Tori Spelling.

I bet you recognized all of these names. Better yet, I bet almost all of these names stirred up images and emotions.

Another quick demonstration:

Arne Duncan vs. Arnold Schwarzenegger

Which name do you recognize? Perhaps both. Duncan is the current U.S. Secretary of Education. You might have heard his name on CNN, but though you recognize it, it holds little mental real estate, and his name is not highly emotive (for most people). Schwarzenegger, by contrast, is a name that practically explodes with images, concepts and emotions for people all over the world.

This is the idea behind becoming a brand. Name recognition alone is not enough. We must use our blogs to drive the power of emotion behind our names.

We use our blogs to connect with READERS on common emotional ground. We craft an experience that is so positive that people not only want to buy our books, but they also want to badger friends and family to buy our books as well. Why? Because they feel they *know* us. They connected with us and, because of that, they are vested in our success; so vested, in fact, that they are willing to mobilize their platforms to help us.

Historically, novelists have had a staggering disadvantage. The only platform they could create was from the fan base for their books. The only brand available was from the books. This was very limiting, hard to control, and even tougher to grow. Now, however, writers have the ability to become personalities with loyal followings before the book is ever even available for sale. The blog is the most powerful tool for doing this.

Chapter 20

APPLYING HIGH CONCEPT TO BLOGGING

OKAY, NOW WE ARE GOING to look at high concept in application. Like I said, high concept is simple but hard. If high concept was easy then every movie, book and blog would be a success. Will we be able to apply high concept to every single post? Probably not. Ah, but if we are mindful to at least try, then we strengthen those writing muscles that are so vital for success in other areas of our writing. Blogging is great practice, and practice makes perfect. High concept will get easier the more we apply it.

High concept for blogging is paramount to blog success. There are bloggers who post every day and never gain large followings. Their subscriptions are less than stellar and they rarely have a lot of dialogue (comments) on their blogs.

What makes the difference? How often they can apply high concept.

Remember, the word cloud exercise? THIS is where you really put that puppy to work. Here is an example of what I would like you to do with those massive word clouds. We are going to use an imaginary friend of mine, Sarah Redding, to demonstrate. She has an impressive word cloud, too, but we're going to look at only a handful of words.

Example 1:

Sarah Redding—horses, romance, Kansas, farm, animals, baby ducks, riding, church, cowboys, history, love, needlepoint, scrapbooking, wallpaper, coffee, simple, honest, salt of the earth, trucks, tailgate parties, Cowboys football, America, Americana, horseback riding, barrel racing, rodeo, George Strait, American Idol, Leanne Rimes.

Doesn't this bundle of words give you a feel for who Sarah is? Doesn't an image form in your mind? Let's take the feel of this group of words and create a log line for her blog.

Sarah Redding's Blog—With Heart from the Heartland

See how this log line gives a feel for Sarah and her writing? A tone that the reader will expect? Are we going to expect racy spy thrillers? No. Because she didn't list those keywords. Also, her log line gives a feeling of home, America, country living, and fresh air. We expect her blogging voice and her writing voice for fiction to be very down to earth, nostalgic, or sentimental. Since most fiction authors draw from their life experiences, we expect Sarah's romance novels to have cowboys, horses, and probably even be set in Kansas.

Now, Sarah is a smart cookie. She read my book before she started blogging so she decided to blog on things other than writing. All her writer friends were blogging about plotters and pantsers and the future of ebooks, but Sarah wanted to stand out. She also longed to connect to potential readers who didn't happen to also be writers.

When we look at Sarah's list of words, we can clearly see that Sarah does a lot of things with horses. Sarah decided that one of her blogging days would be dedicated to talking about her newest horse Blackie and chronicle his training and growth.

See where this blog idea went sideways?

It isn't high concept.

If Sarah goes on and on about horses and uses all kinds of jargon that no one outside the world of barrel racing gets, she has just shot herself in the digital foot. She has narrowed her audience, and she is also treading on dangerous ground of becoming a "horse blog."

How can she make "horses" high concept?

Sarah has to make horses universally appealing and emotional for those outside the horse world as well. She wants her reading audience to feel they can contribute, even if they have never seen a horse up close. Sarah regroups and decides that on Mondays she will post a series known as *Horse Sense*. All types of life lessons she learned from working with horses. Since Sarah knows that, to be high concept, she needs to make her posts emotive and universal, she takes another step. Before she starts writing, Sarah brainstorms all possible lessons she can think of—patience, humility, letting go of control, focus, leadership, trust, passion, compassion, pride, encouragement, love, service, honesty, transparency, defeat, facing failure, regrouping, winning, losing, and setbacks. Why? Because all of these experiences are universal among humans.

Now Sarah thinks back over her experience with horses and marries a story or incident to each of these. Let's start with patience.

Sarah remembers a paint horse, Charlie, that had been abused. Charlie would buck and kick and bite. Though Sarah adored Charlie, his bad behavior drove her to tears. But she kept focusing on his beauty, what this horse had to offer. She kept reminding herself that he was coming from a place of pain. Through this, she learned to trust that time would heal him and, in the meantime, she set her mind to enjoy what Charlie did offer.

Notice this theme is universal. All of us have dealt with a loved one or someone in close social circles whose self-destructive behavior has frustrated us.

Sarah then takes the argument to the next level—that when others hurt us or are destructive, we can fight them, or we can let go and remember that they are likely coming from a place of pain, just like Charlie. We cannot force change.

Sarah has developed the universal nature of the topic and **made it emotional.** Do you see how this type of blog capitalizes on Sarah's strength? She isn't a non-fiction expert; she's a storyteller. Humans are story people. It's how we connect. Not only will this blog capture the interest and attention of those who know and love horses, but it also will invite others to the conversation.

Sarah shares how patience never worked on Charlie. He would never trust and she never could ride him, but being patient allowed Sarah to keep her peace even when Charlie was out of control. Patience allowed her to appreciate broken Charlie despite his poor behavior. **The reader has a positive experience and something meaningful to take away.** It is also highly likely that, if Sarah's writing is any good, this reader will feel compelled to share this post with her network as well.

Sarah finishes her posts by asking the readers to contribute their own opinions and experiences. Most of us might not have ever owned a horse, but almost everyone has had a pet. Animals are a universal and emotive topic. Also, we have all been impatient or in vexing situations that forced us to grow, even if the other party remained unchanged.

Notice how writing about life lessons draws from one of Sarah's many other passions . . . horses. This will keep Sarah far more enthusiastic about blogging because it frees her to tie her other interests and hobbies to her platform. We get to know Sarah as a three-dimensional person, and we feel more connected because she met us, her potential readers, on common emotional ground.

Say Sarah gets tired of writing about horses. Let's go back to her hundred words.

baby ducks

Most of us have seen or held a baby duck. How can Sarah elevate this to true high concept? Apply it to a universal lesson. How about taking time to appreciate small and simple things?

Sarah blogs about holding the baby duck, and even though she should have taken time to enjoy, all she could think about was the laundry and bills and making supper. Sarah elevates the "baby ducks" to all those precious moments in life we need to enjoy. At the end of our lives, will we remember our bank balances or our baby ducks? Focus too much on getting the ducks in a row and we miss out on the beauty of the chaotic moments of life.

Okay. That'll work. But what if Sarah doesn't want to be an inspirational writer? To her, it feels too preachy. She can also go funny.

Sarah can blog about holding the baby duck for an Easter picture and tell how the duck pooped down her brand new dress. She can relay how she spent the entire day trying to hide the poop stain with her purse. Then she can ask readers to share their similar experiences. This engages the readership. All of us have had embarrassing moments and we can laugh and commiserate. High concept.

Some more of Sarah's hundred words:

Tailgate parties → Community. Bonding through BBQ.

Rodeo → Getting back on the horse that threw ya. Never give up. Keep holding on.

Cowboys Football → Love 'em or hate 'em. No football fan is neutral about the Dallas Cowboys. Tenacity of the underdog.

George Strait → Memories. Sarah can talk about George Strait's song *The Dance* playing the night she met her husband. What songs hold the most powerful memories? Share.

See how Sarah Redding starts out as a nobody? Why do we care what she has to say? We don't. She isn't a brand. She isn't Oprah or Ellen. It isn't that we are stuck up and heartless. It's that we only have so much time, so we expect others to work to connect with us. Give us a reason we should care and we will.

Sarah knows that no one (yet) cares what she has to say, so she connects on high concept. Horses, life, love, struggles, recovering from failure, perseverance. Sarah starts a dialogue at least once a week and connects to the readers emotionally.

What happens when others connect with us emotionally?

People care. They become invested. They come to know you as a flesh and blood person who happens to be a writer. You transition from an unknown quantity to a familiar name, bound to excellent content and powerful emotion. Voila! An author brand.

> This tactic can elevate unknown authors to a brand, but it can also humanize an established brand. Back in 2011, James Rollins had fans in a frenzy for his new book *The Devil Colony*. How did he do this? Upon my recommendation, he talked about his love for animals (Jim also happens to be a veterinarian). This approach connected him universally and made fans feel as if they were his friends. Suddenly fans were blogging and tweeting and spreading news about Jim's upcoming book all around the globe. Why? Because Jim's approach was intimate, and made fans feel as if they were helping out a pal. Fans connected to an icon on common ground—love for animals.

As a fiction author, you do not have the job of establishing expertise. Your assignment is merely to start a conversation at least once a week so that followers come to feel as if they KNOW you. The point of a blog is to breathe life into your brand. Your blog is the emotional umbilical cord that connects you with a larger community committed to your success.

How Has the Author Blog Transformed in the Digital Age?

The reason why most author blogs are ineffective for branding is because writers are writing on the wrong topics. Fiction writers keep blogging about plotting, the future of ebooks and the role of Amazon, then they complain they aren't connecting to readers. Let's think about this for a second.

Have you ever hung out with someone who was interested in a topic that bored you to tears? And worse, this person wouldn't stop *talking* about this subject that bored you to tears? Did this endear you to this individual? Did this self-centeredness give you warm, fluffy feelings toward this person? When we blog non-stop about writing, we are expecting readers to care about what we care about. That is selfish thinking. When fiction authors connect through high concept, we are using our strengths—storytelling. We are getting out of the village center of comfort, hanging out with the natives and venturing into the jungle.

Think of it this way. As a novelist, do you write novels about Aristotelian three-act structure? Do you write novels about Smashwords or character development? Do you write riveting tales of Nook versus Kindle? *The Lost Comma. A Semicolon Misplaced. Amazon KDP Adventure.* No? No one? Of course not. You write stories about life, love, family, children, jobs, adventure, triumph, loyalty, betrayal. You connect universally and on emotion. Your readers love your stories because of how they make them *feel*.

Why does this stop when we become bloggers? It shouldn't. We should make readers *feel* so darn good with 250-800 words that they can't wait to buy 80,000.

Another reason most blogs fail to brand a writer is that many have a hard time transitioning from the Old School Journalism-type writing. Most of us grew up in a world where information went one direction. Social media is different. We are counting on others to like us and our content enough to share it with their networks. That is the only way we gain maximum exposure. High concept is how you will gain followers in the UK, Australia and South America. How? You will be connecting with your blogs the same way you connect with your novels—off shared human emotions and experiences. It is this shared emotional experience that compels others to pass on your content to their own networks, their friends and families. This is also how your content goes viral.

Writing a blog is like striking up a conversation at a party. Yet, from the looks of most author blogs, all most of us know to talk about is writing. In reality this is so far from the truth. Writers have been elevating the mundane into magic for thousands of years. Why do we suddenly stop that when we blog? Truth is, we don't have to. We can apply the same creativity we use to build entire worlds and use it to write posts that will connect powerfully with our audience.

Chapter 21

MAKING OUR
AUTHOR BRAND MALLEABLE

YOU NOW KNOW YOU don't want to start a "writing blog" a "horse blog" or "a pet blog." Our goal is to have an US blog. Yet, we do grow and change as we mature. Log lines (or tag lines) help our brand be focused, yet fluid. Log lines are the "themes" of our blogs. We touched on this briefly in the last chapter with my imaginary friend, Sarah Redding. The beauty of a log line is it can give a feel for your brand, but as you grow and change, the log line can be swapped out for something different *without imploding the blog/brand.*

If you looked at the word cloud examples in Chapter 16 and Appendix B, it's pretty clear who these writers are *as people.* When we look to our clouds, we can brainstorm ideas for log lines that go in our blog titles. Since the unifying component of our blogs is not the topic or subject matter, we need to make the log lines fit us and our writing voices. Voice is a product of who you are as a person, what you value, and what makes you emotional. That's one of the reasons those word clouds are so vital for success.

Too many writers are wasting time stating the obvious. They use blog titles like *Red Pen Confessions, An Author's Life, My Writing Journey, The Inky Muse.* All of this is well and good but 1) it's boring and 2) it wastes precious time and space stating the NO DUH stuff. We *see* the blog. We *see* all the black letters on the page. We *get* you're a writer. Really. No brain holding, please. In a world filled with busy people who have the attention span of a gnat on crystal meth, we writers need to take *every* opportunity to hook and be interesting. Bios and blog titles don't get a pass. In the WANA Way, *everything* is put to work. A log line can focus your brand and serve to capture a reader's attention long enough to read your blog.

Let's look at a word cloud, and then I will show you log lines I harvested from this assignment. One of my students, Alica McKenna-Johnson was generous enough to share:

Alica Mckenna-Johnson, writer, fan girl, redhead, mother, wife, daughter, sister, houseparent to kids in CPS care, teacher, homeschooler, cook, gluten-free, vegetarian, high maintenance, home birth, alternative lifestyle, Joss Whedon, foreign films, longs to travel, amazed at the beauty/ power of the human body, cries easily, Comic Con, weight issues, works out, has personal trainer, avid reader, shaman, anti-zen realist, diversity, submissive, sci-fi, knitter, monster movies, everything BBC, foodie, subtitles not dubbing, turns volume up on foreign films with subtitles, Oprah, Fifth Element, science fiction, paranormal, ghosts, romance, YA, judgmental, bitchy, depression, yoga, Pixar Studios, Ghibli Studios, sex, teenagers, drug recognition, foster kids, broken kids, circus arts, purple, green, midnight blue, dancing, belly dancing, alpha males, yelling at/about TV, movies, books, martial arts, hiding who I am, jealous of others, comparing myself to others, obsessed with who I am, constant self-discovery/ exploration, description whore, validation whore, witch, rude, migraines, control freak, banded Rutger Hauer movies, bad horror movies, esp foreign, ethnic foods, good vampire movies and some bad ones—Twilight doesn't count, whiny, American Ninja warrior, So You

Think You Can Dance, Dr. Who, Torchwood, Sherlock, gay romance, snarky, *I Can't Help Falling in Love with You*, love music of all kinds, used to go to concerts, fan fiction, indie author, t-shirt addiction, freckles, hates people (okay just the stupid mean ones), kilts, able to justify just about anything, evil children, wish I had been more supportive of my sister in high school, lived in Alaska-Colorado-California-Arizona, tortured cats as a child by playing dress up. Played Star Trek as a kid—I picked Spock to "save me," love a warm breeze, spunky, crazy, fun, looks at other men –but doesn't touch, loving, picky mother, The Tick, Freakaziod, Last of the Mohicans, fear of spontaneity, ducks in a row, good at understanding accents, tattoos, has become a hermit, socially disconnected, flips people off, funny, you can do whatever. Past Life Regression Hypnotherapist, re-incarnation, loves past lives, loves the differences in how people look, multi-tasking, always surround my children, two stepsons who are one and three years younger than me, Chinese food, anime, Thai food, Ethiopian food, Indian food, Mexican food, fruit, hippie, scared of failure, scared of success, doesn't wear make-up, loves to take personality quizzes, Tarsus, needs my editor desperately, loves to be served, has crazy kids, emotional, Sam Rami, M. Night Shyamalan, Monty Python, musicals, GoCheeksGo, Supernatural, Graphic Novels, Janet Evanovitch, always learning, supportive, a good friend, racing mind, worrier, fears judgment, insecure, afraid I will never be enough, afraid that even if I try I won't succeed, afraid if I read/watch thing that will make me cry I'll never stop, loves too many books, movies, shows, song to count, can't function when the house is quiet, doesn't like to be alone, I have to speak or write things to get them out of my head and process them, wishes supportive- encouraging- always-there-for-me were words my kids had used, had better self-esteem as a teenager than I do now, parents were feminists, mom was in charge, dad physically disabled.

Based off Alica's cloud, these were my suggestions for log lines:

Alica McKenna-Johnson's Blog—Was Queen in My Past Life

Alica McKenna-Johnson's Blog—Diva in My Mind

Alica McKenna-Johnson's Blog—I'm Not Crazy; My Mother Had Me Tested

Alica McKenna-Johnson's Blog—Amazon of ComicCon

Alica McKenna-Johnson's Blog—Phasers on Stun

Alica McKenna-Johnson's Blog—Klatu! Verata! Nickel? Neck Tie?
    Definitely an "N" Word

Alica McKenna-Johnson's Blog—This is my BOOM Stick!

Alica McKenna-Johnson's Blog—Would ROCK the Zombie Apocalypse

Alica McKenna-Johnson's Blog—Where Are We Going?
    And Why Am I in This Hand Basket?

Alica McKenna-Johnson's Blog—Under the Gun

Alica McKenna-Johnson's Blog—Just One More Bite

Alica McKenna-Johnson's Blog—Retired Ninja, Can Kill and Type

Alica McKenna-Johnson's Blog—Falling Over My Feet

Alica McKenna-Johnson's Blog—Embrace the Weird

Alica McKenna-Johnson's Blog—Distinctively Taboo

Alica McKenna-Johnson's Blog—Because Being Normal is Overrated

Alica chose *Alica McKenna-Johnson's Blog—Where Are We Going? And Why Am I in This Hand Basket?* Trust me. It fits. But, looking at the log line, can't you sense the type of content you're in for? You won't go to Alica's blog looking for quilting tips or Christian inspiration or posts about sports. Also, if Alica tires of *Alica McKenna-Johnson's Blog—Where Are We Going? And Why Am I in This Hand Basket?* she can easily switch to

Alica McKenna-Johnson's Blog—Distinctively Taboo and it won't harm her blog or her brand.

Also, go back and look at Alica's cloud. Don't you see conversations jump right off the page? Joss Whedon alone could be a month of content, *and* there are a lot of Whedon fans who are not writers. Alica is not high concept, but *Buffy the Vampire Slayer* is. A lot more people want to talk about *Buffy the Vampire Slayer* than about the advantages of Amazon over iBooks. I know! Shocking, right? This high concept content not only will make the blog far more enjoyable for Alica to write, but it also has a much higher probability of attracting readers. More readers are always good for the ego.

Want to know one of my posts that went viral? I blogged about my addiction to Febreze (I can't seem to stop buying *every* new fragrance). Not only did I get a ton of comments, but the manufacturer of Febreze also wrote me a lovely thank you letter and sent me a box of their new fragrances.

Total enablers.

Chapter 22

IDEAS FOR BLOGS

WHEN WE OPEN OUR MINDS to what a blog is and understand its purpose, we will start bubbling with ideas. One idea feeds the next and the next and the next. We will get far more interest blogging about *Dr. Who, Star Wars,* or trying to make peace with our thighs than we ever will preaching about the advantages of being an indie author. Look to your word clouds and highlight the topics that have broad appeal, then those can give you your starting point. We can take some of the most seemingly mundane topics and elevate them to high concept. There are a lot of blogs that stop just shy of being really great and connecting with others.

Brainstorm Experiences Most People Share

Looking for a job
Getting fired from a job
Shopping
Trying on bathing suits
Dieting
Being sore from exercise
Junk drawers
Messy closets
School

Tests
Failing
First Date
Last Date
Kids
Pets
Weird relatives
Weird neighbors
Strange habits (addiction to office supplies)
Broken down cars
Christmas money
Birthdays
Procrastination
Victory
Sports—being bad or good at them
Dodgeball
Music
Crushes
Food
Celebration
Yard work
Being grounded
Breaking the rules
Bad gifts
Movies
Nostalgia
The DMV
First car
Driving test
Childhood toys (My Little Ponies)
Bad haircuts/perms
Fear of clowns

Do you see how all of these topics are pretty universal? Also, every one of them can easily be made emotive. Positive emotions are best. Even if we talk about failure, always strive to end on a positive note. See how, with these topics, we are connecting via emotion, not information? Too many fiction writers are trying to build a following by sharing information. Why? You aren't non-fiction writers. You are storytellers and storytellers are experts at focusing the reader on ordinary life and assigning greater meaning. Think of your most powerful and vivid memories. Why are they so intense? Emotion. We must employ emotion to be memorable.

Even non-fiction writers can benefit from setting the information in an emotional context. Make sure you are speaking *with* others, not *at* them. If you write non-fiction, try taking a day to post on something high concept. Try setting your information in an emotional context. We are reaching flesh and blood humans, not robots. Our goal should be that we become not only an expert, but also a trusted friend. If we have a choice of ten experts, we will choose the one we feel *connected to*. This past Valentine's Day, I blogged about how our Christmas tree was still up and wondered how long I could leave the tree in our dining room before I was officially "white trash." The comments were hysterical and everyone had fun sharing stories about leaving Christmas decorations up too long.

***The Christmas tree stayed up until the week after Memorial Day. Hubby took it down and totally spoiled my fun. How am I supposed to decorate the tree with pumpkins, now?

My point is that this Christmas tree post had nothing to do with social media, branding or writing, but it made me *real*. Writers (my audience) could connect with common imperfections— or totally feel superior. But my expertise isn't in keeping an immaculate and organized house (or that would have been the *wrong* blog). I teach authors how to be successful, and my goal is to help them relax and allow some imperfection in the right places. How do you get a lot of writing done? Often it comes at the expense of having a Martha Stewart home…or clean hair.

It's okay. We're all friends here.

People are willing to move mountains for friends. They are willing to blog about their books, write reviews and tell everyone who will listen that their friend has a great book. We are loyal to friends from the first book to the last. Bloggers have a unique power to connect to their audiences. When Jenny Lawson (The Bloggess) tried to host a book discussion with fans? They crashed Goodreads.

Can writers blog about writing? Sure. But how many people can we connect with emotionally by talking about plot outline techniques? Also, blogging about the craft is precisely why so many writers burn out a month after starting. We can also hold interviews and review books, but we need more than this to remain fresh and interesting.

Ask Questions

Some of the best blogs are ones that bring up topics we all think about, no one can answer, but everyone has an opinion on. Make your blog about the reader, and then they will shoulder a lot of the burden of providing content. Ask a sticky (yet fun) question. Say what you would do, then open the floor.

If you could travel in time, but only one direction, would you go to the future or the past? Why?

What is the best super power?

If it were possible, would you want to live forever?

Is there such a thing as love at first sight?

Are people born to be artists or is it taught? Nature or nurture?

If you could travel into the past, but bring only ONE modern item, what would it be and why?

If you were stranded on a desert island and could only have three possessions, what would they be?

Do you see how these questions *beg* to be answered. Most humans are living on auto-pilot. We love it when someone wants our ideas, opinions and stories. We *love* to share, so *let us*. The sole onus of being interesting isn't on your shoulders. Good blogs are a conversation, not a lecture. There is a two-way rapport.

My goal is to keep you guys passionate and bursting with ideas for the long term. What you will find by utilizing high concept is that the blogs will be easier to write, because the whole of life is your muse. Also, blogging will make you a stronger, cleaner, faster writer. If you blog using high concept techniques, think how much practice you will have applying the very technique that is at the center of all timeless stories.

Chapter 23

HOW OFTEN DO WE NEED TO BLOG?

I RECOMMEND A *MINIMUM* of three times a week. Before you have a panic attack, just listen. **When it comes to blogging, search engines simply count attendance.** The more frequently we update content, the better search engines like us. Also, the more we post, the more opportunities to go viral or to at least hit that tipping point that changes everything. Blogging once a week is tougher. It seems counterintuitive, but trust me I've tried all different ways. When I blogged once a week, my blog grew so slowly it was all I could do not to give up. After a *year* of posting once a week faithfully, I was lucky to break 70 visits a day. Additionally, posting only once a week made it harder for me to remember to post. I wasn't on the radar of a lot of people, so my blog was easily forgettable for everyone, me included.

Three days a week is a good balance. It will help you with search engines, will help your blog get traction faster, and it will keep you encouraged because you will be able to see growth much sooner. It also teaches you how to work under pressure and learn to meet self-imposed deadlines.

Also, if you write regular high concept blogs, it won't take long before you have enough content to compile into an ebook. Blogging your book is a hot new trend. The blog-to-book is helpful for fiction *and* non-fiction authors. Put the best of your blogs together, add in some new content, and *voila!* You have a book.

This is working smarter not harder. Instead of handing away your fiction for free (indies), give your blog book for free *with purchase of* your fiction. Now you're maximizing all that time you spent blogging. Your blog is a stable, fixed point that won't be as vulnerable to trends. Readers can find you via search engines. You can grow your fan base before the books even come out. You can connect to a network of other bloggers *and* you can harvest that blog later for a *book*. Sell it as a book or give it for free to help the sales of *another* book. Again, put all your content to work and make it work its tail off so you don't have to.

Open Your Mind to What a Blog IS

Remember in Chapter 16 I had you collect images and videos? When I say blog a minimum of three times a week, that doesn't mean you need to *write* all the blogs. One day you can write a post, and on another day post a video. Post an image, then hold a caption contest in the comments. Do a mash-up. Collect a sample of your favorite blogs for the week. Five is a good number. Mash-ups help your SEO and they connect you to other bloggers. Also, if your mash-ups always have good content, people will come to your blog because they look for your recommendations.

The Big Picture of Blogging

Your blog will take time to build a following. You likely won't have a thousand hits a day in two months, but this is why we need to keep a big picture perspective and appreciate the long-term investment. The Bloggess didn't start out with 2-3 million visits a month. She had to build that. But blogging is fantastic author training. The Digital Age Authors who are making the big money? They write clean and they write *fast*. You won't meet more professional writers and they don't need hand-holding because they eat deadlines for breakfast. Blogging is powerful training to become a successful author.

Many new writers can't imagine writing 2,000-5,000 words a

day, six days a week, yet this is a professional pace. Being a career author takes conditioning, just like anything else. If you wanted to run a marathon, you wouldn't lace up your shoes and run 26.2 miles on the first day, would you?

Blogging will train you not only to work faster, it will also help you hone your writing voice. You can gain valuable feedback from your audience. What are they responding to? What seems to hold little interest? Voice gains strength with confidence. In Malcolm Gladwell's book *Outliers* he proposes the *10,000 Hour Rule*. From elite hockey players to the Beatles to violinists to ballerinas to entrepreneurs, there was one common denominator that propelled these talented individuals to top tier professionals.

Practice.

Ten thousand (10,000) hours seemed to be the magical number that transformed the good into the great. "And what's more, the people at the very top don't just work harder or even much harder than everyone else. They work much, *much* harder" (39). Hard work is the key to success, and most of us won't get a free pass. Even when one studies the "geniuses"—Bill Gates, Steve Jobs, Mozart, Wayne Gretzky, Temple Grandin, Martha Graham, Albert Einstein, Henry Ford, Thomas Edison, Frida Kahlo, Toni Morrison—the common denominator is a passion so intense it borders on insanity. If we *love* writing, the way to make it to that top tier of our profession is to love writing so much you're willing to write anywhere, in any form, in the pursuit of excellence. Yes, you can gain your 10,000 hours writing novels, but there's no reason you can't dedicate some of those 10,000 hours into blogging. It's still *writing*, and it's writing that does quadruple-duty: it builds your platform/brand, grows your audience, hones your skills as a writer, and it can later be harvested for books. Bloggers learn how to hook readers early, how to hold attention, and to ship on time. They break free of perfectionism and learn to write for readers. They grow tough skins and can take criticism because they're in the trenches doing what writers do.

They write.

Section 5
SAFE SOCIAL PRACTICES

Chapter 24

HOW TO HANDLE SEX, POLITICS, AND RELIGION

ALL OF US HAVE A FAITH and a political affiliation, but unless we are a religious or political writer we need to be *very* careful. We are counting on others in our social network to help us, to share, retweet and tell people about our books.

When are We Getting in the Danger Zone?

If we hope to build platforms that will reach out and include readers, we need to remember that if we spend half our time calling them idiots, they probably won't be terribly supportive. Additionally, if we have to hide other writers from our feeds because they make our blood pressures spike, then we can't easily support them because we can't SEE them.

What Brand are We After, Anyway?

We must be aware that we can be friends with all kinds of people, and non-stop ranting and name-calling is uncool and a bad way to build a platform, unless our goal is to be known as a political-ranting-hater-jerk. If our goal is to be the next Howard Stern, Bill Maher or Rush Limbaugh then sally forth, but don't send me a friend request.

So if we're NOT political or religious writers, we need to be mindful to not bludgeon part of our support network. Are we running for office or writing books?

BEWARE: The Genie Doesn't Go BACK in the Bottle Online

One of the biggest reasons we do have to be careful of everything we write online is, **once it is out there, we can't control it and it is FOREVER.** If you decide to blog about some politically hot topic because you need to get something off your chest, that's fine, but prepare for some consequences. It very well might be just another of many blogs and life continues on as usual, or it could totally dismantle your platform and irreparably alter your brand. We don't know who is going to read that post, and we can't control where and how it is spread, how it gets twisted and…what if it goes viral?

What takes YEARS to build can take only minutes to destroy.

I was friends with a writer who had a decent little blog following. He suddenly decided to blog about a topic so volatile, it had sparked riots across the U.S. I know he thought his readers would be levelheaded and rational when they read his post, but they were anything but. People were deeply hurt and divided. Fights broke out between commenters, and this writer was inundated with long, emotional, angry emails.

His readers felt they could trust him for a certain kind of content and then he took a weird turn that left his followers disturbed and upset. This writer spent months repairing the damage, and I'm unsure if the harm can ever be completely undone. He never expected this post to be a big deal, yet, once he hit Publish, the genie was out of the bottle and there was no putting it back.

These types of genies also are known to have a wide blast radius. There were very angry people who knew I happened to be friends with this blogger. Trolls made it their mission to attack him, but also come after *me*. I spent days shutting down hate mail for a post I never even wrote and would never have, in a million years, approved of.

We need to remember WE ARE NOT ALONE. **Our actions have consequences and sometimes those actions can inflict collateral damage.** Not only did this writer's platform and brand suffer, but friendships were damaged as well.

Social Media is a Giant Cocktail Party, Yet Not

If you like kittens then you're a moron!

Did that change your mind?

People who like dogs are idiots. Americans spend way too much money on stupid brainless pets when they could be spending it on rainbows.

Did that make you want to give up your pets and spend money other ways? No? What? You didn't like being called names and told what you love and value is stupid?

Most of that hater junk floating around Facebook is not going to change hearts and minds. If that is what we truly seek to do—win people over—then ranting and name-calling is a faulty plan that makes us look like insensitive jerks. Worse still, it's the behavior of hobbyists and amateurs, not serious professionals.

One of the main problems with social media is that it is like a cocktail party...yet it isn't. We have all the expectations of a cocktail party, but there is a computer between us. Most of us would not show up to a party and start ranting and name-calling and beating people up with our beliefs.

On social media, we tend to gravitate to people who love the same things we do—writing, books, kittens, dogs, family, yoga, diets—but that does not naturally presume we are all homogenous on the political and religious front. At a cocktail party we would also gravitate to people who liked talking about the same things—James Bond, scrapbooking, waterskiing—but we would have the benefit of body language to know when we were hurting others or treading into dangerous water with the conversation.

Remember, social media is social but we need to take extra care what we post. We don't have the same social litmus tests online to know when we are alienating others. Often people won't confront us directly. They will unfriend, unfollow or hide our feed, and that isn't going to help us sell books. Additionally, computers don't afford the same social filters. We don't have the benefit of body language or tone of voice. Humor and sarcasm can be taken seriously. I learned this the hard way while commenting on a Facebook thread. I was trying to use humor to debate a hot issue of the time regarding a Hollywood celebrity. Though many people laughed, not everyone did. I took my lumps and lesson and apologized to those I'd unintentionally offended, but I was also prepared to stand by my opinions for better or worse. Hey, I'm always learning, too. That thread was a real eye-opener. It showed me how easy it is for innocent banter to suddenly grow fangs. I do understand we can't please everyone so we don't need to act weird and super-censor all we write. Just remember that arguments can easily get completely out of control and become a runaway freight train that takes out our entire platform. Sometimes, it is best just to not go there.

Social media. Handle with extreme care.

Great Writers Use Story to Change the World

Every time I teach about politics and social media, I hear the outcry about how writers have an obligation to change the world, how we should be doing more than writing about vampires that sparkle. I completely agree. But posting hateful Facebook cartoons is for regular people who are not gifted with the creative power of prose.

Upton Sinclair wrote *The Jungle* to highlight the plight of the immigrant workers who were being exploited. He used story to expose the wage slavery, corruption and horrific practices (mainly) in the meatpacking industry. This book led to the formation of the FDA and was one of the vanguards for social programs for the poor and better treatment for workers.

To Kill a Mockingbird took on racism in the court system and paved the way for equal rights. *Animal Farm* was Orwell's commentary on Stalin, and he showed, through story, how the corruption of leadership was what would poison any revolution. *Brave New World, Uncle Tom's Cabin, 1984, Catcher in the Rye* the list goes on. THIS is how real writers change the world.

Star Trek didn't come on TV and rant about how all races should work together and women were more than secretaries. *Star Trek showed* that world. Gene Roddenberry put the world he envisioned in story form to change hearts and minds in a nonthreatening way, and he did it. Joss Whedon has dedicated his screenwriting career to busting apart stereotypes through *story*.

SHOW, Don't YELL!

Story is very powerful because it harnesses empathy and it draws readers into being part of a narrative. Audiences/readers who are part of something and not being attacked are more likely to be convinced and have a change of heart. We see characters who shatter our preconceived ideas, we get attached and then BOOM! change.

In my opinion, *Terminator 2* did more to shatter stereotypes of weak females than a hundred angry protests. We saw Sarah Connor, were mesmerized by her strength, her power, how motherhood was utterly redefined. She didn't wait on a man, wear lip-gloss, or twist her ankle running away. She learned to rock an AR-15 and use it to defend her boy and to save the world.

AND WE LOVED IT!

Characters like Sarah Connor opened the door for strong female heroes, and the more society was exposed to these daring dames, the more we grew to love and accept them in these new roles. Modern women have the opportunity to pursue professions that once were "Men Only." We now see women on SWAT teams, flying fighter jets, engaging in combat operations and writers helped that happen.

Leave the ranting memes to amateurs and regular people. We are not like them. We are not mere mortals. We are writers, and when we want to change the world, it changes.

Protect the Brand

Social media is a lot of fun and it has a lot of advantages, but as professionals we need to always remember that our brands are accumulations of EVERYTHING we do online. So if we start Twitter fights and rant and name-call and blog about volatile topics, we take a risk. Even when we don't rant, we want to steer clear of topics that can be taken by the opposition as an attack. Why risk it? Thoughtless blog posts have ended careers. In the end, I will never tell you what to write about or not to write about, but this book is about building a platform in a way that leaves time to create. If we're too distracted with Trolls, psychos, stalkers, haters and protests, it's hard to remain focused on the art.

On the other side, if you want to "Like" certain political causes or you want to promote a cause, go for it. People who aren't going to buy your book because they saw you "Liked" the opposing political party are people who probably will always find some reason to nitpick. Don't feel you need to divorce your beliefs, just make sure posts are always positive and *never on your blog*. The only reason I say this is that Twitter and Facebook are less likely to become a giant Troll magnet. Remember earlier we talked about how awesome it is that search engines can deliver new people to our blogs daily. Well, if we blog on something emotionally charged, it can deliver new Trolls daily.

I hope you guys DO change the world. Write books that change hearts and minds, and then use social media to get people to read those books and make the world better. Writers are people, not robots. I get that. I know this is an uncomfortable topic, but it's part of my responsibility as the social media expert for writers to address it. Just remember, words have power. Use them responsibly and professionally.

Chapter 25

DEALING WITH TROLLS

NOW THAT WE'VE DISCUSSED what *not* to blog about, I hope you won't need the advice in this chapter. Ah, but odds are you will. We all get at least one Troll even when we mind our Ps and Qs.

Trolls? Yep. Trolls.

Not the cute fuzzy ones with twirly hair that go on the end of a pencil, either. I am talking mean, nasty, ugly, TROLLS. BLOG TROLLS. Before we talk about how to handle Trolls, I think we first need to discuss exactly what a Blog Troll is.

What is a Blog Troll?

Many writers believe that we should all live in a pink fluffy land of cuddles where everyone thinks our words are golden nuggets of sunshine. Our comments section is not a place for debate. GASP! *Au gauche!* The comments section is a perk for our peeps, to make it easier for them to declare, far and wide, our unrivaled awesomeness.

Duh. Everyone knows that.

You might be thinking. *Kristen! Why are you mentioning this? It's easy to spot trolls. They are the only ones who disagree with me, the only ones who don't affirm how I'm the best thing since glittery unicorn stickers.*

Yes, I do agree that all of you are the best thing since glittery unicorn stickers, but we need to put on our Big Blogger/Author pants and be professionals. Just because someone disagrees or has a different point of view does not automatically make the commenter a Troll. It is HOW the person comments. Disagreement is fine, but it should be respectful.

This point is especially important for the non-fiction folks out there. I know that, as an expert, it can be tough to teach without speaking in general terms. There are ALWAYS exceptions to just about everything. I do blog on writing. I was a copy and content editor for many years and I use my experience to help new authors. Yet, my experience doesn't make me immune from disagreement or attack. For instance, when I blog about how the heavy use of flashbacks can make readers have epileptic seizures, I KNOW I'm going to get the standard, "But So-and-So used flashbacks and she's now a bazillionaire who regularly bathes in diamonds and stacks of crisp Benjamins."

Yep, got it.

I don't mind those comments because I do feel that part of honing our craft is to not just learn the standard, but to go and study the exceptions as well. Why *did* that writer get away with nine thousand adverbs when the rest of us would have been egged and stripped of our Word privileges until we'd read *Strunk & White*? Looking to anomalies is useful. Thus, when readers politely point out exceptions?

No problemo.

We Should be Secure Enough to Defend Our Positions as Needed

If we're blogging on factual things, we do not need to be omnipotent, but we should be competent. This mainly applies to the non-fiction authors. For instance, I'm not the Oracle of All Things Writing/Internet, but if I'm going to blog about the craft and social media? I should know my topics well to defend my position should I need to. I generally don't defend unless I think a commenter has made a point that might confuse readers.

For instance, I posted a blog about hooking readers and how passive goals like "staying alive" or "running away" were doable, but tough to write and tougher to sell. Active, tangible goals are generally superior and will make plotting far easier. A commenter chirped in that I was wrong, and that, *The Great Escape* was a classic and an exception. *The Great Escape* actually wasn't an exception, so I made sure to address that comment. (For those who are curious, the story goal of *The Great Escape* was not to escape or to run away, but rather to create a diversion to reroute the Germans away from the Allied forces—tangible and active.)

Debate is Healthy

Now, I don't consider that commenter a Troll, and I'm happy he took time to bring up that example. It made me think and I believe it was a great example that helped those who were following the comment thread. There are some movies and books that seem like they might be "getting away with" passive plot goals, loads of flashbacks, or any some other literary *faux pas*, but if we look closer we often see the screenwriter/writer is not as big of a rule-breaker as we might have first thought. Or, if the screenwriter/writer *did* break some rules, often we can take a moment to explore *how* the writer broke the rule and WHY he got away with it.

I've had a lot of commenters bring up points that made me think, and the good debate made me stronger. There've even been times I completely changed my position or opinion due to a commenter.

If we aren't learning, we're dying.

For instance, when I first started blogging about social media for writers, I primarily focused on platforms for authors who wanted to go the traditional path. Self-publishing was still in its infancy and ebooks hadn't yet taken off. A retired gentleman, Mike Ragland, who happened to be a regular reader, pointed out that I was biased and that self-published and indie authors needed help, too. Perhaps even more so. This was *excellent* feedback. He was correct. I was (unintentionally) biased, and immediately changed my approach. I'm thankful I did because not long after I shifted my focus, ebooks exploded and the indie movement caught fire and utterly altered the publishing landscape. Because of a thoughtful commenter, I already had established rapport with non-traditional authors so I'm deeply thankful for his honesty. Commenters are *gold*. Sometimes we're too close and can't see the forest for the trees. Commenters can help us get perspective.

All blogs can benefit from *healthy* debate. If a commenter disagrees, take a moment to really understand what she's saying. Sometimes you might be surprised. Blogs thrive and die every day due to the blogger's relationship (or lack thereof) with readers.

Now that we have established that disagreement is good, even healthy, what IS a Blog Troll?

Blog Trolls are Disrespectful

We can disagree without being an equine derriere. Bloggers are human and make mistakes. We all have bad days. I recall a commenter from October of 2011. This guy just absolutely razed me for a handful of typos. Little did that person know that my aunt had slipped into a coma and died the night before. I was exhausted, grieving, and distracted and honestly didn't see the mistakes on my Monday morning post. Yet, there was nothing in my five typos that warranted the vitriolic reaction, which brings me to my next point.

Blog Trolls are Often Emotional

We all get emotional, but Blog Trolls? Trolls get PSYCHO emotional. I once wrote a really funny blog that posited the question, "Are we being responsible novel parents or dead-beat book daddies?" The blog was about writing. It was a humor post, not a commentary on separation and child-custody issues. Aside from the use of my invented term "dead-beat book daddies," I talked about books and writing novels.

Out of nowhere I had a commenter morph into an absolute lunatic. He ranted how I was a man-hater then proceeded to insult every other person who'd commented and even hunted me to Facebook and insulted every person who talked to me on Facebook. Then, when I deleted his comments and booted him from my Facebook, he started his own blog—*Kristen Lamb the Face of Misandry* (which means "man-hating," by the way. I had to look it up, too).

I wish I were kidding.

What to Do about a Troll

Don't take it personally. The world is full of jerks. Look at the bright side. You could be them.

Accept That Not Everyone Will Love You

Awww. I know! This almost makes me cry. To think that not everyone thinks I am awesome? Well, they must be sick, right?

Yeah, I hate to say it, but there is no law of the universe that dictates everyone must love us. No matter how hard we try, there will always be a percentage of people who just don't like us. For me, it is a far, far, far, almost statistically meaningless percentage...like a mere .000000001%...okay, yeah. I know I can't please everyone.

For the non-fiction authors who want to use blogging to establish establishing expertise? Just expect the commenter who tells you that you have the brain of a monkey and that you're a loser–poseur-fake. My favorite comment like the one on the following page?

Actual Comment:
Kristen, you have to actually BE an expert at something before you can claim to be an expert.

Yeah. OUCH. Oh well. It happens. I don't necessarily count a comment like this as a Troll, just a jerk. But both Trolls and jerks will help you grow the thick skin necessary for the professional author.

How Do You Handle a Blog Troll?

Start with being kind. Few things diffuse someone who has blown an emotional fuse quicker than a dose of kindness. Just like that guy had no idea I'd had a death in the family, I have no idea what might have been falling apart in his life. This is one of the reasons we shouldn't take things personally. It really isn't about us. That nasty rant likely has more to do with the pile of bills, sucky job, or nasty divorce than it has to do with us or our content. All of us have shown our butts at one time or another. If we want grace from others, we should be quick to offer forgiveness and patience.

If you make a mistake, be quick to admit it. We're writers and bloggers, not God. Yes, being writers make us feel a lot like The Big Guy but, unlike an omnipotent being, we err. If someone points out where you're wrong and she's correct? It's embarrassing but not the end of the world. Just politely thank the commenter and take the *mea culpa*. Most people won't remember if we messed up. They will, however, remember if we messed up and then spent three weeks arguing and trying to cover or defend our mistakes.

The Troll who personally attacked me about five typos? He did have a legitimate complaint, kind of. The blog was about editing, and I had several glaring typos (granted the post was actually *not* about line-editing, but rather content editing). But, I corrected the *oopses* and thanked him for his diligence…and then watched with a huge grin as my loyal commenters pounced on him, slapped him around and made him mind his manners.

Don't Feel the Need to Approve Haters

Your blog can be set up so you have to approve a commenter's post before it can actually become a comment. If someone is emotionally out of control and disrespectful, don't feel the need to let them in. Commenters need to feel safe to voice an opinion and Trolls can make people afraid to comment. Relationships are about setting boundaries. My friend Piper Bayard, a fabulous author and blogger, emails Trolls and tells them she has trashed their comment, but then tells them that if they will voice their disagreement in a more respectful way, she'd be happy to approve them.

Good fences make good neighbors.

Don't Defend Unless You Need to

I have a saying, "People have the right to be wrong." Sometimes a commenter is way off base or rude. Just move on. Many times your loyal commenters will pop the offending Troll on the snoot and remind them that piddling in the comments section is rude.

Focus on the Positive

Trolls offer us perspective and humility. Like leeches, turkey buzzards, and ticks all serve a viable part of the Earth's ecosystem, Blog Trolls offer balance to the blog ecosystem (like scaring away the uncommitted). But, just because cockroaches and hyenas serve a purpose in the Circle of Life doesn't mean we should include them in the petting zoo. Same with Trolls. Focus on all the kind and supportive people. They deserve our attention more anyway.

Chapter 26

STAYING SAFE ON SOCIAL MEDIA

EVERY NEW TERRITORY COMES with splendors never seen, resources never tapped, and powers never before harnessed. Yet, with new opportunities come new predators, eager to take advantage of the naive.

I can't explain why there are those in this world who will hurt people they've never met or steal with no concern to what devastation they might create. But, these crooks are there, they are a real threat, and this chapter is to help you guard against attacks. It does you no good to follow all the tips, steps and advice in this book, just for a hacker or phisher to devastate what you've created.

Hackers and Phisers Use Emotion

One common tactic used by hackers and phishers is they seek to get us emotional. We might get an e-mail that we won something and all we have to do is "click this link" to claim our prize. Thieves will also use scare tactics. If they can frighten or momentarily panic us, we're far more likely to part with sensitive information without thinking.

Frequently they'll tell us our account has been suspended because we have been breaking rules we haven't broken, like friending people we don't know, or friending too many people or even that we have been reported as spammers. Of course, if we just "enter our password" they will get it sorted straight away.

Uh huh.

They want us to think, *Not me! I follow the rules! This is a mistake! I need to get to the bottom of this RIGHT NOW!*

When I see this, I log out then back in and often the message goes away, and then I report them. Facebook or Twitter can't get these guys if we don't blow the whistle. Be a sheepdog. Sheep either get eaten by wolves (hand over password) or they go back to munching grass (playing Farmville). Digital sheepdogs run to alert those in charge that wolves are sniffing the perimeter.

If there are suspected bots on Twitter, we should block and report them. If they try to phish our account, we need to report them. If we get odd emails that seem like phishing on Facebook, we must report it.

Digital Wolves WILL Wear Digital Sheep Clothing

Thieves will try to upset you. They want you emotional because it serves their end game. One of the ways they can get this reaction is by posing as an authority. For instance, I had this pop up on my Facebook:

Now, 99% of the time I'm multitasking while a toddler is trying to scale the back of my head like the jungle gym at Chik-fil-A. Do you see how EASY it would be to catch me off guard and hack my account? Looks official, but look closer.

See how they tried to embarrass and upset me? These creeps know that most of us are good and decent and follow the rules. We were the kids who would have cried if we were threatened with a visit to the principal. These bottom-feeders use what is good and noble about us to manipulate us, then attack. They will use our respect for authority against us if we let them.

I've also had a pop-up appear when I went to get on Tweet Deck. The pop up from "Tweet Deck Security" was there to inform me that my account had been suspended for suspicious spamming activity, but that they were sure it was all a misunderstanding. If I just typed in my password, they would make sure everything was sorted and my account would be unlocked.

I closed the window, logged out then logged back in. My account was fine. This was an attack.

If They Can't Bait You with Bosses, They'll Bait You with Buddies

Another common ploy is to come disguised as our "friends." (The image and website address have been altered.)

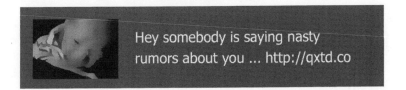

Hey somebody is saying nasty rumors about you ... http://qxtd.co

The friend (phisher) will send a direct message about rumors about you or a nasty review or wild pictures and a link. The phisher is disguised as a fellow member of the herd. Baaaahhh-hhh. Someone is saying baaaaaad things about you.

I'm your friend so I am discreetly telling you so you can go tell them what for.

No, they're a phisher, and, if you hit that link, your computer is toast. Malware will be all over you like digital fleas on digital sheep.

If you get a direct message like this, be a sheepdog. Look out for your peeps. Tell them you are getting strange messages and alert them to change their passwords. (Something more than seven digits with a number is a good choice.) DM them back, but even if you can't? No one will mind a, "Hey, I tried to DM you but I can't. You might want to change your password. Getting weird DMs from you."

This Also Applies to Email

If you get an email from a friend and there is only a link, DO NOT CLICK. If they write a message that seems out of character, DO NOT CLICK. REPLY ALL and alert everyone on the email that this is likely a phisher and tell the sender to change her password immediately. Put in the subject line Re: THIS IS A PHISHER!!! DO NOT CLICK THE LINK!!!

Either the sender will come back and verify he really did send just a link; it was for a dancing squirrel and he hit *Send* before he typed a message, or he can change his password and keep phishers from getting in any deeper.

If a friend emails for help because she is stranded (and you are unsure if this is really the person), feel free to email back and tell the friend to call you. Since you are friends, then she should have your number.

DO NOT Foreword Cutesy Emails

Ever get those messages with a picture of an angel and you have to send to 25 friends in the next ten minutes if you want a miracle, but if you don't forward the message the note promises that you will be hit with some form of bad luck? DO NOT PASS THESE ON. Hackers use these types of messages to get a hold of addresses.

How else could that cousin in Uganda who wants to will you a million dollars find you?

If you do get some super cute story in your email and you really want to pass it on, just copy and paste into a new email. Thieves already don't work for a living. Why make their life on Easy Street easy?

Play Games at Your Own Risk

There are all kinds of games on Facebook. We can join causes or keep up with high school peeps, but often it requires granting permission to an application to have access to our information. Not all of this is nefarious, since if the purpose of the application is to connect alumni, it requires that kind of information.

But these applications are gateways for hackers and phishers, too. I don't play games like Farmville for that reason (it's also because I don't have time). But any of those games are a risk, so be alert and don't just grant access to anyone. I rarely join anything that wants access to my account information, even if it will make life easier.

We must always do the cost-benefit analysis. Sure we can have fun, or an ease of access, but we can also grant fun and ease of access to thieves.

Don't Use Tweet Validation Services and DO NOT FOLLOW People Who Do

We've already mentioned this in the chapter about Twitter, but here's a reminder. I don't like any service that directs people to an outside page. Anything that directs us off Twitter is vulnerable and can be hijacked. We could be redirected to a copycat site that is there to capture information. We don't need validation services.

It is not THAT hard to unfollow bots. If someone follows us and then they spam us, it takes two clicks to report and block them.

If I follow someone and I get A DM that I need to click a link to prove I'm a real person? I move on. That's a good way to get phished. Since I don't like people making me vulnerable to attack, I just make it my policy to not open others to attack as well.

Update Your Plug-Ins

Update your plug-ins regularly. Flash, Java, Adobe all make browsing and social media better, but those updates—while often annoying—frequently are to improve security and keep hackers and phishers from having a portal into your life so they can wreck it.

To sum up:

1. Never give information to any unconfirmed source.

2. If a message makes you emotional, calm down before clicking any links or providing any information. Thieves want us reactive. Remain CALM AND PROACTIVE. First try logging out, then back in.

3. Never click on any outside link sent from someone you don't know. Even if you receive a link from someone you know, trust but verify. Take a second to message back and ask if they sent the link. For all you know, their account could be compromised. Ignore validation services. There are plenty of people who won't throw you to the phishers who'll befriend you.

4. USB/flash drives are classic tools for getting malware through a firewall. If you don't trust where a drive came from, don't insert it into your computer.

5. Always report any attempts to gain access to your information or accounts.

6. Keep an eye out for friends, family and members of your network. Alert them if it seems their account has been compromised.

7. Do NOT USE any outside validation services. This opens those in your network to phishers.

8. Use solid passwords that you can REMEMBER. Include

numbers and punctuation. Your Facebook and Twitter passwords could be something as simple as: FacebookGoHornedFrogs! or Mommyeats22cookies or Ilovewriting2000wordsaday!

9. NEVER post your actual birthday. Birth dates are a great way for thieves to gain access where they don't belong.

10. Turn off the Geo-Tracker on Facebook. This function let's you "check in" and tell everyone where you are. Great! Then thieves will know they can rob your house in peace. People don't need this much information.

Social media is, above all else, *social*. It's far easier to relax and have a good time if we aren't having our bank accounts emptied and our identities stolen. Remember, they call those people con *artists* for a reason. They will be cunning, clever and quick, but we can be educated and work together.

We can be authentic and real on social media without parting with sensitive information. Revealing that I love science fiction movies, Xbox, and Bikram yoga is personal and tells others a lot about who I am. I don't need to tell the world my birthdate and home address to come across as a human being.

Technology keeps changing and thieves are always coming up with new ways to steal, so I hope this section will keep you safe. Yet, as an additional precaution, WANA International has Internet security expert Jay Donovan who teaches classes regularly. If thieves are always upping their game, we need to stay two steps ahead. Jay is also currently writing some Internet security books for WANA Publishing, so keep an eye out for those as well.

Chapter 27

SUMMING UP

THE WORLD WE ONCE KNEW is gone, and technology has infiltrated every aspect of our lives. We can't go back, but we can choose how we move forward. Social media is more than necessary for the Digital Age Author, it's also a gift. When we use social media properly, we lay the foundation for a long-term, successful career doing what we love most. Writers finally have multiple career paths and far greater control of their destinies. Whether the big publishers die or reinvent, their fate won't change the fact that modern audiences will gravitate to authors willing to seek them out and begin a dialogue. Human audiences crave human connection.

The rise of the machines marks the return to our human roots. The glow of the campfire has been replaced by the glow of our Facebook pages and Twitter feeds. We still long to talk, share, bond, and make friends and that never changes. When we sit in silence and feel the flow of the digital tides, we're connected to the eternal.

By this point in the book you should:

1. Have an understanding of where we fit on the timeline of human communication.

2. Understand the fundamental changes that technology creates, societally and biologically.

3. Have a grasp of the new world of publishing and an idea of what path suits you best.

4. Know that failure isn't the end. We can try new things and learn.

5. Appreciate that there are predatory publishers on the traditional *and* indie side. We need to do our homework.

6. Understand why agents and publishing attorneys are valuable. Never sign anything you don't understand.

7. Know why marketing alone is virtually invisible. Ads, promotion and PR alone will have depressing results. Give the PR people something to work with. An established author platform built on solid relationships will make any marketing more effective, thus a better investment.

8. Appreciate the difference between market norms and social norms and why it's risky when we blend them together.

9. Embrace that *everything we do* on social media is part of the brand.

10. Understand the pitfalls of automation.

11. Have a grasp of why an author brand is fundamentally different. Books are not tacos and writers are not car insurance.

12. Have a more open view of who "readers" are and know that the fat part of the bell curve ("non-readers") is where we will see the biggest successes.

13. Have an idea how you can make your posts more "sticky." Be memorable by being different and open to new groups of people.

14. Understand you are not alone. Successful social media is a team effort. Connectors, Mavens, and Salespeople are everywhere, but we can't befriend these powerful allies unless we're present.

15. Grasp the basics of what it means to "go viral" and focus on content that will more easily spread.

16. Avoid drag. Streamline everything you do on social media. Make it easy for people to follow you, share your content and find (and buy) your books.

17. Use your author name (the one printed on the front of your books). ONE name only, please.

18. Ditch any cutesy moniker. Search engines can't help you effectively if your author name is a secret.

19. Possess a basic understanding of social media terms.

20. Have a fundamental grasp of how search engines work and what behaviors earn their favor.

21. Understand why tags and keywords are vital and how to use them to your advantage.

22. Possess a written list of clear, attainable, actionable goals with deadlines.

23. Have an idea which social sites will fit best with your brand and author platform.

24. Open accounts on at least the main social sites (Facebook, Twitter, LinkedIn, Flickr, Pinterest, Google+, YouTube and Goodreads). You won't need to use all of these sites, but you want to at least own the digital real estate in the event of a major change (e.g. MySpace's demise).

25. Create a friendly author headshot. Use www.picmonkey.com if you need to.

26. Have a massive and detailed word cloud (and keep adding to it).

27. Have written bios of four lengths—Long, Short, Shorter and Twitter Short.

28. Upload your author picture and appropriate bio (saturated in tags and keywords) on all the main social sites (even ones you don't use).

29. Make sure you have a contact email on all your social site profiles.

30. Have a place to blog. Ideally this should be your author website or a free WordPress site with some variation of *your name* as the URL.

31. Have a Flickr account with any images you've uploaded tagged accordingly. If you contribute to WANA Commons, make sure to change the licensing so we can share.

32. Have a Pinterest account with boards (folders) of your favorite images to use for blogging, graphics, or memes.

33. Maintain a Word document with the embed codes for a minimum of 15 videos. Recruit your spouse or kids to help if you need it. Let them be part of your success. Kids are great at finding fun videos. Just give them some search parameters and watch them impress you.

34. Have a membership on WANATribe (optional). It's a great place to connect with other writers who can offer guidance and emotional support.

35. Understand the basics of Twitter and how it can benefit you in more ways than simply advertising your books.

36. Have a basic understanding of how to organize Twitter using TweetDeck or HootSuite.

37. Know the behaviors that not only are unproductive for your brand, but that can get your account suspended/deleted.

38. Possess an understanding why Facebook is a vital part of a successful author platform. Never underestimate *weak ties* and never dissect your platform. Everyone is a potential fan, even the illiterate (there *are* audio books).

39. Understand the difference between a profile page and a fan page, the advantages and disadvantages of both, and why authors really need both types of pages (at least initially).

40. Appreciate the power of images. Use your images to create memes or graphics of your own.

41. Know Facebook behaviors that can hurt your brand and get you in trouble with Facebook (suspension or deletion).

42. Understand the basics of High Concept Blogging.

43. Refer to your word cloud for tags, keywords, log line ideas, bios and topics.

44. Appreciate how much a blog can do for you. It offers stability, discoverability (via search engines), and can later be harvested for ebooks to sell or use for marketing. Blogs play to a writer's strength . . . writing.

45. Know that blogging helps us hit the golden mark of 10,000 hours of practice far faster and offers many advantages beyond "selling books."

46. Know how to handle sex, politics and religion. We don't have to lose our beliefs to be successful, but we must handle with care.

47. Never to blog on volatile subjects. I only suggest this because blogs are so enduring and thus, Trolls will harass you *forever*. Obviously, this is your call. Personally, I'd rather be writing more books.

48. Know how to spot and handle Blog Trolls. We all get one eventually, and usually they are a sign we're doing something right. They don't have any power we don't give them.

49. Have a basic understanding of best practices for a safe Internet experience. We can't enjoy and grow a platform that's infested with phishers, bots and hackers.

50. Remember to have fun!

Thank you for taking this journey with me, and I hope you feel excited about your future as an author. We have more power and control than ever before, but with great power comes great responsibility (all the *Spiderman* fans cheer). Yes, it's a lot of work, but nothing worth having is easy. If you build your platform the WANA Way, it will be far more fun and effective and it can grow and change as you grow and change. Your efforts will be focused, so the returns will be greater. You won't be spread so thinly that you have no time for the most important part of the job . . . writing more books. You'll be part of a team, so you'll have support and help as the paradigm continues to change.

These days, we need our tribe. It's a dangerous world, filled digital dingoes and virtual vultures. With enough hard work and perseverance, we can all enjoy the riches of this uncharted land, but it's imperative we stick together. We need all the help we can get. Yes, to be successful you must have a solid author platform, but no one ever said you had to build it by yourself.

WE ARE NOT ALONE!

* * *

LIFE GOAL EXAMPLES

Example B: Stuart Sheldon's Goals

BIG LIFE GOAL(s)

I live exclusively and luxuriously as an author and fine artist. At least 5 books published. Am *a New York Times* best-selling author in both adult fiction and non-fiction. Speak at conferences, including TED. Teach a writing class at least once at a prestigious university. Live in many exhilarating places amidst iconoclasts and thought leaders of every stripe.

5 Year Goal(s)

I have at least two books published. Am working on my best book yet. I speak all over the world. My books and artwork generate thousands of dollars of income each day. My blog has a million followers. I am commissioned to write essays and articles for *The New Yorker* and *New York Times*. My kids, wife and I live abroad for at least six months and spend much of our time in philanthropic pursuits helping others in real time each day.

3 Year Goal(s)

I have one best-selling book and 100,000 followers for my blog. I earn at least $100,000/yr from books and art sales. I write a column for *Vanity Fair*. I write at least one article for the *New York Times* and *The New Yorker*. I'm invited to speak at top writing and art conferences and universities.

1 Year Goal(s)

I sell my first book to an enthusiastic publisher who puts some real muscle behind promotion. I get an advance north of $25,000. I complete a first draft of my second book. I have 20,000 followers for my blog. I sell a magazine article to the *New York Times* or *The Atlantic*. I am invited to speak for the first time at a conference or prestigious place of learning.

6 Month Goal(s)

I find an agent that I love and the search for a publisher kicks off with gusto. My blog has 10,000 followers. My blog is perfected with a dynamic dialogue amidst my fervent readers. I post a minimum of once a week. I am part of a robust blogging community and we actively engage in lifting one another's fortunes. I get 50-100 pages written in my new book. I get a column in a local magazine.

Example C: Sarah Brabazon's Goals

Since we have permission to aim for the stars:

BIG LIFE GOAL(s)

My books entertain millions of readers and film adaptations captivate audiences in many cultures worldwide, the earliest ones are considered classics. I am known for my insight into the human heart and the many paths that lead to true happiness.

I wisely invested my earnings from the first royalty check so that now I am independently wealthy. My family company has a venture philanthropic arm. I travel the world for pleasure and research. I can order breakfast in twenty languages, and drink in forty.

In my fifties, I became a licensed pilot and learned to tango. One of my sons is an interplanetary colonist, the other is working for *Medecins sans Frontieres*, although I would be equally happy if they were 'still finding themselves' or 'between careers.'

5 Year Goal(s)

I now write category romance only for fun. My rights will revert soon, and I plan to renegotiate my contracts with the more favourable modern Harlequin clauses. I have three full-length novels published and have completed the first ms in my SF series which combines 'Master & Commander' with 'Avatar,' with a twist of 'Fifty Shades of Grey.'

I struggle to find the time to blog, so I go into partnership with some of the bloggers that I met in WANA1012, with whom I have remained friends, to guest-post on each other's blogs, reducing workload while reaching a much wider audience.

I now live with my family on a canal barge somewhere in Europe. I attend writing conferences for fun and rejuvenation, and also reader conventions, where I am heartened by stories from readers of how my novels have enhanced their lives.

My sons have decided what they want to do in life and taken charge of their own education to achieve this. They choose careers based on fulfillment, not earning capacity.

3 Year Goal(s)

My debut novel won the Golden Heart competition. I have ten category novels published, and several of them have won awards. I am able to complete four to five category-length novels a year and have time off (and income) to take traveling holidays with my husband and children where we do not bunk with extended family. My investment strategy is on track.

My full-length novel was recently requested by several agents; I don't know it yet, but there will be a bidding war. I will go with the agent most likely to foster my long-term business plan.

Blogging is as natural as having a conversation. I have a loyal group of readers who talk about my books and promote me to their networks. I have friends among this group who have crossed the electronic boundary to be face-to-face friends.

My homeschooled sons take increasing charge of their own education, I take on more of a mentoring role than lecturer, allowing me more time to focus on writing. My eldest is taking an active interest in his own investment portfolio.

1 Year Goal(s)

I have a signed contract with a traditional print publisher, or my e-first publisher has earmarked me to be print published. My contract includes reasonable terms for rights reversion and ensures that I continue to have control over my career.

I have strong plots for all 10 of my partial manuscripts, and story ideas continue to flow to me from the ether. I am working towards completing a polished manuscript every two months, but I am not compromising on writing compelling stories to do so.

My blog is known as the place to go to discuss real and imagined relationships between strong women and alpha heroes. Despite gaining significant social interaction from social networking, I resist the urge to bombard readers with excessive blog posts/twitter updates/facebook posts.

6 Month Goal(s)

My epublished erotic short story is selling well and I have banked my first royalty cheque. I easily navigated the gnarly reef of applying for an ITIN with the IRS, having paid attention last financial year when all the Romance Writers of Australia members had so much trouble.

My blog has 1,000 regular visitors, strong comment response and I am enjoying it as a creative outlet and adjunct to Morning Pages. My personal word-count is pushing 700k.

My category romance has been submitted as per request with Harlequin Mills & Boon, and instead of waiting 11 months with no reply, I notify them that if I don't hear from them, I am submitting it elsewhere in four months. I don't hear from them. My partial submissions (requested) to Penguin Destiny and Harlequin Escape both result in full requests.

I get an aggregate score higher than 90% for my category romance entries in the RWA (Australia) First Kiss and Selling Synopsis contests.

Appendix B

WORD CLOUDS

Example A (continued):
Jennifer Fischetto's Cloud

...down-to-earth, real, happily-for-now, hates artificial sweetener, dislikes stereotypes and judgmental people, Halloween, Santa Claus, Scrabble, positive things, thoughts become things, dream hope believe, dandelions, thunder and lightning, body acceptance, family, secrets in the family, betrayal in family, danger in family, horror movies, ghost stories, scaring people, CSI, Law & Order SVU, darkness inside, candy, hyperbole, overly dramatic, HUGE potty mouth, Easy Bake Oven as a child, stop violence, hopeful, The Walking Dead, Long Island, ex-New Yorker, lived in GA and hated it, wish I was a better singer, reader, daydreamer, super great hearing and sense of smell, double-jointed thumbs and asked to perform as a kid, uses creative curse words, dislikes travel, Buffy the Vampire Slayer, Charmed, the original Charlie's Angels, stop negative talk, don't teach daughters to hate their bodies, buy bigger jeans instead of changing your body, self-love, self-nurture, inner child, women's body shouldn't sell products, racism, sexism, sizism, someone's size doesn't depict their health, someone's health is none of your business, what you think about me is none of my business, Snickers, The Exorcist, Carrie, The Omen trilogy, Bad Seed remake, The Birds, Crowhaven's Farm, Audrey Rose, driving by Amityville Horror house, storyteller, hate hate hate the summer, hate the heat and humidity, dislike sunlight, love clouds, love wind, flowers, snow is okay, cold is fine, love night-time, love sparkly things, can't swim, semi-afraid of heights, won't go under water, love being a hermit, modern, dislike history and old-fashioned things, contemporary, like gadgets, want to learn how to sketch, dislikes a lot of processed foods, love trees, not a dog person, dislikes all kinds of rodents, decaf coffee, don't agree with the craze over Starbucks and shoes and naked male abs, not girly but like dainty things, can't stand Disney and prissiness and vanity, laughter is key to life, lazy housekeeper, ignores dust, hates cleaning, not your typical mom, anti-organized religion, spiritual, Universe, liberal, just because you have an opinion doesn't mean you should always share it, dead bodies, fat bodies, female bodies, bodies of color, menopausal bodies, middle-aged bodies, a handful of stories don't include dead bodies, contemporary YA, real-life issues surrounding dead bodies, life of a hermit, dislikes crowds, social anxiety, wacky, no tolerance for ignorance or hate, loves office supplies, getting books and notebooks makes me feel like a child, painful past, bitter, sometimes still angry, believes in hope, looks forward to the future, what if..., no regrets, my kids are my world but not my life, dislikes mainstream anything especially America, supports minorities of all kinds, believes in equality for all, resents American history, no longer a victim, single mom, never married, oldest child, half-Italian, slight left-over NY accent, dislikes the radio, hates the news, walks around house in dark, never afraid of dark, dislike all rodents and reptiles, hate vampires and werewolves, sick and tired of books about fey and fallen angels and girls who suddenly get powers, never learned how to drive, think greeting cards are a waste of money, love cute and cuddly things, prefer vegetables over animal, no books or movies truly scare me, love psychology, very psychologically enlightened and informed, never finished college, lives way below poverty level, homeschools, unconventional homeschooling, looks forward to no longer homeschooling, uses way too many smiley emoticons, comfort over appearances, as important as my beliefs are I'm not comfortable teaching, prefer to laugh and make others laugh, also serious, practical, logical, idealistic, daydreamer, realistic, fat people aren't cheery-we're humans, trying to become Zen Jenn, fear of abandonment, prefer to read about real women than perfect ones, cherry iced tea, hate the colors brown and gold, love things make of glass and rhinestones, distrust people mostly, easy for me to open up, honest and direct but polite, "inappropriate" conversations with kids about cat poop and zombies and most anything, don't believe in shielding kids for the most part, love short days and long nights, love falling snow but hate shoveling, love trees and flowers and grass but not dirt and bugs, could never camp, can't pee outdoors, can't pee in front of anyone, super shy bladder, did I mention chocolate, love deep conversations, serious, broad-minded, dislike celebrity mania, celebrities shouldn't make as much money as they do especially when teachers make crap, celebrities aren't special and I can care less about their personal lives, love and admire characters not the people that play them, hate superficiality, love houses, favorite thing on Sims is building houses, love decorating, love plants, dislike above 70 degrees, would love a garden, love brainstorming, favorite part of writing is brainstorming-creating the characters and story, most of what I do is about the story-TV stories-movies-books-writing-Sims 3, my days are filled with make-believe and stories-not much else, once upon a crime (used to own that domain), equality for all, marriage equality, equality in entertainment and media, even the dead deserve equality, honest to myself, always striving to be better as a person and author, love learning, new adult, while I will have three adults books pubbed my passion and interests are solely with young adult, love Christmas lights, not a holiday person, not a traditional person, prefer doing things my own way, refuse to follow, get annoyed by how many people follow everyone else, interested in conspiracy theories but don't know much about them, dislike vanity, accept myself the way I am-wrinkles gray hair and all, YA books, YA themes, various topics these great books discuss, YA issues which aren't always YA but have that underwhelming sense of needing help coupled with the need for independence, feeling out of control.

Example B: D.J. Parson's Cloud

Daughter, aunt, great aunt, sister-in-law, wife, animal mom, look forward to girls night out, let hair down with Beck's dark beer or Negra Modelo (it only takes one), DAR member (not my cup of tea, but mom insisted), Southern Baptist bloodline, active in everything church until a few years ago, retired church secretary left disillusioned, reference letter said I was an angel, they never knew me, swear like a sailor and sneak cigarettes, received Bible degree from Liberty U. to see for myself, degree not BIG degree, no letters after my name, however received A's and can spar with the best on doctrine, certificate on wall gave confidence, miss my church, know and love old hymns, would save Bible commentaries over jewelry in case of disaster, Scriptures teach life but a vapor, history very important to me, love historians, but cannot understand where they are, and why not screaming warnings, Bible teaches nothing new under sun, history repeats, wondering where behavioral science professors are who study behavior, mannerisms, facial expressions, can we not tell when someone is lying, or do we care…, like to work behind the scenes, am the BEST number two man, one reason why I like WANAs can be myself, late bloomer, married first (only) time 43, husband took on two Dalmatians, three cats and a bird, they are gone now, last cat 23, need to take to Vet for last trip, but cannot bear it…yet, Robert Ludlum enthusiast, one bookcase dedicated to intrigue, will take break at

Christmas, and read another, love the seasons in Missouri Ozarks, rolling hills, hillbillies, privacy, famous Country Club Plaza two hours north in Kansas City, to get away and remind myself I'm really a fashion model, now modeling fuller-figure camouflage pants, and long underwear tops, sequin jacket and black turban ready, just in case, old hippie, old Trekkie, Sci-Fi Channel relaxes me, husband recites Gunsmoke, I recite ancient Egyptian pyramids, Bolivia, Peru, France, English megalithic sites, so old we can't date the stones, whoa!! MAJOR interest! also Old Testament Ezekiel witnessing visitation from skies, with loud thundering and waterfall sounds, the Lord's voice, Enoch raptured, beam me up Scottie, Sumerian writing on bowls found indicating Sumerians interacting with space men, absolutely astonishing, dinosaurs not extinction, but extermination, annoyed at unreturned phone calls, speaks volumes, today's business manners bug me, business etiquette not what it used to be, terrified of what to tell my hair stylist as to why I'm moving my business, hope she won't cut my hair off, or should I just not show up to appointment, found out she is voting against women, ignorant of what women had to do to own their own businesses, own property, obtain a mortgage, not get thrown into the streets if they were pregnant, reminds me of mentor Dorothy Sayers, Christian humanist 1883-1957 her work and amateur sleuth Lord Peter Wimsey described as first feminist mystery novel, Sayers ignored social mores, lived with someone without marriage he broke her heart and stormed out leaving her pregnant, she was a good friend of CS Lewis, JRR Tolkien read her novels, Sayers was also credited with coining the phrase "It pays to advertise" and was offered doctorate in divinity she declined, perhaps one of our WANA friends will be the CS Lewis we all knew, my first website, abortionmisnomers.com, its time is still to come, maybe useful soon, Tina Fey and Meryl Streep brave to speak against men with rape on the brain, and movie stars reputations on the line,

Madelyn Stowe, Kathleen Turner, keeping women healthy, we
are not alone, here, either, the beautiful Lake of the Ozarks
100 feet below my office, water glistens and sunset reveals Creator, not happenstance, others won't have a home, or clothes,
and missing family, missing babies, horror, is there a God after
all, rising water, drought, firestorms, earthquake, where did At-
lantis go, the Mayan cut their penis to beg the Gods for rain,
told my husband hope it rains soon for his sake, he didn't think
funny, neither did I, purchased twelve acres with trees for fuel
with two wells, pantry stocked, but for how long, my second
website gobagmeals.com good idea, snack meals in tote for easy
access in case of disaster, wish East Coast had seen my website
but no one saw it, conceal and carry class, hand could fall off,
Ruger .38, haven't touched case since, but confident if necessary, husband keeps his truck gas on empty, maddening, hasn't
he seen the lines at the pumps, eating less, smaller portions,
what if there was not enough, we waste so much, embarrassing
to see hungry children TV faces, sickens me, can't understand
why them, not me, not athletic, wish I was, boycotting Walmart and McDonalds, local writing group for seniors on Mondays, love them, good day for Staples and Starbucks, husband
plays cards Tuesday nights, laundry done, solace, Coke, 70%
dark cocoa, civic education lacking for kids, kids can't tell myth
from fact, or lies, easy for politicians to say anything, students
must be able to read history, spot propaganda, how do we
build kids who can make good decisions, and skills to be good
citizens, world views changing, multi ethnic politics, 45% polled
do not know what Supreme Court does, or if corrupt, baffled
who wants to cut public education, afraid to fly, haven't been to
airport since pre-9/11, when hate is on the loose, you can't
contain it, why were Jews chosen to play their part in the
human drama, how can Muslims be sure they are not Jewish, or
vice versa, without a DNA test, pictures on bookcases of Lisa
Beamer, wife of 9/11 hero pilot, "My faith wasn't rooted in

governments, religion, tall buildings, or frail people, my faith and my security were in God"…and, Anne Rice, Vampires to Christ, who handed over her vampire empire to a successor, and chose Biblical research over money, could I be so lucky…to be one of those, maybe could rent a car, but cannot drive in traffic, lost my cosmopolitan, love the women born in the 70s, women extraordinaire, will probably save the world, Rula Jebreal, Italo-Palestinian journalist, proponent of Middle East peace, Nina Turner Congresswoman Ohio, fighter against voter suppression, Chrystal Ball, news anchor beauty and brains, Joy Reid civic scholar, Lena Taylor Wisconsin Senate, Jackie Speier 12th District California, Michelle Bernard, Pres. Independent Women's Forum, Joan Walsh, author What's the Matter with White People, Karen Hunter political commentator, Meghan McCain the Daily Beast, Professor Melissa Harris Perry, Governor Jennifer Granholm, CEO Gina Bianchini, I was surprised to see Ning at the bottom of WANA webpage, didn't know what Ning even was, but saw her interviewed, coincidence or Divine appointment, I want to praise and encouragement these women, Dead Sea Scrolls enthusiast, church wrong Galileo jailed Earth ROUND, church wrong Inquisition MURDERS, Columbus ship manifest in Hebrew, so amazed I took 18-week Hebrew class, can't speak it but can read a little, opened new world to me, church wrong again Germany, executed Pastor Dietrich Boenhoffer witnessed 70% of clergy siding with Hitler and the complete failure of Protestant Church, Marcia Gay Harden in *The Mist*, convinced others the monsters were punishment from God, so easily fooled…sheep will follow anything, Middle Ages literature depict UFO sightings, often in conjunction with Biblical narrative and art, prominent minister Cotton Mather saw flying light through telescope, NASA has records, 16th century Zurich wood carving of war in heavens, Thomas Payne attacked by Christianity wrote The Age of Reason, the Plurality of Worlds were all agreed to by Ben Franklin,

Thomas Jefferson, and John Adams, what would Michelle Bachman say, poor girl, Chaco Canyon and Hopi ruins astrological sites cannot be explained, intriguing, rogue waves, won't be going on any cruises soon, prophesynewswatch.com, Mayan calendar true, end of eon, the new paradigm, social media and everything else, not Armageddon, not anti-Christian, but more God, Bible teaches separation of church and state and government hangs on His shoulders, I'm preparing to hang on to the right side of history.

Example C: Stuart Sheldon's Cloud

Ingredients:

Man, funny, gentleman, father, quirky, handsome, clever, passionate, compassionate, lazy, dreamer, liberated, free, eager, hungry, engorged, hell-bent, confident, wise, happy, content, husband, generous, capable, erudite, educated, traveled, silly, raunchy, goofy, loving, loyal, nostalgic, driven, childish, childlike, frustrated, healthy, middle-aged, experimental, open, meditative, surfing, ocean lover, nature, ballsy, courageous, ridiculous, arrogant, true, real, meditative, optimistic, sad, grateful, disappointed, lucky, frisky urbane, casual

Songs:

Radiohead—Weird Fishes—uplifting, fresh, free, mathematical, clever, unhinged

Stones—Girl With the Faraway Eyes—funny, irreverent, satirical, melodic. College, driving on country roads in northern Florida

Eddie Vedder—Big Hot Sun—vastness, loneliness, freedom and melancholy. Open space in the mountains

Beenie Man—Dem Sugar—happy, joyous, primal, dancey, undeniable. Teaching children at art camp. Dancing like a madman

Boston—Long Time—junior high, anthem, uplift, launch.
Rocking out as a young stoner.

Stevie Wonder—Evil—richness, heart, truth, compassion,
hope in the darkness. The rare talent of one tapped into the
root of all beauty and pain.

James Taylor—Sarah Maria—teen angst, love, simplicity, clar-
ity. Late nights lying in bed wondering when I would be happy

Jackson Browne—A Song for Adam—wistfulness, sadness,
loneliness, timeless love. Summer camp. Teen angst and long-
ing for love.

Rod Stewart—Gasoline Alley—70s, my mom's old record
player with the wooden cover

Lynard Skynard—Sweet Home Alabama—first fave song.
Turn it up!

Barbra Streisand—Don't Rain on My Parade—Hey, Mr.
Ornstein…HERE I AM!!!

Things that make me Laugh, Cry, Angry, Disappointed:

My naked children laughing, Tina Fey, 30 Rock, The Office,
Burning Man installations, watching people embrace loved ones
at airports, baby animals, pristine parts of Kauai on the Kalalau
Trail, gospel music, a well-sung national anthem, warm earth
tones, bright orange, sky blue, Pulp Fiction, Les Mis on Broadway, the movie Rent, Obama's oratory skill, any child in pain or
need, anyone sad, nostalgia, my body deteriorating, impatient
drivers who won't let you in, technology, shaving nicks, my
three-year-old's tantrums, my kids' whining, my dad's lack of
sophistication, my siblings' obstinacy, ice on the sidewalk, pol-
lution in the sea, Miami's lack of surf, being rejected by a publisher or gallery, watching an old friend dance, watching my
children sleep, political gridlock, racism, religious intolerance,
wasted potential, stupidity, meanness, hypocrisy

Things that interest me make me think or wonder:

Live volcanoes, political deftness, surfing, salsa dancing, the passage of time, the awareness of now, how are siblings born with such different personalities, what makes one artist succeed and another toil in obscurity, how can societies scapegoat groups of people, what makes a child prodigy able to play piano by ear, do animals feel emotion, what is life like on other planets, do psychotropic drugs really open doors of perception, can people levitate, what makes wisdom, is life driven by sexuality, why is reality TV a thing, why are vampires popular, Johnny Depp, Natalie Portman, Paul Newman, do we choose to succeed or fail, the importance of luck in success, is it better to be vegetarian, is gluttony really a bad thing, when will I sell my just-completed debut memoir!

Appendix C

AUTHOR BIOS & LENGTH

Example B: Cole Vassiliou

Long Bio

Cole Vassiliou suffers from re-entry shock after being kidnapped by aliens when she was seven. She spent six years living among a strange spiritually enlightened race before being banished to a secluded island occupied by bogans and fellow immigrants, locally known as Down Under. It is rumored she was punished for her rebellious determination to find a way to have her cake and eat it too—by repeatedly throwing herself off the deep end.

On one of her many island escape-attempts, Cole narrowly survived a perilous time travel voyage aboard a mythical tall-ship crewed by trolls. During an attack by a fleet of cyberpunk fairies, Cole strapped herself to a barrel of rum-flavored fairy-dust and floated back to Down Under.

Delirious with hunger, she stumbled ashore and agreed to an arranged marriage with a descendent of a Greek king in exchange for a lifetime supply of roast lamb. She's now plotting her next island escape from her apartment in the infamous convict colony Sydney, this time with her husband—an abnormally hairy engineer who builds and fixes anything she wants.

Cole is an expert in useless life lessons and dystopian advice. In spite of this, she continues her pursuit of literary awesomeness.

A little-known useless fact about Cole is that among various phases of study, she undertook a subject on classical elfish litera-ture—which she somehow passed even though she can't read, understand or speak the language of elves. She therefore thinks she may possess undeveloped paranormal superpowers.

Fortunately, Cole doesn't have any pets, offspring, or neigh-borhood trolls.

Short Version

Cole Vassiliou suffers from re-entry shock after being kidnapped by aliens when she was seven. She spent six years living among a strange spiritually enlightened race before being banished to a se-cluded island occupied by bogans and fellow immigrants, locally known as Down Under. It is rumored she was punished for her rebellious determination to find a way to have her cake and eat it too—by repeatedly throwing herself off the deep end.

Cole is an expert in useless life lessons and dystopian advice. In spite of this, she continues her pursuit of literary awesomeness (and bending spoons using only her mind).

A little-known useless fact about Cole is that among various phases of study, she undertook a subject on classical elfish litera-ture—which she somehow passed even though she can't read, understand or speak the language of elves. She therefore thinks she may possess undeveloped paranormal superpowers. Still work-ing on the spoon thing.

Shorter Version

Cole Vassiliou suffers from re-entry shock after being kidnapped by aliens when she was seven. It is rumored she was punished for her rebellious determination to find a way to have her cake and eat it too—by repeatedly throwing herself off the deep end.

Cole in an expert in useless life lessons and dystopian advice. In spite of this, she continues her pursuit of literary awesome-ness.

Twitter Short

Cole Vassilliou is an expert in useless life lessons and dystopian advice. In spite of this, she continues her pursuit of literary awesomeness.

Acknowledgments

A HUGE THANKS to the WANAs for supporting me through this project, and a special thanks to those of you trapped in WANA Hotel California (you know who you are). I appreciate your patience and your contributions to this book so others can learn. That was very a brave and beautiful thing for you to do.

I'd like to thank the numerous beta readers, in particular Laurie McClean, Wayne Ude, Piper Bayard, and my husband Shawn. I'd also like to thank Duke and Kimberly Pennell who helped edit this book. I couldn't have done this without their keen eye and ability to spot how much I just LOVE the word "just."

Thank you to my family. You have been so patient with a tired, frazzled and rarely bedazzled mom, daughter, sister and wife. Hey, can we hang out now? I have at least a day until I start something new.

Finally, I want to thank two people I owe a HUGE debt of gratitude. Thank you Bob Mayer for giving me a chance, for opening the door. You're an inspiration and mentor to so many. Also, I thank his business partner, Jen Talty. It was her brilliant mind that came up with the title that became a movement that will one day become legend.

Hey, we can hope.

WANAs would not exist without her bit of genius. Cool Gus Publishing was so good to me and I'm eternally grateful for their care and that they believed in me. I wish them all the success they so deserve.

Bibliography

Ariely, Dan. *Predictably Irrational*. New York: Harper Collins. 2010. Print.

Bennett, Shea. "Twitter On Track for 500 Million." *Media Bistro*. 13 Jan. 2012.Web. 8 Apr. 2013.

Buhner, Stephen. *Ensouling Language*. Rochester: Inner traditions. 2010. Print.

Constine, Josh. "How big is Facebook's Data?" *Tech Crunch*. 22 Aug. 2012. Web. 8 Apr. 2013.

Deahl, Rachel. "Amazon Bids on Dorchester Assets." *Publishers Weekly*. 28 June 2012. Web. 8 Apr. 2013.

Gladwell, Malcolm. *Blink*. New York: Little, Brown. 2005. Print.

—. *The Tipping Point*. Boston: Back Bay, 2002. Print.

—. *Outliers*. Boston: Back Bay, 2011. Print.

Godin, Seth. *Linchpin*. New York: Portfolio, 2010. Print.

—. *Unleashing the Ideavirus*. New York: Hyperion, 2001. Print.

Greene, Robert. *Mastery*. New York: Penguin, 2012. Print.

Lindstrom, Martin. *Buyology*. New York: Broadway, 2010. Print.

Maass, Donald. *Writing the Breakout Novel*. Cincinnati: Writers Digest, 2002. Print.

Postman, Neil. *Technopoly*. New York: Knopf, 1992. Print.

—. *Amusing Ourselves to Death*. New York: Penguin, 1986. Print.

Radwanick, Sarah. "More than 200 Billion Online Videos Viewed Globally in October." *comScore*.14 Dec. 2011. Web. 8 Apr. 2012.

Rossio, Terry. "Mental Real Estate." *Wordplayer*. WP42 . Web. 8 Apr. 2013.

Scalzi, John. "A Contract From Alibi." *Whatever*. 6 Mar. 2013. Web. 8 Apr.2013.

Shapiro, Stephen. "Sobering Statistics About the Book Industry." *SteveShapiro*. 3 Jul. 2006. Web. 8 Apr. 2013.

Strauss, Victoria. "Second-Class Contracts? Deal Terms at Random House's Hydra Imprint." *Writer Beware* blog. 28 Feb. 2013. Web. 8 Apr. 2013.

Trachtenberg, Jeffrey. "Barnes & Noble's Nook Falls Behind." *The Wall Street Journal*. Web. 28 Feb. 2013.

About the Author

A HUGE THANKS to the WANAs for supporting me through KRISTEN LAMB is the author of the #1 best-selling books "We Are Not Alone—The Writer's Guide to Social Media" and "Are You There, Blog? It's Me, Writer."

Kristen has helped thousands of writers find success using social media. Her methods are responsible for selling hundreds of thousands of books. Kristen has helped all levels of writers from mega authors to self-published unknowns attain amazing results. She's the founder of the WANA movement, the CEO of WANA International and creator of WANATribe, the social network for creatives. Kristen has dedicated her life to helping writers and artists reach their dreams and achieve the impossible.

In her free time, Kristen trains sea monkeys for the purposes of world domination....when she isn't trying to saw through her ankle monitor.

Contact Kristen:
Email: kristen@wanaintl.com
Twitter: @KristenLambTX
Blog: warriorwriters.wordpress.com
Facebook: www.facebook.com/authorkristenlamb

10800992R00198

Made in the USA
San Bernardino, CA
27 April 2014